TIMELY AND PROFITABLE HELP FOR TROUBLED AMERICANS

40 people
9 out of 10
sign up

100 down
people

ino

Charge
shipping

70%

7 levels down

1) PBS
in Phil.

$3 sales kit

2) yellow pgs- fund-sign fund raisers
raising up

They're k'ing
w/diff. men

non-profit
signup - Church does not have
To buy product

Republished by overwhelming public demand from across the nation as ***a new, larger edition*** with "Recipes from Our Mountain Home."

vitamins
shampoo
books
sporting goods also sporting sports

Ed Shorly - Phil.

rolls over

5 weeks

purch $10/mo
keep your people

2nd mo. lose your org.

Advisor - Enhance
$1,000/mo To keep bonuses
or lose people

A contemporary Thoreau, Schneider is an advocate of the rural life. — — Chico *Enterprise-Record*, Chico, California.

Sympathy and concern for an American populace headed toward what he feels is another period of "hard times" prompted Hans J. Schneider to write *Timely and Profitable Help for Troubled Americans.* — — Medford *Mail Tribune*, Medford, Oregon.

Schneider forecasts a dark future, which "will see the United States in a far worse recession and depression than we have ever experienced before." . . . America is headed on an irreversible course toward runaway inflation, more deficit spending and stronger central controls. It will soon cause a crippling depression. — — Red Bluff *Daily News*, Red Bluff, California.

It is concerned with the total life and how to live better today and be more prepared for tomorrow — — Ashland *Daily Tidings*, Ashland, Oregon.

Hans J. Schneider and his family live on a ranch . . . practicing what he preaches in a new book calling for a return to a simpler kind of life. — — Klamath Falls *Herald and News*, Klamath Falls, Oregon.

(Turn to the back of the dedicatory page and book for Reader's Comments and more complete book reviews which partly reflect what stormy, nationwide welcome this book has received.)

TIMELY
AND
PROFITABLE HELP
FOR
TROUBLED
AMERICANS

by
HANS J. SCHNEIDER

Illustrated by Roy S. Wathne

Published by

WORLD WIDE PUBLISHING CORPORATION
P.O. Box 105
Ashland, Oregon 97520

FIRST EDITION ....DECEMBER, 1976
SECOND ENLARGED AND REVISED EDITION....OCTOBER, 1977

Library of Congress Cataloging in Publication Data

Schneider, Hans J.   1935-
    Timely and profitable help for troubled Americans.

    1. Finance, Personal. 2. United States--Economic
conditions--1971-   3. Wilderness survival.
I. Title.
HG179.S293   332'.024   77-89938
ISBN 0-930294-12-2
(formerly 0-89036-066-9)

Printed in the United States of America

This book is dedicated to the friendly and most generous people, the Americans, with the hope that they may gather from its pages new courage to face the chaotic times descending upon us.

• In your book TIMELY AND PROFITABLE HELP FOR TROUBLED AMERICANS you told it like it is.—H. L. C., Goodlettsville, TN.

• If it is 50% as good as you say, it will be worth reading.—C. M. V., Detroit, MI.

• It is the best book I have read on the subject.—Dr. Marjorie Fry, Editor, Castle Rock, CO.

• I marvel at your experiences and your comprehensive understanding of National and International developments in their relationship to Bible prophecy.—E. L. M., Editor, Harrisonburg, VA.

• Your book is most appropriate for these days. Runaway inflation and civil disorder are just around the curve. Your chapter on unconventional Methods in the Absence of Medical Facilities will be most valuable in the coming days. I have seen the positive results of mud packs for swelling, splinters etc. TIMELY AND PROFITABLE HELP FOR TROUBLED AMERICANS is a good prescription for those of us who no longer expect any help from the failing institutions of this world and recognize that we must work out our own salvation—physical, mental and spiritual. Best Regards.—John R. Andrew, M.D., Ellijay, GA.

• Started your wonderful book yesterday and could not give it up until daylight failed. What a mission you have to perform to get this message to the poor fearful people. Isn't it great how your book came to help me to look up and it inspires such hope. It is truly an inspirational gift—thank you.—Mrs. M. H., Necedah, WI.

• Don't start reading the book until you have time to finish it. Once started you will not want to quit. —K. L. N., Entrepreneur, Talent, OR.

• Your two books were received a week ago, and although I do not recall ever having read a book through before taking up another one, I finished TIMELY AND PROFITABLE HELP . . . in four or five days! It is very interesting, and I laughed as much as I cried over your revelations. It is difficult to imagine anyone with as wide and varied experience as yours, but it shows up in your writings. Be sure to send me a notice if you write anything further. I want to reread your TIMELY AND PROFITABLE HELP . . . over again as it was so interesting, and I want to impress some of it on my mind. Our friend in the South Pacific wrote that he had received your books as well.
—N. McC., Hamilton, MT.

• Having received your book TIMELY AND PROFITABLE HELP . . . , I must say first that it is not only the <u>soundest</u> survival book I have read, but is marvelously entertaining, while presenting the horrible truth in a rational, delicate manner, it presents easily attainable, as well as alternative ways of weathering out the impending and inevitable storm to come. The book cannot help but bring inspiration and hope to all that read it. The beginning of your book was so exciting, and I wished you had written much more, but I realize your intent was not to write an autobiography. The travels and anecdotes interspersed throughout certainly made for lively and informative reading.—P.N.M., Researcher, Joseph, OR.

• How nice to hear from you and congratulations on finishing your book. Of course we want it. Enclosed is order and check for same.—B. and L. B., Veteran United Airline Captain, Reno, NV.

• Your books are just great.—F. H., Cusseta, AL.

• Your writing is brilliant, altogether different. Your book has freeflowing ideas that are not bound . . . Enjoy the book very much, its super logic, knowledge, perception, keen observation, and also your talent at drawing parallels from life, history and natural patterns of the universe. Language is fluent and vivid, structure of book marvelous. The cover of the book is excellent. I have high respect for your intelligence in many fields and on many subjects . . . —G. F., Roy, UT.

• As to your book, it was most interesting as well as instructive.—Mrs. A. M., Hillsboro, OR.

• I heard your interview on KRED in Eureka a week ago. I really enjoyed your talk. I also would like to read your book. Could you send a copy C.O.D.?—D. C., Crescent City, CA.

• I was overjoyed yesterday when I received the package from you. . . . Please ship me another 10 of your books for . . . TROUBLED AMERICANS. I believe I have 5 of them on the way now but I have practically sold all you have sent me.
—J. A. M., Memphis, TN.

(More comments in back of book)

A WORD ABOUT THE AUTHOR

In recent years good selling books on financial and food-storage preparations for an oncoming crash have increasingly appeared on the American market.

It is refreshing now to see a book written not by a "theorist," but by one who has actually lived through such conditions and who has predicted these very times now upon us in his lectures all over the United States and around the world since 1961.

At last we have a comprehensive, practical, easy-to-read and understand survival manual written by a world traveller, lecturer, pilot, and world-wide expert on survival tactics. The author is also a practical authority on economics because of his experience in that field in various nations and having attained high commercial skills of trade in foreign commerce seminars. He does not deal in complicated theories or many statistics that make boring reading, nor in quoting much other reference material, but instead relates his very own practical, simple, down-to-earth, proven experiences. The information included in this book will be of immediate value, no matter what the political or economic conditions might be.

Mr. Schneider survived two merciless dictatorships, a complete economic and political crash combined with monetary chaos, an almost fatal illness and many encounters with death while piloting small planes on dangerous missions in various parts of the world—all this through personally gained practical know-how.

In 1958 the author again left behind a re-established life in West Germany with weekend house, sailboat, financial prosperity and immigrated to the United States, starting from "scratch" in a new land without friends or connections this side of the Atlantic. He later lived under survival conditions on his journeys through nearly 100 countries of the world and two-year extensive criss-cross trips through his new home country, the United States, on only pennies a day.

As you relive the author's life—he is referred to by his friends as having lived seven lives—in perusing the following pages which are written from his heart and bubble at times with a lively humor, you will be spellbound to the end.

HANS J. SCHNEIDER RETURNING FROM ONE OF HIS EXTENSIVE INTERNATIONAL SPEAKING TOURS.

Posing for a newspaper interview, the author unravels a portion of his 130 airline tickets representing a two-year trip through 44 countries around the world. (Statesman photo)

PREFACE

As the shadows are lengthening all across the "land of the free", time is running out as we see the dark clouds and hear the roaring of the thunder. I strongly desire to share in this form the great wealth of knowledge gained in various vital fields with the people of my adopted country while there is yet time to put it to use for their benefit now and in the darker days to come.

Some might think that all troubles will magically vanish into oblivion, but this book makes clear beyond any shadow of doubt why we are headed for a drastic depression with a devastating effect upon our present economical and political systems. History has proven many times that after hyper-inflation or depression a country is usually not free any longer.

Warning voices have been heard in increasing strength in recent years and a number of good books have appeared on the market dealing with this problem, most specializing in certain areas. Many of them point to economic collapse and chaos in the near future. A few others concentrate along lines of physical survival as related to you, your home and provisions. A great percentage of you are not able to buy and read stacks of various books, each on a separate topic, as there would be so many to study. As conditions grow worse you already will have a struggle to stay alive and therefore have even less opportunity available for research. However, a good knowledge in only one area would be of no avail to you. A chain always breaks at its weakest link. The knowledge you have must be comprehensive and complete or it will not benefit you. What good will it do if you guard your wealth but are not able to keep alive due to lack of food, clothing or shelter? What good will it do if you are well sheltered in these things but are not able to help yourself in the case of sickness? What good will it do if you have a great amount of storage food and security in one place but are not able to maintain yourself when driven from that spot? Now you can see that it easily can be a life-or-death matter to have a fairly good working knowledge in the entire field under survival conditions. Also, not much time is left. Therefore, we have a great need for a brief, all-encompassing and up-to-date manual with practical application, preferably written by one who speaks from personal experience. Naturally, such a book is extremely difficult to come by as it would take an author who has lived many extraordinary lives in many different places. It doesn't take much thought to realize that there must only be very few such people alive and, of those few, none might care to write about it.

I have discovered the need for such a book. Many times I have looked for one but without success. It would have made things a lot easier for me throughout the years and could have saved me small fortunes, much waste of time and aggravation of mind.

My keen awareness of the need for an all-inclusive volume on such vital matters has caused me finally to write one. It has been quite an endeavor, and I am deeply thankful to my wife, Inger Marie, and our five children for their faithful help and patience throughout the time of my research and writing and my oldest son in particular, who has enthusiastically contributed his thoughts on this book. I would especially like to express my gratitude to a friend, my secretary Polly M. Updegraff, who has assisted me in an untiring effort in this laborious task for over three solid months. Without her invaluable help, the writing and production of this book would have been impossible. I also appreciate the willingness of her son to assume many extra burdens in order to permit her to spend the necessary time on the book.

I therefore dedicate this book to my wife, Inger Marie, my children, my friend and co-worker, Polly M. Updegraff, and the American people in general.

In this book you will find the practical knowledge acquired in many years of extensive travel in nearly *100 countries*. A great number of interests have brought about the enormous amount of events which have transpired in my life. When occasionally remembering the many outright dangerous times I experienced, I often wonder that my life has been spared. I believe there are reasons. Perhaps one is that this book could be written and made available to you, the reader.

You will learn about my experiences under two dictatorial rulerships and a total breakdown in between while living in Europe. You will receive valuable information as to what we did to survive these crucial times—information which once again should prove extremely valuable as we are now confronted with the very same conditions right here in America. Along the way you will be amused by some of the comical episodes.

In 1950 I was able to leave the eastern territories of Germany, finding again a more comfortable life in the western part. Finally I settled in America, giving up business and many influential connections and friendships in the old country.

There is a tendency for writers to make certain subjects too long. I have read books in which the author discussed the same topic endlessly and rehashed it in addition. I have tried to keep each matter brief and to the point and references are included along with the text rather than relegated to a bibliography. There was no need to expand the book artificially, as I had difficulty in covering all the topics I wanted to include.

Reading this book should be a rewarding and enriching experience. It will be just like taking a hike on a winding trail through the mountains with new vistas opening up beyond each curve of the path, or like listening to a symphony with pianissimo and fortissimo variations galore, and keep you interested and spellbound to the end—this is, if you are intelligent and perceptive. Such important topics as economics and survival tactics under many conceivable conditions are covered with special attention and a world-wide scope. This is important at a time of large international involvement, constant movement of people (even on a global scale), and increasing problems everywhere.

You should greatly profit from this study under any circumstances—crash or no crash. It contains a multitude of important down-to-earth advice for all kinds of lifestyles under various conditions which can make your life easier, more joyful and meaningful. It should not only save you money and hardships but, in fact, increase your wealth and bring greater blessings in your family's life and health.

Because of its tremendous scope, this book is of permanent rather than temporary value (even though there are a few brief passages which will be superseded by changing conditions). Endeavor to read it in its entirety first in order to receive a better and much-needed all-around knowledge and understanding. Then, because of its detailed partitioning, you will always be able to refer quickly to the chapters, parts or sections you want to study further as the need arises. There is a unique combination of needed up-to-date material and much more information which will not become obsolete. It has an immediate appeal with a long-range potential and will not be a "here today, gone tomorrow" volume.

In my extensive speaking engagements across America and the world I have usually included a "Question and Answer" session at the end of each meeting. This has given me a good understanding of the needs of the people and what interests them. I have "zeroed in" on these very matters and included others which need to be known.

It is my sincere belief and hope that you will extract much worthwhile material from a careful reading of this book and that it may challenge you to the core for the rest of your life.

I have written this "mini-encyclopedia" in an effort to help the Americans to help themselves while they are still able to do so.

Hans J. Schneider

INTRODUCTION

Bitter night winds, approaching hurricane velocity, are sweeping over the entire globe. These winds, screaming with fury and filled with foreboding, are whipping to tatters the storm flags flying above every realm of present-day life. Storm signals are now fluttering so wildly that no person with a minimum of moral discrimination can fail to understand their unmistakable warning. We are living in a night of total crisis. Evil men are seeking to dethrone God from His place in the universe. Two global wars have brought men—not to their senses—but to the brink of penultimate disaster. Revolution and revolt flame almost everywhere, while men are watching—watching—as global night comes on apace.

How much longer will this country last, and how much freedom will prevail? These are thoughts which come to me as I look out of the windows of our mountain home this early morning of a beautiful, crisp, refreshing day. There is absolute calm and quiet. No branch moves and no leaf trembles. It seems that nature around us radiates a calm permanence so much unknown in our world today. What my eyes see as they scan the majestic forest and the clear blue sky seems to be in sharp contrast to the confusion, strife and bloody turmoil many people of this land find themselves in. Our cities have become crime-infested horrors. Dreams have turned to nightmares. The economic and political condition is more unstable than ever—men everywhere are bewildered. Where will it lead?

Reflecting upon these things, my memory goes back many years. As I compare the many events in my past life—the life under two dictatorships and one complete economic and political crash—many striking parallels come to mind. At this point we concern ourselves with what we can learn from those lessons of the past as we find ourselves in an almost identical situation today, although on an even more global scale. It has been asserted many times that if man could learn from past historical events he would be much better off, as history continually repeats itself. Therefore, in the following pages which will unfold before you, dear friend and reader, you will find *my very own* experiences and lessons learned as a result of situations similar to those we are facing now and in the immediate future. I will endeavor to concentrate on the main issues we are concerned with at this stage as I try to set down as many of my comprehensive experiences as I possibly can within the pages of this book. It will not be easy. My life so far has been an extremely full life and has encompassed a multitute of avenues.

TABLE OF CONTENTS

PART I
A DRAMATIC
BACKGROUND—MY
TEACHER

WHAT'S AHEAD?

Complete change of weather patterns with disastrous results on our food and industrial production?

Financial rape of the middle class through runaway inflation, increasing taxes and Federal budgets out of control with final monetary collapse?

Another dramatic stock market decline?

Rapid developments of the Electronic Funds Transfer Systems (EFTS), ushering in the "checkless-cashless society"?

Famines and shortages in fuel, electrical power, and in general?

Increasing bank problems with catastrophic effects on the Federal Deposit Insurance Corporation (FDIC), which was created for normal rather than crisis times?

An atomic war?

A world in constant tremor caused by an increase in the frequency and destructiveness of earthquakes?

Socialized medicine and other ruinous governmental welfare programs?

Chapter 1

What's Ahead?

Please forgive me, dear reader, if from bare necessity I am starting this book by painting a true but rather somber and ugly picture. If it is more than your nerves can take, you particularly need to read this volume because what would you do in such situations if just reading about it strikes the heart with panic? Unfortunately, this world we are living in is not always a pretty place; but to accommodate you, just imagine that it is merely a bad dream. Cheer up, though, for there is a lot of help offered for such tragic times as these in this volume.

Now visualize yourself, for a moment, under the following circumstances.

It is a beautiful time of the year and life is going on as usual. Suddenly a relatively calm environment is turned into an inferno as the pre-dawn hours are shattered by sirens howling, apparently everywhere. Frenzied and confusing radio announcements chase one another in a vain effort to keep the populace briefed about the many horrifying events crashing down upon them like a thunderbolt out of the blue sky. The latest bulletin, read in a trembling voice, discloses that inter-continental missiles armed with nuclear warheads already have been launched from an overseas nation and are ready to strike the United States momentarily.

Still dulled from sleep and spellbound into temporary inactivity, people wonder what to do next. Earsplitting explosions thunder and clash, with smoke mushrooming into the sky wherever they look. Confusion is reigning. The entire machinery of a once-powerful empire has ground to a halt and the wheels of commerce have ceased turning. Men's own civilization has largely destroyed them and life has now become a nightmare to those few left who are acquainted only with the hereditary soft and comfortable life their culture offered.

In some places the heat is so intense that six-foot persons are reduced to corpses about three feet long and thousands of persons seeking shelter in subways dissolve into a single pool of liquid. One woman with her baby in her arms is melting into the street, forming a tar statue.

Finally the sounds of strife are stilled, although tendrils of smoke still rise here and there from the ruined cities and prostrated towns. Many hours later, after the "close-in" fallout has abated, you find yourself amid the following scene.

Vandals, hunger, disease and countless other scarcely imaginable horrors are stalking the land. Some people are cooking their food in wash pails over the still-smoldering fire of what had once been their home. True, some survive, but the toll is tremendous. Those remaining are barely able to drag themselves around and they are still too stunned to comprehend the enormity of the disaster that has overtaken them.

You find yourself moved back into the stone age. Your wife and daughters are endangered by the invading armies or some sadistic countrymen. Pestilence and plagues are spreading rapidly in the absence of sanitary utilities. No medical or hospital facilities are left intact to serve the remaining few badly injured, burned survivors and the sick. Some have friends familiar with the healing arts, but there is no way to call them as telephone lines have been destroyed and it is questionable whether those friends are still alive. The remaining skeletons of ruined cities have become ratholes of infection with mobs running wild, plundering and smashing the last few worthwhile remnants. There are no stores left in operation so you cannot buy food or clothing. The transportation systems and the communication media are entirely broken down.

Famines are prevalent; men can barely remember the last time they sat down for a meal. The most pitiful sight is that of emaciated children with sunken cheeks and hollow eyes stumbling along the streets barefoot in the snow and dressed only in rags as they beg for a scrap of food or a drink of water.

Under the monopolistic terror regime, which is now holding dictatorial sway over this beloved land after it had already conquered much of the world with its coercion, crowds are gathered every so often into big public squares. Despotic government agents patrol the homes to make sure everyone attends, for the word has gone out that whoever does not show up will be very severely punished. After the crowd has assembled, executions take place before their eyes in order to strike fear into everyone's heart.

There are no schools your children can attend. Everyone— including children—must work in order to survive. When you arise in the morning you never know where the next meal will come from.

All your possessions have been confiscated and you are employed in the business you once owned, making a monthly wage equal in value to a loaf of bread.

You must make your own clothing and shoes from whatever materials you have handy or can find. Some garments are patched so much you can hardly tell what the original material was. Often shoes have become only a memory and people wrap their feet in rags.

The place where you dwell is bitter cold as fuel for heating is practically unavailable. Some persons live many feet below the ground in caves that are dark and damp as well.

There is the constant uncertainty of what will happen next and whether some agent will come and drag you off to an unknown destination. Perhaps you will never see your wife and children again or know what fate overtook them. There seems to be no hope anywhere in sight. The only things visible are desolation, torture, sickness, fear and want.

"Impossible!" you say.

But you have just read actual life experiences of people in Europe and Asia in recent years, only then we had to contend with bomber squadrons rather than intercontinental missiles. What makes you believe these and worse things could not happen in America, especially after you have seen many definite warning signs right here in the very recent years with campus riots, rising crime, prison turmoils, hijackings, kidnappings, the burning of cities and a runaway inflation only barely and temporarily abated!

In addition, the United States has already fallen well behind the Soviet Union in military strength. In sharp contrast, the Soviet Union is straining its economy to increase further its military superiority over the United States. Former Defense Secretary Schlesinger said in his February 5, 1975 annual report to Congress that the Soviets "outstrip" us "in Strategic Offensive Forces by 60%."

In signing the SALT I agreements, the United States adopted the incredible Mutual Assured Destruction (MAD) theory and agreed not to defend its civilian population. *This is why all surface-to-air missiles in the United States were dismantled.*

General L. D. Clay, Jr., Commander-in-Chief, North American Air Defense Command (NORAD), in a November 13, 1974 speech declared, "We no longer have as our primary mission the air defense of the North American continent." General Clay said that NORAD would still provide warning of a strategic attack, *but he added the chilling comment that "...the nation as an entity and every citizen in it may measure longevity from the instant warning is received."*

These facts have been released by government officials, yet most of the same officials feel politically restrained from publicly admitting that these facts add up to the Soviets having already gained military superiority over the United States.

A comparison of the following figures will give you a shocking picture of the monumental imbalance that exists:

	U.S.	U.S.S.R.
Strategic heavy and medium bombers	498	860
Sub-launched long-range cruise missiles	0	314
Tanks	9,000	40,000
Artillery	6,000	20,000
Heavy mortars	3,000	10,000
Interceptor aircraft	532	2,650
Surface-to-air missiles	0	9,800

The following quotation is also very illuminative: "If the Soviets were to launch an all-out nuclear attack on American cities and industrial centers, *the American death toll would be 100 million or higher,* the Pentagon has said." *(Defense/Space Daily,* September 18, 1975).

Whether you realize it or not, you are at the threshold of such earth-moving and mind-boggling calamities that stagger the imagination. Nuclear-warfare-induced earthquakes and volcanic eruptions (especially around the Pacific circle of fire) will cause such giant earth movements and coastal collapses that the globe will literally shake at its foundation and reel to and fro with mighty tidal waves changing the geographical outline of every continent worldwide.

Craters and fissures will spread across the land from the Pacific to the Atlantic. The atmosphere will be so filled with smoke, fumes and other contaminants of warfare that the moon will actually appear red and the sun turn dark. There will be distress upon nations and men's hearts will fail them for fear as they are looking at those things coming upon the earth.

It will be a gloomy day of trouble and anxiety with once-inhabited cities lying waste and the pomp of the strong having ceased. Every heart will melt and tremble in sorrow, all hands will be feeble, every spirit faint and all knees weak as water on account of the fury laying the land desolate.

There are a few, however, who have foreseen a tragedy like this, provided for such a day spiritually and moved back into the mountains and other wilderness areas before it struck, storing up food and clothing and furnishing shelter ahead of time. Their habitations are like isles in a raging sea of a drowning humanity. They are the ones who were laughed at like Noah of old, but now the tide has turned and those who once mocked are gone into oblivion. They are no more—their foolishness has brought them to an abrupt end. Their joy suddenly has been turned into mourning and their dancing into tottering. Gone are their festivals of old.

It is precisely for this reason, dear reader, that this book has been written. The very fact that you are reading it proves there is yet time and countless things you can do to prepare. Begin *now* to utilize the opportunities that are left and use the information that is set down in the following pages. If you do, the chances are that you will never be sorry for having done so; if, however, you neglect these all-important arrangements, bitter remorse will most likely soon follow.

Chapter 2

Why Germany Was Ready
for a Demagogue

One of the most needless and foolish wars mankind ever fought—the decimation of the white race through the greatest and most tragic blood-spilling between kindred men—finally ended by an armistice on November 11, 1918. According to indoctrination, it was a war to end all wars. The affinity between the United States and Germany, cemented even further by close racial kinship, was propagandized to death—a sad fate if one realizes that the basic blood line of English descendants living here is closely related to the Germans and that about a fourth of the early twentieth-century Americans were actually of German stock.

Germany, once America's good friend, lay prostrate at the feet of its supposed wartime enemies thanks to the treaty of Versailles (June 28, 1919) which intentionally saddled a poor, humbled, bankrupt and broken nation, already in shambles, with an impossible load of reparation payments in the amount of $33,000,000,000. In addition to this, the defeated country lost all colonies and much of its own land to the various European nations. Because of this overwhelming situation, a terrible suffering began to spread across the land among its helpless people, especially in industrial areas and cities.

Germans actually had to scavenge food from garbage cans behind hotels. A cup of coffee, for instance, soared in price from one million marks to two million marks in two days as Germany was in its death throes when inflation reached its peak in 1923. It all kindled a deep, slow-burning fire of bitterness inside the people and the stage was set for the entrance into the world spotlight of a demagogue by the name of Adolph Hitler.

It has been rightly said that an inflation to this degree, with the complete loss of the value of a currency, strikes a more devastating and widespread blow throughout a nation than virtually any other calamity. Prices rose 10% an hour and the mark plummeted to 1/1,000,000,000,000,000 of its former value. Backing for paper money flooding the country from 84 printing presses working around the clock was non-existent. Artificial government manipulation of money has always been proven to backfire upon the country employing this means of propping up a failing economy. Furthermore, freedom and control cannot co-exist, so when controls increase, as is the case in such times, freedom decreases.

A whole wheelbarrow full of money would not even buy a loaf of bread with the inflation at its zenith. Workers were paid in the middle of the day so their waiting wives could hurry to stores with the money before prices rose further. A book purchased at 9:00 in the morning for 72,000 marks cost 180,000 marks only five hours later. Prices on restaurant menus were meaningless as prices rose from the time one ordered food until paying the bill.

Obviously, people's savings vanished quickly. An investment in government bonds in 1916 of $100,000 (400,000 marks) would have been worth only $10.00 seven years later. A match was worth more than a German mark.

Speculation was much indulged in as inflation grew. Many people were hypnotized into believing they were profiting, but only a few were aware of the true situation. One industrialist invested more in businesses after having made a fortune in inflated paper money. He became deeply indebted, but the continual downward trend of the mark's value cancelled out the debts. However, he did not know when to stop, and lost everything when inflation was finally brought to a halt.

In such times miseries multiply because the resulting inflation, as has been historically proven, has a debasing influence upon the populace and the way is paved for wars, depressions and such men as Napoleon and Hitler. The latter was enabled to rise to power in Germany because the hardships inflicted upon the people were such that they were ready to snatch at anything promising to bring better times.

The Dawes Plan of 1925, the Young Plan of 1929, President Hoover's one-year payment suspension on war debts and reparations in 1931 and the 1932 Lausanne Agreement induced slight temporary relief upon a suffering nation. But when the world depression settled on Europe around that time and an unemployed and hungry German people became desperate again, the smoldering wrath that had been dormant within the people broke out afresh and they were finally ready to listen to a despot.

Soon a more deadly World War II pushed mankind to the brink of disaster and made an unwilling American populace more acceptable to joining the United Nations after they had rejected the earlier model of it, the League of Nations. Thus, world government was brought within the grasp of everyone. The plans of a small cadre of international monetary racketeers was working well.

The above account is a very timely message and of immediate interest to all Americans. As you will see later when reading the chapters *The Present State Of The Economy* and *Investment Suggestions*, we are rapidly heading for a situation similar to that of Germany in the 1920's. May I, however, invite you next to accompany me through some of the actual bone-chilling experiences made while personally living under two dictatorships and a crash. I am certain that there will be much you can learn for the times ahead.

HOW WE SURVIVED BEING LASHED BY A CRASH AND USED OUR WITS UNDER DICTATOR- SHIPS

Chapter 3

How We Survived Being Lashed By A Crash
And Used Our Wits Under Dictatorships

Life Under Hitler

Pre-Crash Grandeur

It started when I came into this world as the son of a multimillionaire industrialist. All of my father's industrial plants, properties, fleet of cars and our suburban estate with large landscaped gardens which formed the background of my early childhood were located in the part of Germany now east of the Iron Curtain and, in fact, east of East Germany; or, in other words, east of the Oder-Neisse line. The years of my early life were blessed with many of the world's comforts. My parents' residence was furnished with many gadgets which would seem ultra-modern in our day and age, even though that was about 40 years ago. It was at that time one of the most modern houses. The floor in the kitchen as well as in the bathroom was constructed with a built-in electric heating system covered by beautiful tiles. The central heating system was fueled by gas. The huge picture windows in our conservatory could be lowered out of sight into the wall. It had air raid shelters with fresh air ventilation systems and steel pipe ceilings. The floors were of terrazzo tiles. The first floor was of parquet. Closets were built in and were moth proof. There were two large balconies and one terrace which was partly open and partly covered. The house had an attached double garage, built with pits under the flooring to enable more efficient servicing of vehicles. The outer gate as well as the front door was served by a remote control system and an intercom. The house, which was built in 1936, was visited many times by the professors and pupils of the architectural school in Breslau, because it was unique.

My childhood years were enriched further by the beautiful classical music, such as famous operatic arias, etc., of my mother's lovely coloratura soprano voice as she accompanied herself on the expensive grand piano. The grounds were furnished with stately evergreen trees, a vast expanse of well-kept lawn and colorful terraced rock gardens. A scenic river adjoined the estate.

The extravagant life of those years was especially expressed by occasional parties held on the premises as well as other outside engagements. I can still picture the famed evenings at our home while guests from the social elite gathered and my parents entertained them. On those occasions my mother would bring enjoyment to the gathering with her beautiful voice accompanied by instrumental music while my father brought up the most delicious, expensive and aged wines from his own private, built-in wine cellar. Luxurious fur coats and fur pieces, maids, gardeners as well as a fleet of cars with chauffeurs were the order of the day. This was the world I knew then.

Threatening Shadows

This life, however, did not last too long. Dark shadows were spreading themselves over Adolf Hitler's promised millenium. I still remember when they drafted my brother into the Hitler Jugend, even though he was at that time only about twelve years old.

Also I remember how occasional air raids were conducted over our territory, accompanied by howling sirens, the sound of flak in the distance and the flash of exploding shells and bombs rending the night sky. The realization that such fighting took the cream of the European populace made us feel very uneasy about the war maneuvers. Some of the most intelligent and wonderful young people we have known died in the war. This draining away of the prime lifeblood of Europe as well as other nations' populations has been of very sad consequence to our civilization, especially since many combatants were related either directly or remotely.

Shortages became more and more noticeable as the war continued, and I still remember how my parents started saving certain items such as concentrated fruit juices. There was an almost complete absence of imported items such as oranges, bananas, pineapples and coconuts as the foreign supply lines were almost nonfunctioning toward the end. Naturally, there was a great shortage of gasoline and the available resources had to be used for priorities.

I also remember the time our metal garden fences were dismantled in a desperate effort to keep the war machinery going. Very soon the cities of Breslau, Berlin and Aachen were declared forts. At that time the German government ordered an immediate evacuation of the private citizens of our home town, Breslau. But even before that occurred, I became seriously ill—even unto death. There was no hope for me and the worst was expected. I eventually recuperated partly after a long hospital stay and although I was still physically very weak and unable to walk, we were then immediately driven by my father to a smaller town some distance from the big city of Breslau as part of the evacuation move.

I still remember how five German tanks, loaded down with weapons, came rolling through that little town we were then brought to, wanting to defend it. The people of that town, not willing to see any further destruction, strictly advised against such a move. The end of a vanishing empire was seen as German women stood on the sides of the road and waved goodbye to those last German forces.

The end of Hitler's regime was at hand and the complete political and economic crash was right before us.

Life During the Crash and Under Communism

The Changing Scene

Just hours after the Germans left, a different sight appeared. Two Russian officers were walking down the main street ahead of an endless column of very antiquated vehicles, many of which pulled obsolete cannons with Mongolians sitting on them. It was a sight to behold; it looked as though we had suddenly dropped back in time to the Middle Ages! Right before the arrival of this column a few German soldiers were passing by some of the hillside residences, laying down their uniforms and heading for the mountains. The two Russian officers heading the column aimed at them and others as they lifted up their guns, pointed toward the surrounding hills and shot.

It was an amazing sight to see the very same German women who had waved goodbye to the last departing German forces stand on the streets again and wave to the arriving Russian forces!

A Lonely Woman's Search Through a Ruined City

When the war had come to an end, my mother decided that she would look for her husband who was in the City of Breslau, which had earlier been declared a fort. He had been committed to stay to the end in some civilian capacity connected with supplying food to the remaining garrison. For three or four months we had not heard a word from him for that was about the period of time that city had held out.

My mother and another woman one day started out on the road, hitchhiking, as all transportation systems had broken down. A Russian truck stopped and picked them up. After telling the driver where they wanted to go, the women climbed into the bed of the truck. It was not very long before the ladies discovered that the Russians were not driving toward their destination and immediately perceived that they were deliberately being taken away. My mother at once shouted in a loud, stern, deep voice, "STOI!" (STOP!), and the army truck driver, thinking it was an officer on the street someplace, immediately brought the truck to a halt. My mother and her friend jumped off and headed for the nearby trees and escaped. They hiked the rest of the way (very many miles) to the City of Breslau, spending the night in an old ruined shack, one of the few remnants in a completely devastated city (about 80% of Breslau was destroyed). My mother, who had become a God-fearing person during those terrifying days, spent all of the night crying and praying while her friend slept.

The following day my mother decided she would simply walk around the ruined city, past rubble and dead bodies, looking for her husband as she didn't know what else to do. While walking down a street, she saw a man approaching her. As he had a long, gray beard, she thought to herself, "My, isn't that an old man!" As he came closer, she recognized him to be her husband! I guess it would not have to be mentioned how impressive this occurrence was when she met him on the very day after her arrival in such a big, ruined city, especially since her friend's husband who was imprisoned by the Russians together with my father for the same cause (civilian participants in the nation during war) was kept in prison for one further year.

Humorous Episodes

The times that followed were a mixture of humor and terror. The following occurrences will be unbelievable to the people in this civilized country, but they do show the condition Russia was in as a whole at that time.

A Russian soldier on a good bicycle saw a German boy riding down the street not using his hands on an old bicycle without tires. As he rode from the opposite end of the street and approached the boy, the Russian soldier thought this boy must have a very special bicycle since he could ride it freehandedly. He traded his bike for the boy's bike, and the boy very delightedly took off fast on that good bicycle. The Russian, on the other hand, started to pursue the boy freehandedly with the other bicycle. He went a few feet and crashed to the ground. He hollered furiously after the boy, who happily waved goodbye to the Russian soldier. After he arrived home, the boy found a box of gold watches on the back carriage of that bicycle.

Watches in those days were largely unknown to the Russian people and many collected them as a hobby—by the trunk load—as they were novelty items to them. One evening as we were gathered at that little mountain home we were living in then, having dinner with a circle of friends, a banging was heard at the door. As we opened it, two Russian soldiers came in, motioning for my mother to get up from the table and come to them. Not knowing what they wanted, we expected the worst. My mother, having no choice, stepped toward them. They grasped her hand and took off her watch. After this one soldier said, "Thank you, madam," bowed slightly and they left.

During those years my brother tried to contribute to the small income of the family by repairing watches. One day a Russian soldier entered his little repair shop and brought in a watch, indicating that it was broken. My brother opened it in the presence of his customer and, to his amazement, a dead bedbug fell out! The watch contained no mechanism at all. Apparently some German had played a joke on that soldier, having taken the mechanism out of the watch and substituted the bedbug. When the Russian customer saw the dead bedbug fall out, he exclaimed in surprise, "Oh, maschinka kaput!" (machine broken), for he thought that the bedbug indeed had been the mechanism of that watch.

On other occasions Russian soldiers getting their water from faucets when thirsty, thought that was a good deal. They broke the faucets off from the walls and saved them for future use. When they came to other places that did not have faucets and without water, they would stick the faucets they had saved into the wall and turn them on, thinking water would come out.

For the fun of it, I will add another amazing incident.

One day two Russian officers came into the house of some friends with several fish in their hands. They indicated that they wanted to wash the fish and walked into the bathroom. They immediately saw the old-fashioned toilet facility with the water tank mounted below the ceiling which was activated by a pull chain hanging down. They laid the fish into the toilet and pulled the chain, endeavoring to wash their fish. However, that was the last they saw of the fish, for they had left that facility as the soldiers discovered when looking down into the bowl. Upon close examination the soldiers found that the big outlet pipe of the bowl went through the floor. Immediately they left this apartment (which was on the second floor), ran downstairs and speedily demanded entrance to the apartment below. As soon as the door was opened they rushed into the bathroom, thinking the fish had arrived down there!

I mentioned the small repair shop of my brother and might add that it was extremely hard in those days to obtain repair parts and even harder to obtain repair manuals, which were very much needed items for his work. It was impossible to buy any regular toilet paper and we had torn up newspapers and other paper as a substitute. We had a big, long, curved hook mounted in the lavatory upon which we hung all those pieces of paper. It was usually my grandfather's job to take care of that particular supply. One day my brother visited that facility and almost fainted when he saw his very valuable repair manuals nicely parted and cut up in small pieces hanging from that hook! Needless to say that this produced quite a verbal conflict.

The True Face of Communism

Unfortunately, though, not all our experiences were of this humorous nature, but rather they were much in the minority. There were many raids upon the homes of the German people by Polish, Czechoslovakian and Russian people. Especially feared were the Mongolians and thereafter the Czechoslovakian and Polish people. There were visits by Mongolian soldiers to German homes where women were alone, their husbands having died during the war. Many times there were cries in the night, as some of these women were raped, their pregnant bodies split open and football played with the remainder of the little child's body after its legs and arms had been torn off.

An old couple was dragged into the snow-covered street in the middle of winter. An old chair leg was used to club them down until they were lying in the snow, bleeding. Their torturers waited until the elderly people gathered enough strength to rise and then bludgeoned them repeatedly. Their crime was reading the Bible in their home and praying. It had become a criminal offense to hold religious meetings, to pray and to read religious books of any kind, and people had better not be found doing those things.

In another case two Communist soldiers entered a German home, herded all the eleven inhabitants into a corner of the room and machine gunned them down. One little child of that family had rolled underneath the bed, escaping the massacre and was later instrumental in the apprehension of those merciless killers.

This all happened after the war had ended and unarmed people were at the mercy of armed soldiers moving into their territory. Many a day we trembled for our lives.

At this point I would like to emphasize, however, that it is not the belief of this author or his intent to imply that all people of some nations are bad and all the people of some other nations are good; rather, it is his belief that there are good and bad people wherever a person goes, no matter which country it is. To deal in generalities is foolish and childish. It would be just as wrong to say that all the Russian people are Communists as it would be to say that all the Cuban people are Communists just because they happen to live under those particular dictatorships. It would not be very farfetched to state it could be possible that there are more people who are in favor of Communism in the United States of America than there are in Russia, for in Russia the people know what it is and most of them are longing for the day and hour when they could be free. However, in America many people have no idea what it is like to live under Communism.

For those who favor the Communist system, we might mention that under that system you have no freedom of travel, no freedom of choice as far as jobs are concerned, no religious freedom, no freedom of speech and no freedom to assemble. For those who are impressed by the so-called "progress" of Soviet Russia we might mention that much or most of that has been accomplished by the vampiric feeding of the Soviet empire on its satellite countries of the East Bloc—or shall we better call them Soviet slave camps—and by the vast amounts of money and know-how extended to them by Western nations, especially America. While again visiting East Germany some years ago, it was distressing for me to see how the people were literally starving, without the bare necessities of life, standing in long food lines and making very little money, as usually totalitarian or other repressive governments such as Communism keep their people in bondage by not allowing them time to think, to meditate, to arrive at their own conclusions or to be individually creative. They keep their people working for eleven or twelve hours a day with little food. They know that hungry people can easily be kept under control as those people will constantly consume their energies and time in an effort to supply even the most necessary items to satisfy their hunger pangs by standing in long food lines. They know that under those conditions people are unable to have thoughts of their own. Furthermore, they can influence the masses in certain ways by increasing or restricting that food supply.

At the same time the industrial output of East Germany was partly represented at the Leipzig Fair for export purposes, most of the products were unavailable for the people themselves but they were rather used to bring more funds for a Soviet empire. Certainly Soviet Russia therefore could not afford to let the people progress very far in their demands for freedom as they did in Hungary and East Berlin some years ago. Instead, they saw the need to smash that resistance against their tyrannical set-up immediately. There were none of the freedoms which people would relish during the five years we spent under Communism; we had to struggle to keep ourselves supplied with the bare necessities of life.

These five years were mostly filled with trials, persecution and hardship. The territory we were living in was settled at that time by the remaining German people, Russians and mostly Polish people, as the Russian people gave that territory as an extension to the Polish people because they had been resettled by them earlier. In the beginning the Communist governments drove out the German people, who left by the millions for East and West Germany. They went by foot and horse-drawn vehicles in the middle of a severe winter and many thousands died on the westward trek. About twenty million people were resettled at that time and Albert Schweitzer called it one of the greatest crimes ever committed on humanity.

The fact that those eastern territories were completely turned over to the Russian and Polish people is not a commonly known fact in the United States. In effect, Germany had been practically split up into three major divisions: West Germany, East Germany and the territories east of those two areas, which were completely lost.

Being a native of Germany, I have been unable in the past to understand why a large, important part of Germany, abounding with mineral resources, was entirely given to the Russian people and then, in turn, part of that territory went to the Polish people, necessitating the evacuation of twenty million people. Furthermore, I could not understand why vast industrial areas and centers of German military industry such as Peenemünde were permitted to go into Russian hands at the end of the war and why commands were given for the withdrawal of American forces which had advanced further than the present West German boundary lines suggest so that Russian forces could take over that particular territory after it had been conquered and paid for by the blood of American soldiers. West Berlin being created an island as the result of such a move caused many further problems and difficulties.

Today, after much research work on these matters, I do not any longer marvel about those moves for I have become aware that there is a pattern followed by certain interests which in turn dictate their policy to the "powers that be" in Washington, D.C. and then many of the disastrous moves and confusing strategies which end up in the usual defeats for America open up as a move in the overall strategy of those very power-hungry elements. (For further information read *Roosevelt's Road to Russia,* by G. N. Crocker.)

When considering the snarled mess Europe is in because of interwoven politics, commerce and treaties caused by controlled American intervention, we can see that the views the early leaders of this country held still are true today:

> *"I have many reasons to think that not one of the European Powers wishes to see America rise very fast to power.*
>
> *"We ought, therefore, to be cautious how we magnify our ideas, and exaggerate our expressions of the generosity and magnitude of any of those Powers.*
>
> *"Let us treat them with gratitude, but with dignity. Let us, above all avoid, as much as possible, entangling ourselves with their wars or politics.*
>
> *"Our business with Europe, and theirs with us, is commerce, not politics, much less war; America has been the sport of European wars and politics long enough."* (John Adams).

"I am for relying for defense on our own army and on our own Naval force to protect our coasts and harbors. I am for free commerce with all nations; political connection, with none; and little or no diplomatic establishments.

"And I am not for linking ourselves by new treaties with the quarrels of Europe; entering that field to preserve their balance. For us to attempt to reform all Europe and bring them back to principals (sic) of morality, and respect for the equal rights of nations, would show us to be only maniacs of another character.

"The first object of my heart is my own country."
(Thomas Jefferson).

The problems we had in the aftermath of the Second World War were largely contributed to by the infamous agreements at Potsdam, Teheran and Yalta.

The people who run the show behind the scene; namely, the international monopoly capitalists, in reality are very unhappy people because as long as they feel it is their job to set themselves up as masters of everyone else they will never be able to be happy. In the midst of all their fervent strife for power and their imaginations of splendor and feeling themselves destined to lead all humanity, they are very unhappy persons indeed. We find after all that their international industrial interests and power aspirations have built a house of cards over their heads which will fall over and bury them in the final analysis.

After the initial forced evacuation of the German people from that territory the Polish and Russian people saw that they had made a mistake, for they did not know how to run the remaining industries. My father, along with many other German people, was held back and forced to work as a manager in one of his former plants. He earned an amount of money in one month equal to the cost of one pound of butter.

Adverse Conditions Teach Improvisation

In those early years after the war there was almost nothing available to be bought as practically no stores were in existence. Our moral and economic survival came under test at that time.

We found that a person learns many things which he never thought he would or could do when he is put under the acid test of survival. He loses his specialization and branches out into many different areas of making a living. Under such circumstances people really learn how to improvise, and this is one of the great arts of life which will always come in handy.

We were able to secure a limited amount of wool for knitting needs by unravelling old socks, mittens and sweaters after cutting off the worn-out areas. We would end up with a pile of small pieces of wool which we would knot together and roll into a ball. Then we were able to knit new woolen garments.

We actually made our clothes out of potato sacks. We fabricated our own shoes from old automobile inner tubes and tires and various other items we could lay our hands on. We built our own bicycles out of various scrap parts we found lying around the countryside and on rubbish piles. Those bicycles were made from parts of many different types of bicycles. We did not have the comfort of riding on inflated tires, but had to ride them on the rim and on cobbled streets. Can you imagine what a rattling that made! However, even that seemed like paradise for us children.

People who lived in an area where there was good snow cover in the wintertime found skis, snowshoes and sleds very helpful. Some were able to use a large dog such as a St. Bernard, a goat or a cow as a draft animal.

Joys of a Simple Life

We found that the simple life brought along with it many joys that in a more sophisticated environment were not so much part of us. Smaller things took on a new meaning and we became more thankful for the little things of everyday life. It was not long until we started to improvise by cutting old garden hoses apart, filling them with sand and putting them on the bicycles securely by sewing them together. Riding those bicycles with the hoses really made a difference—and what an experience that was!

Our Unconventional Methods in the
Absence of Medical Facilities

Earlier in this book I mentioned my encounter with serious illness—an illness which would trouble me for many more years. While spending our five years under the Communist terror regime there were no medical facilities we could call upon whatsoever. Fortunately, my aunt had a knowledge of herbs and curing diseases by simple home remedies. To our amazement, the sores on my foot and troubles which I struggled with for many months received greater and faster relief through the herbal treatment than they had through medical salves and treatments. We used narrow-leaf plaintain which we washed in pure water and dried with a clean towel. After this we crushed and rubbed it between our hands and then pressed the juice into the wounds. It produced an immediate healing of wounds which had been running for a long time. Since small bone splinters had been left in the foot from the operation quickly performed under emergency conditions at the very end of the war, the foot would swell up and reopen after terrible pain, so there was a need for cleansing and purification of the inner system of the foot.

Later, while I suffered terrible pain again when no medical help was available, an old forester about eighty-one years old visited us. He told my mother that there was no need for me to suffer in such a way or for her to go through those agonies with me. He advised us to go to the forest and dig loam or mud (because loam does not contain any stones) after removing the upper layer (about half a foot thick). Then we took that loam and mixed it up with water until it became a thick, pasty substance and applied it on and well around the afflicted part about the thickness of two fingers. Then some clean cotton cloths were wrapped around it, bandages placed over the cloths and left on until the mud had become dry. The dried mud was removed and fresh, moist mud applied. This treatment opened the pores and produced a suction which pulled out impure substances from the body through the wounds and pores and gave me definite, immediate and great relief. At times when there was a danger that the soil might be impure, I would put a small piece of gauze over the open wound before applying the mud.

Our Unconventional Methods in the Absence of School Facilities

During these five years there were no schools available to the German children. There was hardly any time left for school as the available time was occupied by jobs and various tasks needed to survive. The only schooling we received during those years other than the practical, everyday life was some teaching my grandfather gave a number of German children (myself included) in various subjects.

When thinking back on the amazing way my grandfather handled the education of the remaining German children in the territory, I still marvel at his endurance. Day after day he would ride long distances on his bicycle, as this was the most that was available for us as far as transportation media was concerned. He would do this summer and winter, even though the streets would at times be covered by deep snow and he would only be able to ride at times and push the bicycle throughout portions of the way. He would have alternate routes and take care of various areas on different days. He did this in spite of getting close to eighty years of age. Since there was no textbook material available, he would collect and accumulate all kinds of various old textbooks he could lay his hands on and then he would make many handwritten excerpts from various books which he then would distribute to the children and also have them copy some of the same in order to provide them with textbook material. I might add at this point that this educational material was far superior to that which is being handed out in the schools today. This also helped the children to appreciate the textbooks more because of their personal participation in their production (unlike the situation of today).

Grandfather was always active with his mind. He would be thinking, writing or reading, and no doubt this also kept him young. We find when people keep active with their minds, learning, improving and finding new and better ways in life, this keeps them younger. When a person starts to stagnate in his mind, this is usually the time when the body will also stagnate, which is only logical, as our entire body is being controlled by our thinking mechanism.

At a later time when coming to West Germany we found that the lessons provided by my grandfather, combined with the practical life and training we had received during those years, were not so bad after all: it took me only about half a year to catch up, and this after approximately six years without formal schooling!

There is an important lesson for us here as we are now living in a day and age where employers request more and more papers and certificates of their employees and where universities and schools engage in a theoretical study, leaving out the practical aspects almost entirely. We find that an education of theoretical things in combination with practical things has a very great value.

Solving Our Food Problem

The food situation would have been a catastrophe to supermarket shoppers. There was practically no food to be bought in those days. We found our supplies by picking berries and mushrooms in the mountains. We had a small garden where we had various fruit such as currants, gooseberries and cherries, as well as strawberries, potatoes, tomatoes and many other products. We used nettles as spinach which, by the way, is very healthful and very tasty if prepared properly. We used dandelion leaves and other wild edible greens for our salads. We had one goat and three chickens which supplied us with milk, meat and eggs. It was important to have only economical animals as there were no resources for fancy livestock and no time available to invest in that type of undertaking. Such easy-to-care-for animals provided people not only with food but also with leather, which they could prepare with just a few added items.

All of the foods I mentioned were fresh products, and from those we could conserve for the wintertime. Many of the mushrooms we sliced into thin pieces and hung on a string in a warm room or in the sunshine to dry. They were later added to meat dishes and made into delicious soups. We also were able to dry some fruits and vegetables, such as pears and apples, in a similar way. Many other vegetables, such as potatoes, carrots, etc., would keep through the winter imbedded in some soil or sand in specially constructed bins in our cellar.

We were able to secure wheat by gathering the heads from the fields after the grain had been harvested. We rubbed them on an old-fashioned washboard placed in a container so the kernels would be separated and collected. Then on a windy day we winnowed the wheat by slowly pouring it into another container placed about two feet below. These wheat kernels were ground for bread, cereal, etc. Even a simple coffee grinder will do.

Behavior Patterns of People Under Survival Conditions

We experienced in Germany that when the system broke down, uneducated people living in our mansion just absolutely messed up everything. Honey pots were placed on the grand piano and honey dripped into the inner parts of the piano and onto the genuine Persian carpets. Things were banged and smashed up and the formerly beautiful estate was completely demolished and had become almost unrecognizable.

A very important point to realize in the case of a general breakdown is that men will become worse than beasts when they do not have food for their bellies, and they will be ready to pounce upon their neighbor, tearing him apart for just a piece of bread. We have seen under Communism how even our own relatives and apparent friends betrayed us when it came to a showdown. For instance, my father was able to bring with him a number of suitcases with the most valuable items in our household in Breslau such as genuine furs, jewelry, good clothing and good shoes, as he made several trips between Breslau and our small mountain hideout house. Those personal effects were hidden in the center of a woodshed on the premises and firewood was stored around those belongings. We thought that of course those items were perfectly secure from theft or takeover by the foreign troops invading. One day two Russian Communist soldiers questioned my uncle about those very belongings and it was hard for us to understand how they had knowledge of them. They took a gun, turned it around and started knocking down my uncle, threatening him if he would not tell them where those goods were stored. Naturally, before surrendering his life, my uncle told those Communists where the items had been stored. They immediately ordered him to remove the firewood and left with all those goods, after telling my uncle that they were told about them by relatives of ours living right next door. Therefore, as you make survival preparations, do not disseminate information to more people than you absolutely have to.

On the other hand, we found that Russian soldiers gave German children bread thickly spread with butter and other good things. One Polish person gave me dried meat and a supply of cookies in a kind gesture.

Generalizing

This again will prove my point that we cannot draw national boundary lines when we talk about the good and bad character of people. We find there are good and bad people scattered everywhere and I find no discrimination in myself against any certain nationality. I have met a lot of wonderful people wherever I have travelled around the world in nearly one hundred lands, although there have been a few who were unsympathetic.

It seems a tragedy when we remember what was done to the Japanese and German people in general in the United States during the Second World War, for instance, much of it in a propaganda effort to fuel the war machinery.

A NEW LIFE

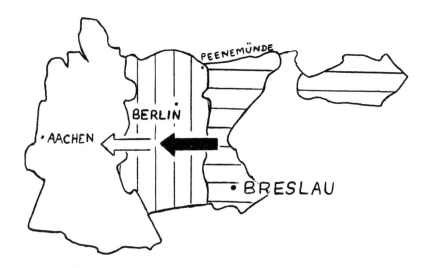

IN WEST GERMANY

 East Germany

Ceded to Russia and Poland during the Yalta and Potsdam Conferences

Chapter 4

A New Life
in West Germany

In 1950 we were finally able to make our way to West Germany in a train sponsored by the Red Cross. For eight years after this, German people could not leave the Polish-occupied territory of former Germany. When arriving in West Germany, we had not much more than just the clothes on our backs. Again we had to start from scratch.

Ethical Business Practices Pay Off

This time it was my father's good reputation among his former business associates which helped us to get back again on our feet very quickly. It was remarkable how my father was able to keep his good standing with his business friends especially in the countries of Holland, Belgium and France, all of which countries were heavily involved in the Second World War. There had been much resentment against German people or Germany as a whole by the people of those countries because of that war, and my father had been the civilian administrator under the German government of the textile industry in these occupied countries which made his situation more critical.

At a time when we were in great need of friends for a new start in West Germany, many former business associates remembered that my father was one who had never sued anyone, never gypped anyone, always been fair in his dealings and always been ready to stretch out a helping hand to a person in need. A very rich business friend in Holland gave my father an automobile at a time when we did not even have any necessities of life, when we had just arrived from under Communism. This enabled my father to start immediately covering the West German territory in order to make contacts and restart his import-export and wholesale trading company in textiles which he had had in addition to the factories in the eastern territories.

A Free Enterprise System
Brings New Prosperity

Fortunately, the years in West Germany were blessed years businesswise because at that time we had an able Finance Minister by the name of Ludwig Erhard, who permitted the West German economy a freer reign. Many of the dampening influences, multitudes of which are now put upon the American businessman, were kept out of the German general market; in fact, there were many encouraging means initiated for that market. It was mainly because of this and of the encouragement of the spirit of individual enterprise in the German market plus loans from America (later repaid) that West Germany was able to recover from the disastrous blow of a Second World War so quickly, even in spite of the extensive dismantling by England, France, etc. and the tremendous reparation payments. Of course there was also the fact that Germany had rebuilt with new machinery and more modern equipment while England, for instance, had trouble competing on the market with its old and outdated equipment. Here the selfishness of those nations turned to their own detriment.

Breathtaking Experiences as a New Pilot

As West Germany moved ahead in its reconstruction and as people became more wealthy and materialistic, they also became more and more shortsighted and complacent. Probably because of my past experience, I was unable to find my place in a complacent society. I continued to live a dangerous, different and unorthodox life. As soon as possible I became one of the first pilots in West Germany after the war. While living in Belgium for some time, I chartered a 65-horse power Aeronca Chief from an aeronautical club. With this plane I started on a mission around Europe down to Africa. On the first leg of the journey I got into bad weather and found myself flying for half an hour over Paris at an altitude of about 240 feet. After I had followed the Seine River for a while, wondering how much longer I would live, I was able to make an emergency landing at a naval airport. Nearly every flight was another survival trip. Only old, outdated charts (1:1,-000,000) were available. On a flight to Gibraltar from Seville, Spain, I received red rocket signals which meant strictly no landing. With almost empty tanks I barely made it across the Mediterranean to Africa.

One flight took me around the northwestern corner of Spain by the name of Cape de Finisterre. The air turbulence was such that the plane became uncontrollable and again I met near disaster. On another flight I made an emergency landing at a United States Air Force base in France. I was greeted by machine guns pointed at me. When taken up to the tower I was overwhelmed by the impressive array of an international warning system.

A 150-pound friend who accompanied me on these trips was so badly shaken by all those experiences that he lost weight and was reduced to only 100 pounds when we returned home.

Constantly On Guard

These trips taught me once more how fleeting life actually can be, and to a certain extent you lose fear of death when being brought into such situations frequently. The need of being on guard daily in order to survive was constantly before me. If in some of those flight situations while piloting the plane I would have been negligent for even a moment, it could have meant my sure death. As our present society is lying in its death agonies, we again will face the need of being continuously on guard lest we perish.

Methods Learned Under Adversity Prove Helpful Again

Now in West Germany while I pushed myself in an effort to make up lost school knowledge, the trouble with the osteomyelitis in my foot started to flare up once more as I did not get sufficient exercise. I had shoved the natural way of life into the background, for we had again entered a more sophisticated way of life. I was finally taken into a hospital as the pain I was suffering was unbearable and I was becoming so weak I could hardly carry on any longer, being unable to sleep nights at all. I spent two weeks in the hospital under the treatment of a famous professor. During that period of time I was given forty injections of aureomycin, streptomycin and penicillin. My body was honeycombed with injection scabs and I was given alcohol poultices. My condition was not improving, however, and as a result the medical staff decided they would perform an operation on me.

At this hour of trouble I remembered the simple things I had learned in my past life. We told the professor that I was not going to be subjected to an operation as I knew I would be bedridden after this for a long period of time and then go on crutches for another long period of time if that were to be performed. We made it clear that I was to go back home and that we were going to apply the loam poultices as we had done in years gone by, telling him how much relief they had given me before. As my mother pushed me out of the hospital in a wheelchair to bring me home, the professor warned her, saying, "Mrs. Schneider, I am warning you, it is dangerous what you do." He said further, however, that if those loam poultices helped me they would apply them in the hospital.

After coming home I applied the above-described poultices for three days and three nights continuously. After the three days and nights I was back on my feet, restored to health. One of the first things I did was to visit the hospital, and while entering I saw the professor standing down the hallway talking to a lady. As soon as the lady left, I approached the professor. His eyes opened wide in amazement and he said, "Mr. Schneider, I cannot believe it! May I see your foot?" I was glad to show it to him. However, there were no mud poultices applied in that hospital as he had promised. Simple treatments, such as this, would bring no glory or money to either the professor or the hospital, so apparently the promise was conveniently forgotten.

NEW START

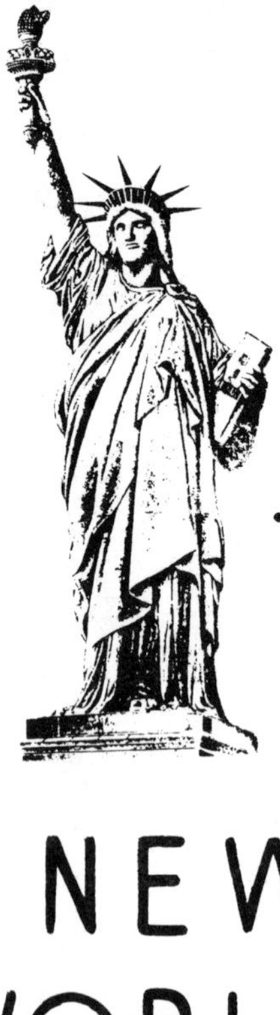

IN THE

NEW WORLD

Chapter 5

New Start in The
New World

An Immigrant in New York

I now arrived as an immigrant in the United States and a new life began in New York City. I found a job the first day I looked for work. When working in the office of a forwarding agency as an assistant import manager, I was left alone at my desk as the manager had left the office for a rather lengthy period of time. Many calls kept coming in on the telephone and I had quite a time conversing with the callers as I had not had time to ground myself in the English language. I was able to manage somehow and a few months later I had obtained enough working knowledge of English to get along nicely. I held a couple of secular jobs in addition to starting a business of my own, which I knew did not give me fulfillment for the rest of my life but were just bridges for making money quickly to enable me to move on to something better. I had thoroughly detested the pent-up feeling and the rush-rush style of a life in that big city; however, I tried to make the best of it by frequent outings to the Metropolitan Opera, beautiful museums and other points of interest this city had to offer.

New York—Goodbye!

Soon after having saved up some money, I was on my way again—this time with the Volkswagen "bug" I had bought and remodelled by taking the right seat apart, coordinating the front seat with the back seat as a bed, filling in the back seat with a wedge-shaped pillow. In this way I had a "home on wheels."

I was on a survival trip, which further added to my knowledge of how to get by with just bare necessities and living extensively off the land. I travelled over five months for $160, which included my outlays for gasoline and infrequent car repairs. No sooner had I left the big city behind where a person does not even know his next-door neighbor than I ran into the friendly folks living in smaller communities and the open country. I became a guest in many different homes. Once while following up on an invitation, I was greeted at the door by the head of the household who had just been playing with his many children on the floor, saying that it was a lot of fun to play with the little children. This lieutenant commander really made me feel at home, saying, "Stay as long as you want."

My Individuality Finds Greater Expression in Life

I soon found out that by leaving a pre-patterned and established life in Germany behind, I had found a much more interesting life. While still living with my parents in Germany I was pressed into their particular lifestyle, their social activities, including all the various boring friends of their higher elite. This made it nearly impossible for me to develop my own interests and to find true fulfillment and development of my own ideals, hopes and dreams. Now I was travelling in this big, beautiful land, finding new challenges and experiences daily. When I got tired of visiting with people I would head for some of the beautiful national parks, monuments and national forests such as the Shenandoah National Park. There I would pull my car in some lonely camping spot, staying away from the overcrowded camping facilities. I would bed myself down for the night, opening the little sunroof of my car. My eyes

would look right into the firmament and the last impression I received before falling asleep would be the myriads of sparkling stars with the background of a dark sky. Upon waking up in the early mornings I would have another look into that magnificent scenery, the birds singing all around me as if to join in with my joyful heart to greet another lovely day.

It was in moments such as this that my life was automatically revalued. Things which seemed to be important to me earlier dropped into the background for I came to look at them in a different, and may I say greater, perspective; therefore, they lost their appeal as now I had found things which interested me more and which enveloped my being more fully.

Nature Provides

I would develop a deep interest in nature around me. I would watch the animals such as deer and notice how they obtained a ready food supply to keep them going. There were certain mosses growing on trees relished by those deer. I would try them and find them just as delicious as nuts. More and more I would develop a pattern of living off the land, just as nature provides it. My food bills would get smaller consistently. Extra food which was needed was obtained in supermarkets as I did not go to the expense of eating in restaurants. There were many products I would find in the open country such as nuts, apples, oranges and mangoes—all free of charge. These items were found along the wayside at vacant homesteads and in abandoned orchards. Many times I would not drive very far and I would find places where food in abundance would be scattered on the ground under some trees. I would take some boxes and load them up with those products and again I would have a supply for days. Once while travelling in Florida I ran across a forgotten tree with most of the beautiful mangoes lying on the ground and a few left on the tree. Again I loaded in and drove off with the little Volkswagen filled with boxes of precious, golden mangoes with a beautiful fragrance and an ever-so-sweet taste. For days I ate nothing but mangoes. I felt much better for it. What a way to cleanse my body!

Estranged From the Land

It is hard to understand why people will rush to a super-market to buy preserved food which has been demineralized through heat treatments, conversion and chemicalization while in their own yards the nuts, apples and other products are lying underneath their trees loaded with fresh vitamins and minerals. No wonder the hospitals are filled with sick people! It brings to mind a statement a doctor friend of mine made some time ago when he said that the disease of cancer will spread in such catastrophic proportions right here in the United States that it will make the bubonic plague of the Middle Ages look like a picnic!

Roaming the Great Outdoors

On this five-month journey I would roam the mountains, study the plants, visit with interesting people, hike in beautiful parks and botanical gardens and swim in many lovely lakes and rivers; I just went from day to day as I pleased. What an interesting way to live when a person never knows what the next day will bring, yet each day would be filled with new and exciting experiences.

The Dolphin—Man's Protector From Sharks

On a visit to the marine park in St. Augustine, Florida, and other various marine parks in the Florida Keys, I watched the antics of the dolphins and marvelled about some of the tales told about this mysterious aquatic creature. The scientists declare it to be the most intelligent creature in the world and the U.S. Navy has even used it in underwater warfare! I was told that an elderly lady once paddled out in the ocean in a small boat and dolphins pushed her boat safely back to shore. Another time after a small child had fallen from a boat dolphins appeared and brought it back to the beach.

The dolphin is one of the greatest enemies of the shark. It is comforting to know that if you swim in the ocean where dolphins are present you won't have to fear sharks as dolphins will immediately attack any shark that ventures in the area. A

dolphin can kill a shark very quickly by swimming with great speed and piercing the soft underbelly of the shark with its flint-hard nose which penetrates some distance due to the momentum gathered in the dolphin's approach. It will also ram the shark's gills.

I have seen a dolphin leap as high as twenty-one feet out of the water. At another time I swam in a small manmade lake with a dolphin that has been featured in many movies and is claimed to be the highest-leaping dolphin known. I was warned that barracudas were in the pond, but I felt fairly safe because of the presence of the dolphin. Soon after I started swimming, the dolphin came and began to play with me, swimming and rolling all around me. It dove under me and leapt around, shouting like a child. After a while I "played dead," breathing quietly, to see what the dolphin would do. At first I noticed an increase in the sweet-sounding cries of the dolphin. Then it became quiet and nipped at my hand, like a dog seeking attention. I knew the dolphin had come to see whether I was really dead.

The Fabulous Undersea World

Another time I marvelled at the fantastic undersea life I found while diving around coral reefs at such places as Lu Key off the east coast of Florida; Penecamp Underwater State Park, Florida; Papeete, Tahiti and the Outer Barrier Reef, Australia. This world-famous barrier reef is one of the longest coral reefs in the world, reaching from around Brisbane, Australia, to New Guinea, and suggests that at one time in earth's history these areas were connected. It is also suggestive of the possibility that at one time the six thousand islands of Indonesia were connected to Asia, making a chain from Asia to Australia. Since animal life in Australia is completely different from animal life in Asia, science is unable to corroborate this.

As I dove into the sparkling water, I saw many beautiful tropical fish and other forms of marine life. The colors were vibrant. I could see many lovely shells and watched sea animals, anemones and sea worms waving and bowing with the movement of the sea. It was a magnificent sight—an entirely different world!

At some areas I encountered swordfish, swam among barracudas and much other fascinating marine life.

The American Rut and Ensuing Chaos

The least desirable life I could think of is the patterned life so many people live—everything is planned a long time ahead in detail and every day is about the same, no changes, no excitement, just everything in a dreary rut. No wonder there are so many uninteresting individuals around! They are victims of a commercial and political propaganda machine which has stamped out a lot of mechanical puppets who are dancing to the tunes, whims and fancies of that small cadre. Sad to say, but most of them don't even know it. When flying over some city in my small plane, looking down upon some main street plaza and seeing the rushing to and fro of many people like ants in an ant hill, I wonder what it is all about. What are those individuals trying to attain and are they attaining what they really want? I sincerely doubt it, because most of them are engaged in a debilitating effort to strengthen and maintain their economic situation—a situation which has already had a severe shaking and which soon is going to turn into a nightmare for those who have not taken time to familiarize themselves with the underlying causes and trends for the oncoming monetary and economic disaster and therefore will be caught unprepared.

PART II
HEARKEN AMERICA!

A
EUROPEAN
SYMPATHIZES
WITH THE
AMERICAN
PEOPLE

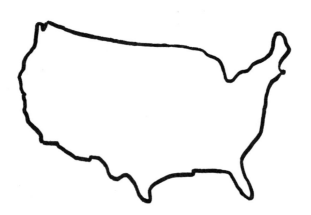

Chapter 6

A European Sympathizes
With
the American People

A Plain Comparison

At this time I would like to draw a parallel. Many of you will remember the giant ocean liner "Titanic" which at that time was the pride of the British Empire. It was declared to be unsinkable as it had been constructed in such a way that the various sections of the ship were divided into various chambers which could at any time be closed off should the ship develop a leak anywhere along the hull. One day that vessel was on its maiden voyage from England to New York, endeavoring to obtain the blue ribbon which was given to the ship making that crossing in the shortest period of time. Some of the wealthiest representatives of society were aboard on that particular trip. There was a very festive mood aboard; everyone was enjoying life to the fullest. There were parties, big dinners, concerts and dances to entertain the passengers. No one with even the slightest sprinkling of imagination would have at that time believed that the journey would end as it did. Everything was going fine and according to schedule. The boat was well on its way to achieve the prize and there was certainly no reason for pessimism.

At some point during this trip, however, warning voices were heard. It was made known that there were giant icebergs seemingly obstructing the path ahead of the vessel. Those voices of warning were unwelcomed and it seemed as though they were considered to be spoilers of fun and the great hope for achievement. Repeatedly the captain was cautioned of the danger ahead. Drunk with overenthusiasm and overconfidence, however, he constantly ignored the warnings. The entire power of that gigantic vessel was concentrated in him and it would have been a simple act of command on his part to reduce the power in order to slow down the ship and look out for the icebergs ahead. Unfortunately, this was not done and there were no precautionary measures taken whatsoever until the catastrophe suddenly hit. The most illustrious ocean liner the world had ever seen collided with an iceberg. It found its watery grave on the bottom of that great ocean, taking with it more than two thirds of the people aboard. The fantastic undertaking ended in a sudden tragedy.

This time I would like to compare the United States of America with the "Titanic." For a long time the United States with its war machinery, economy (industrial might, American dollar, etc.) and great resources has been looked upon nationally as well as internationally as indestructible. But for some time now many warning voices have been heard—warnings by people who know that it is impossible to keep pouring out American life blood by continuous wars on foreign soil, big foreign-aid programs, stifling socialistic programs at home and mushrooming welfare programs without any ill effects. Historians have pointed out that there has never been an empire in the history of the world with such high rates of taxes, delinquency and divorce which still kept standing.

A country found itself the dominant nation of the world but more by chance than by plan. It found it difficult to aid so many other nations; the strain upon its own economy was increasingly greater. It was necessary to increase taxes time after time in order to finance its programs. The increased taxes forced prices up and wages followed suit. The working man was not able to compete with products manufactured by cheap foreign labor and demanded high import duties. The government was forced to subsidize the workers to make up the difference between the value of the products they manufactured and their wages. Eventually many workers realized they could live off the subsidy and quit work altogether to live a life of ease. Those who continued to work demanded shorter hours and even higher wages. All these things became more and more complicated and eventually the average man could not comprehend it and he turned more and more to the spectacular shows promoted by the power elite.

I have spoken of Imperial Rome just prior to its collapse. The conditions are parallel to those prevalent in the United States today.

Edward Gibbon in his book *The Decline and Fall of the Roman Empire* pointed out five major reasons why Rome fell:

1. Higher and higher taxes, the spending of public money for free bread and circuses for the populace.
2. The undermining of the dignity and sanctity of the home, which is the basis for human society.
3. The mad craze for pleasure and sports, becoming more exciting, more brutal and more immoral each year.
4. The building of great armaments when the true enemy was within; the decay of individual responsibility.
5. The decay of religion; faith fading into mere form and losing touch with life and losing power to guide the people.

It is very clear that those five conditions have been in existence in the United States for many years now. The powers in control in America as well as the general populace have consistently ignored those warnings. They have thought, and many of them still think, that it is impossible for a nation such as America ever to fall—just as the captain thought on board the "Titanic." Those who still live in plenty, having no lack of food, having sufficient finances to purchase their needs, seemingly see no reason to panic. However, the possibility is great that the great splendor and might of this great nation will come to just as sudden an end as in the case of the "Titanic". The results of this will be every bit as dramatic or fatal. America has been referred to as "the land of the free" and when it falls the repercussions will be felt in every empire around the globe.

I have issued warnings along this line in my many lectures within the United States as well as abroad since 1961. Some thought it to be impossible in those years, but with the events which have transpired within just the last few years, many of those persons have seen the need to re-examine their stand and have come to a change of attitude. Fortunately, past events, as tragic as they have been for the United States, have not yet led us to sudden and complete chaos; but there is still some time left for those who have awakened to prepare at last. The present monetary system of the United States, as well as our economy, will fade as surely as night follows day, yet it might still be hard for some to see. It will take some research in economics and history to enable a person to get a plain and overall view of those facts. There are some very excellent books on the market which will give you an insight into the necessary economic understanding, such as the books written by Harry Browne, Harry Schultz and Franz Pick.

As the repercussions from the money manipulators' mismanagement of the economy continue to increase in number and magnitude, more persons are becoming aware of how vulnerable the United States—and, indeed, the entire world—is to economic adversity. No nation is "depression-proof" as political and economic leaders would have us believe, and continuing inflation will only hasten the inevitable consequences of long-term fiscal folly.

About half of the time the average wage earner works to pay his hidden taxes. During this time he is a financial slave to the nonproductive international monetary speculators and their various international and national (government) agencies which hand out the taxpayers' money wildly for their own egocentric and power-hungry programs. The idea that the worker is being exploited by the capitalists serves as a fine hideout for the real powers behind the scene. Part-time wage-earner slaves who might be satisfied and therefore more productive are a greater asset to that power elite rather than full-time slaves, such as in the Soviet Union, who are not satisfied and therefore much less productive. They endeavor to strip the common man of as much as they can as long as he maintains full production.

The American public is kept in a state of permanent confusion by means of continuous propaganda and counter-propaganda by an endless parade of crusades, issues and conflicting viewpoints and by economic as well as political smokescreens. It is therefore especially necessary for any person who does not want to become part of the crowd being buried in this avalanche to take the time to keep himself abreast of the inner workings and machinations in order to keep his overall view.

What is Your Perspective?

Some time ago I flew with my small plane close to one of the Caribbean islands. There were some beautiful coral reefs; a number of small pleasure boats had anchored and people were swimming and diving in the area. While circling over that territory I suddenly discovered several sharks right close to the people in the water. By continuing to circle over them I tried to warn them, but they did not understand. I knew the fatal danger those people were in, but they, not knowing their danger, continued with their recreational activities because their view was limited. Because of my altitude, I had a much further and panoramic view and was able to see many more things than the people in the water. There is a great need for many folks today to get out of the small environment in which they have entrapped themselves and to get a further-reaching view by studying and understanding the real issues of the day. *Then after a person receives this perspective he will know how to plan the various details of his life, deciding which things to eliminate, which things to change and which new directions to take.*

The Big Overpopulation Myth

Coming from Europe, I became very much amazed that in the United States we would hear so much about the problem of overpopulation. That seems outright ridiculous to me. If we consider that America is eighty-one times as large as Germany, only has three times as many people and there are countries which are even more densely populated than Germany, then we will understand the silliness of this artificially created anxiety of being overpopulated here in America.

In the United States the population is concentrated only in certain areas such as the northeastern part around Chicago, Detroit, Philadelphia, New York, Washington, D.C., the east coast of Florida, certain portions of the Gulf of Mexico area and the southern portion of the west coast of California. Much of the rest of the United States is still vacant land which could support many more people. In fact, there are many areas in the world which could support and which are or have been looking for more immigrants such as New Zealand, Australia, Canada, Argentina and Brazil.

It is a scientific fact that if we were to use the know-how and finances which we are spending in expensive and destructive wars in an effort to irrigate many of the arid areas of the world, such as the western deserts of the United States and the Sahara Desert, then the earth could support yet many more lives. If we speak of overpopulation then we should direct our attention to India and China, since each country has between 600 million and 900 million people. Even at that, both countries would be amply able to support their populations if it were not for the preferred way of life and poverty as a backlash from the antiquated religion in India and for the proven fallacious Communist set-up in China. We find that Taiwan, the free part of China, a relatively small island, is well able to support its 16 million inhabitants and its economy equals, if not even supersedes, mainland China with its 830 million inhabitants.

Wastefulness

When travelling through the American land of vanishing plenty, I still get heavy hearted when I see how much waste there is. The food which is presently being thrown away in government and other installations, clubs, restaurants and schools every day could feed a vast portion of the poor people of this world.

When we add to this all the products which are being wasted in the farm belts of America and the many vegetables and fruits which end up rotting away on the ground because of lack of pickers or because of low prices, you could probably feed the world. At times when visiting university campuses I nearly get sick when I see how much of the food which the students carry to the tables on their trays remains uneaten and also winds up in the trash can.

Wastefulness has never brought any good, and unless we are willing to mend our ways it would almost seem that a crash would teach us some valuable lessons. It is amazing how fast we lose wastefulness when we start to go hungry and when we do not any longer have the necessities of everyday life. Under those conditions a person starts to utilize almost everything, just like the Indians. When they killed buffalo they used every little part of it, including the bones for arrowheads and even the sinews as thread, until the white man came and boasted of the numbers of buffalo he could kill in a day.

Breakdown of Family Life

Divorce is rapidly on the increase in the United States, an average of one divorce for every two and one-half marriages. This involves children in about sixty per cent of the broken homes, two thirds of whom are under ten years of age. Frequently these children are exposed to delinquent influences and many wind up in juvenile hall.

Many mothers now work, either as a result of divorce or to supplement the family income. With mother working, hundreds of thousands of children return home from school every day to an empty house. They must fend for themselves the best they can and the wholesome home atmosphere is missing altogether. The children feel insecure and do not know how to cope with problems that arise in the parents' absence. They turn for companionship to other children in the area or to the television set.

Most television programs during the late afternoon and evening hours feature violence. Such programs exert a powerful influence on children and teach them a set of moral and social values about violence which are not consistent with the standards of a civilized society. It is up to parents to remove this demoralizing influence and replace it by a wholesome, favorable home atmosphere.

As a European, I am used to finding lovely classical music or soothing and joyful popular music at any time of the day on the radio without interruption by commercials, so I find it particularly vexing to my spirit to find scarcely one good piece of music all day while dialing back and forth on my car radio. Knowing what tremendous influence music has upon the character and development of a person, it will not be difficult to understand how much the American radio has been used as an instrument to indoctrinate its listeners with the base motives of the powers behind the radio networks. It will indeed be difficult for a people subjected to the loud, insistent beat of African jungle music day after day to maintain a superior cultural pattern of life such as behooves our populace and not to find themselves eventually brought down to a behavior level such as we find in the dark jungle areas of Africa. We have a famous saying in the old country which states that "a person is formed by his environment." You cannot expect culture and sophistication from a chimpanzee; much less can you expect high hopes, dreams and aspirations from a people who are exposed to such a degrading media bombardment!

It is astounding how all the inventions of the white man have been turned as weapons against him, including his printing press, radio and television. It seems that the backward areas of this world, consisting mostly of African and Asian areas, are large recipients of our industrial plants which hopefully will not be turned against America and Europe after those continents have been toppled by one means or another.

The "United States" Reflects America

It was autumn of 1959. I was on board the ocean liner "United States" returning from a trip to the European continent. We were fighting heavy weather, waves billowing, storm howling and misty water blowing across the bridge of the mighty ship which was rolling and yawing heavily. Lack of depth in the fairly light ocean liner which could be converted speedily into a troop transport did not give it enough stabilizing effect. People on board were rather sick and unable to maneuver about properly. While visiting the rest room, I noticed another utterly sick passenger standing at the urinal freely vomiting. I was taken aghast by this pathetic sight, and although I addressed the man, he was unable to communicate other than by just grunting a four-letter word spelled "Hell." I had to smile as it properly described the situation.

While I sat on the promenade deck looking over the wild sea, an impressive array of past and present empires passed visually through my mind. My thoughts finally turned to the empire carrying the same name as the ship. I could see a similar rough sea ahead for that fair land. I could visualize people as sick and faint as the man I had met in that rest room, not any longer able to maneuver about sensibly. Knowing that there is very little equity for anything the American people own; that their financial and economic structure has steadily been eroding through massive foreign give-away programs, high tax structures, many wars and the Federal (private) Reserve System; that their spiritual life has suffered because of the continually increasing pressure of meeting their financial obligations, I realized the shallow draft of the ship would indeed be comparable to the shallow foundation left under our empiric system and suddenly it dawned on me how fast this entire structure could be overturned by even a minor storm.

Intravenous Feeding

We have already seen the effects of government-managed economy in numerous shortages and long-term deliveries for which the government is trying to place the blame on business. This time the crash is being held up far beyond the time it would have occurred as the international banking system exerts much more complete control today than it did decades ago. It is now using its power to delay the economic readjustment horrors to a time of its own choosing so it can use this in combination with other trickeries as mentioned elsewhere in this book.

As a whole, the United States people are very poor—most of the things they possess are being paid for in installments while the real capital is owned by a few and much of it has been shipped abroad. In Europe people have jewelry, libraries, brick houses and other valuable items. The United States market was able to endure more adversity because of our many resources than the much more dependent market of a small European nation.

Blessings of Oil

Some students of the American monetary system might wonder why the dollar has been able to keep from falling apart completely. Fortunately, America has many points in its favor. One point is the enormous oil resources we have in this country. One of the reasons why Switzerland still accepts United States dollars is that it feels the dollar might not fail so quickly because in further confrontations with foreign oil-producing countries the United States will continue to be backed by its own power supply while many of the European countries, including Switzerland, have practically no oil. This would leave Europe much more vulnerable in that field which naturally would have its reflection on the currency. No matter how great the United States resources are, however, they cannot continue to make up for the irresponsible fiscal policy being followed by the United States Government.

Recession!—World War III?

Bankruptcies in 1975 reached the highest rate since the 1930's; in fact, public opinion polls indicated that people looked at the economic outlook with greater gloom than at any time before. As unemployment in the United States in 1975, for instance, had reached 9.2%, consumer prices were up considerably and there seemed to be much unemployment ahead (unless we again go to war, which is a distinct possibility), it is understandable why many people were discouraged and ready to give up.

How close we came to a war is to be seen by a statement from a European source: Some policies of the United States have served to widen the breach in the Middle East rather than heal it. It was reported that military intervention against the Arabian states was already planned. American and English aircraft carriers had been stationed in the Persian Gulf for weeks. Verbal threats were issued only after the plan had been discarded (apparently temporarily). The reasons for the discarding of the plan were to be seen in the position France took and in the facts that the American leaders started to realize that Europe would not go along with such a plan and that the Arabians would blow up their oil wells.

King Hussein made the statement that this time the war in the Middle East will be a total war. Both sides have terrible weapons and the big powers will most likely be involved. The United States will fight on the side of Israel in such a conflict—a war caused by a combination of interests such as the monopolistic powers and international finance (both also behind Communism) represent. Some of the international monopolists cannot stand to see the Arab nations prospering through oil at the expense of the international industries which they control. Any genuine nationalization of foreign holdings, such as foreign oil companies, on the part of the Arabian national governments takes tremendous fortunes and money controls out of the hands of these international vampires. Therefore, through the nationalization of such oil companies on the soil of Arabian countries they are not able to exert the direct control they have been used to for a long time. It is easy to understand that they would be in favor of an arms engagement against these Middle East countries. Zionist national as well as international forces will be glad to join in for similar reasons (such as the Arab-Israel conflict). The way for American popular support has been prepared through the artificially created energy (oil and gas) crunch in the United States. Further conditioning of the American mind in this regard is continually being done. At the same time the most militant and exclusive of the world religions will be weakened and brought to a readiness of cooperation when the coming economic-religious world dictatorship appears on the scene.

Rise to the Challenge

There are many incentives open to the individual who wants to rise to the challenge rather than being overcome. In order to do so, he will have to have a good understanding of the true overall aspects of the economy and other related matters in order to survive the coming rough waves which are ahead, just as a swimmer must be a master in that sport in order to keep himself afloat when the sea gets rough. To draw another example from nature, an eagle which encounters head wind on his flight could let his wings hang down and stop struggling with the elements and find himself pressed to the ground; but rather than this, an eagle will rise to the challenge by turning his wings upward into the head wind. Instead of being pressed lower, he is being pushed higher and higher; the higher he flies, the better view he receives. An overall perspective is the all-important one in order to maintain yourself in a national and global oncoming crash.

So if you as an individual look at any of the difficulties which confront you now and in the future with the attitude of using them as stepping stones to better things rather than submitting to them in defeat, then you will find that those difficulties will turn to your advantage instead to your destruction. This is a secret which nearly all great men in this world, whether they have been great men in the spiritual realm or in the financial realm, have applied. Unfortunately, the former idealistic way of being a self-made man—following your personal incentive by complying with your own individualistic ability in bringing this also to an expression in your job (often being self-employed, thus having more of a challenge and your own disposition of your time)—has gone.

Which Form of Government?

Many words have been written in defense of one form of government or another. Some believe that a democracy is the right form of government, others a republic and others an anarchy, monarchy or dictatorship.

While travelling in so many countries and observing, I have come to the conclusion that it is wrong to set a general pattern and to tell the whole world that just one particular thing is the right one just because we have found it to be so. I find that there is a need for variety of government because there is a great variety in the mentality of people. For example, a free form of government which has been the government of the people, for the people and by the people has been and is the most ideal form of government for the inventive, productive and individualistic type of people which have for the greatest part come to the United States. Therefore, this type of government has been a great blessing. This type of government, however, might not be the right type in countries where people do not have this type of character. In areas where people are rather lethargic and lazy in their mentality, a dictatorship by a good man can be of great value and benefit for all involved because that type of people need a firm hand as a motivating force. Then achievements and a higher standard of living will be reached there also.

A Provocative Question

May I raise the question here: Would it not be tragic if the mentality of the American people would become (or rather has become) such as not to deserve their former type of government any longer? Could it be that here we see some of the true reasons for the decline and fall of our great republic? Maybe we should say in the final analysis that each nation ends up with the type of government it deserves.

Assessment

Having observed the fast-changing pattern of our national government, I have concluded that there has been a rapid change in the American mentality. The latter, of course, is very obvious even to a casual observer.

We could therefore conclude that the only feasible and workable way of a return to a sane government is by having a big enough return of people to this inventive and creative pioneer spirit. If such spirit is strong enough, then it will be impossible that this will remain unreflected in the national government. However, it may well be possible that this is hypothetical since a people who have left such a spirit might not be able any longer to come to the conclusion that this is the ideal set-up to be sought after and therefore might not initiate such a move. That may well be the reason why practically every empire in the history of this world was not able to rejuvenate itself after it had passed the zenith of its power. We would hate to pass the conclusions of history as an unconditional indictment upon this fair land.

Depression, Dictatorship and Monopoly Capitalists

History has shown us over and over again that some of the most destructive results of a depression, inflation and inflationary depression have been a serious moral decay of the people under its influence and such countries have finally ended up in dictatorships. It is a dictatorship which is favored by the international monopoly capitalists who, by the way, are bitter enemies of free enterprise because such totalitarian governments form an established captive market for them. Any student of factual historical records and books with an in-depth study of the underlying factors involved in historical makings will know for a fact that Communism would have been a failure soon after its inception if it had not been consistently sponsored, financed and diplomatically recognized by those very monopoly capitalists in free western nations, especially in the United States. (For further study on this read *Wall Street and the Bolshevik Revolution*, by Anthony C. Sutton, *The Naked Capitalist*, by W. Cleon Skousen, as well as many other books on the market.)

Again the large monopoly companies profited through the fixed exchange rates which kept the American dollar artificially high. This made the importation of products much more lucrative than if the exchange rate had been set by the general market, because in this way they were able to sell their products more cheaply on the American market. Only large companies, which could afford having branch companies in various foreign cheap labor countries, were the ones that profited from the situation. They produced abroad and then imported their products to the United States, which at the same time also hurt local factories, the local labor forces and the balance of payments. This might have been one further reason why the devaluation of the dollar had been held up as it was.

At a point when the government (secretly run by the monopoly capitalists) does not any longer represent the interests of its people, you must not any longer confuse it with your country. They have become two different entities. For many years our freedoms, standards and material blessings have been nibbled away, bit by bit, by some of the double-minded persons in positions of leadership or influence. They have pretended to be modern "Robin Hoods," stealing from those who work for a living and giving to those who arc too lazy to work, by means of higher taxes, inflation and various social programs. Many government leaders who seek to control others believe that the general public is too dumb to care for its own affairs properly. If the general public cannot handle its own affairs, how can the government—which is made up of individuals from the general public—properly control others' affairs? Mongrelizing of races has been encouraged, yet these same people take pride in the pedigrees of their pets and livestock. Those who stand up for what is right are booed and discredited. Criminals are coddled and their victims persecuted. Busing of school children to distant schools and the increasing use of pollution devices which gulp gas are insisted upon even though this nation experiences a gas shortage. Big businesses are greatly favored by laws that work a great hardship on small businesses and individual endeavors even though the government is supposedly trying to help the little fellow. There is a vast difference between government ventures and individual ventures in the economic realm. When a venture of an individual person fails, only a small number of people are affected; but when a government venture fails, as has happened many times, its effect can be disastrous upon the entire economy. Freedom of religion is preached, but yet the fundamental Christians are attacked and belittled. Money is taken from many collection plates all over the country and given to enemies of Christianity, even to groups who have not stopped at murder. (Doesn't the Bible state, "Thou shalt not kill?") Instead of seeking leadership from the choices offered to us by the Republican and Democratic parties, we should rather seek some honest, moral, God-fearing men who understand and believe the Constitution, and help them to become leaders even if it cannot be accomplished by either of the two major political parties. Let us not continue in a manner which can only lead us to complete destruction, but instead let us unite and shake off the things that pull us down and restore our nation to the greatness it once had!

We can rest assured that the selfishness of today's monopoly capitalists also will turn to their own self-destruction, and most assuredly the house of cards which they have built will fly apart and bury them in the not-too-distant future. We can compare the small elite of international monopoly capitalists, who have set themselves up to rule the world, with a chess player. His constant aim is to outwit the other person. He finds himself entangled in a spiderweb of thoughts, plans and possibilities. Out of my own experience when playing chess I have found the following to be true: When finding a definite pattern and possibility to beat the opponent (having thought out a good move to defeat the other fellow), all of my attention then is centered on that particular stage of the game. This very easily and many times does take my attention off some potentially dangerous moves of the opponent. Then, usually before completing my strategic moves, the opponent will have outflanked me and taken one or more of my chess pieces, in a surprise move.

It is a known fact of life that as a person becomes very sure of himself in certain things, his downfall soon follows. You might have heard the proverb "Beware of him who standeth lest he fall," and consider well that the fall usually coincides with the time period of a person feeling most secure. According to the pattern of life, therefore, we would conclude that this self-esteemed clique spoken of above will find themselves in quicksand just at a period of time when they believe themselves to be on safest ground. They will find just as the chess player has found out that while they were busy devising and implementing their devilish schemes, opponents suddenly will have outflanked them.

It will not be possible for them to suppress permanently the spirit of a Patrick Henry, for instance, who cried out, "Give me liberty or give me death." It is practically a proven fact that countries such as Soviet Russia and its satellites could not have continued their barbaric oppression of the people if it had not been for the help of western nations such as the United States, especially. Many times Communist Russia was put back on its feet by financial help and other recognitions from the United States. There is a very strong possibility that the international power brokers have permitted the American freedom, even though it is mostly a paper freedom these days, to continue thus far as they needed the know-how, the individual creativity and the freemarket system with its tremendous industrial output in order to support their slave camps and captive markets in other areas.

It has been a philosophical contention in those ranks to see how great a degree they can drive the American people with their various oppressive methods such as excessive taxation, inflation, red tape, various oppressive legislative regulations and many other harassments until it renders our system completely non-functionable. According to my understanding, it will be that time—that is, when we have reached the moment that our point of no return becomes fully assessable and noticeable to the people in the form of a final crash or sufficient monetary chaos—which will constitute the most critical period for these international pirates. There are several reasons for this:

1. If there is no nation or system on this earth left where the only true functional system, that of a "free general market," is any longer functional, then those international financiers will not be able to use the know-how and industrial capacity of such an individualistic society as their financial and materialistic back-up tools to keep this world under bondage. In other words, those international monopolists were especially able to place themselves into leading positions in some of the most influential western countries and by doing so could control just about the entire wealth and power capacity of those nations as they are trying to do for the enslavement of the rest of the world. When they do not have those productive societies any longer at their disposal, they will have a hard time maintaining a global enslavement. A tool only becomes valuable in its application on something else.

2. There are, fortunately enough, a fair amount of people left on this globe with the spirit of a Patrick Henry as the previously mentioned uprising in East Berlin and Hungary proved and as we can notice among a few of the American people. The more oppression people of this type encounter, the more their spirit of liberty and freedom increases and strengthens, just as the muscles in our body become stronger when being used. Then this oppressive system will not have the resources of a free society to call upon in order to suppress such an uprising as there would be only enslaved subjects left, and enslaved subjects cannot maintain sufficiently strong economics.

3. Enslaved people, such as the Russians, will not any longer wait and hope for other so-called "free" nations like America to come to their rescue as then there are no such phony "free" nations left. There is nothing worse than placing your last rays of hope on false objects. It also delays your own struggling actions which could have led to success.

4. At this time the uprising will be on a more global scale since there will be freedom-loving voices heard everywhere as all nations are oppressed.

In a way it has been more difficult for the American people to come to a full unfolding of their capacities or powers because in our status quo we have maintained a system of apparent freedom and there has been no full showdown which has brought the opposing powers to a direct collision course. This has also prevented the liberty-seeking elements in this country to come to a complete development of their powers and full co-operation against the common enemy. They so far have been persecuted in individual cases by "hit and miss" tactics, but not yet as a common front. This, however, is quickly changing. The utilization of the powers of free societies has been the leverage the international power brokers have used in their total enslavement of other countries or societies. In case of a global enslavement this leverage will be gone. Even though the international vampires wanted to bring it to a complete showdown for some time, it might be that this is the reason for their not doing so thus far. But when they finally do so, they will find that their long-thought-out and intricately planned strategy will boomerang, delivering them their own death blow.

The people who are now preparing for the showdown seem to be those who are the strongest supporters of Constitutional government, personal freedom and sound currency. Because of their understanding of sane principles, they are the ones who see the crisis coming.

It is encouraging to know that history finally will be on our side, no matter how discouraging it may look at the present time. Even though the sky is clouded on our political and economic horizon, the sun will break through one of these days soon, as certain as day follows night.

IMPORTANT POINTS FOR:

1. A REWARDING LIFE

2. SAVING TIME

3. SAVING MONEY

4. GETTING OUT OF DEBT

5. SUCCESS

PERSONAL APPLICATION

Chapter 7

Important Points For
Personal Application

Man's Limit

At one period of my life I delved deeply into the study of philosophy and different religions in my search for knowledge and understanding of life. I buried myself so much in this study that often friends who were philosophy students warned me that I might someday lose my mind if I continued studying at the furious pace and depth I had been maintaining. As I tried to figure out all the problems of mankind, I would find that when I had come up with the answer to one problem, ten new problems came to mind. I would then be faced with ten new problems to solve, and as this process continued I could see that I was on an ever-widening road without end. I had to agree with the Greek wise man who said, "The more I know, the more I realize that I do not know anything!" Even if a person spent his whole lifetime studying just one subject under one branch of knowledge, he would not be able to understand one two-thousandth part of it at the end of his studies.

Fresh Momentum After Inward Reflection Reassessing Life

Try to stay as free as possible from the many intricacies of our modern civilization. At times it will be very difficult to reassess your life, come to a certain decision or even develop new thought patterns. In that case you are in definite need of a time away from your place of daily routine. Find some quiet location such as a cabin up in the mountains or an oasis in the desert or some peaceful place where you will not be disturbed (by the telephone, activities of the family, visits, noises of neighbors or other such things). When you have found that quiet location, try to make your mind a blank. Do this, and remain in that state for perhaps a period of several days until the many impressions and voices still lingering with you drop definitely into the background and you feel a calm and peace steal over you. At that time let inspiration take over and work for you. You will find that if properly done, this system will be a definite asset in your life and once you have experienced it in operation you will never want to do without the same. It is an excellent way to sort out important issues from unimportant issues, to reassess your life and to obtain new inspiration which is very much needed as a motivating factor and stimulant in life. During this time try to stay away from rich or strong foods and possibly eat less or even fast a few days, and you will find that this will contribute greatly to calm down your mind and body as a whole.

Be sure once you have received specific guidance by means of the above system and are very certain about it that you act immediately upon it, or otherwise all the good you have received will easily be dissipated by a new turbulence in life coming toward you. Valuable inspirations and understandings received in such a manner can quickly drop into the background and be forgotten or lose their perspective and importance if not used very soon.

Beside days or weeks away from your daily routine for the purposes stated above, you should also have more frequent intervals in which you give your dreams and ideals free realm to unfold. You can do this in combination with hiking, swimming, camping, observing nature or hunting. Usually time you spend with things you like, such as listening to beautiful music, will be very contributive in this way. I always find tremendous inspiration while listening to my favorite music, such as the Italian operas, the Vienna Boys Choir, Serge Jaroff's "Don Cossack Chorus," Neapolitan folk songs, mariachi music, etc. It is during times of such great uplifts when joy settles all over you that inspiration can really lift you up afresh and carry you on to a refreshing mood and cheerful manner. I think that in life as a whole we need more of this. Men everywhere are too much depressed and imprisoned by circumstances rather than climbing above them. I think of them when visiting a zoo, for instance. There are creatures such as lions, zebras and eagles which are imprisoned in little, manmade cells constructed of iron and concrete. These poor creatures were created to roam the open country and the challenging wilderness. You can literally see their still-yearning hearts when standing before the cages as their eyes seem to pierce right through you, gazing into the distance. The same is true of man as a whole in our world today. He is encaged in small apartment buildings in some noisy, confusing city—or shall I say jungle of concrete and gasoline stations! It seems to me that man was made for higher things. He was made to roam a great world of prairies, forests, mountains, lakes and oceans. He was made to rejoice at the nightly firmament or the lonely howls of the coyotes. He was made to marvel at the setting of the sun or to sing with the birds in the air. It was the frontier life of early America which created great noble characters. People settled in the wilderness, built their own homes and found their own food. Their children grew up in a natural environment, learning the tactics of genuine natural survival early in life. While sitting before the fire in the evening they could dream and reflect about a life which had meaning, joy and fulfillment.

Today man has built his own prison house by what is called civilization—not to call it a culture—which some of the old empires had. It seems that the more civilized we get, the more destruction we bring upon ourselves. The more computerized we get, the more vulnerable we become. The mightier the construction of man and the higher his Babylonian Tower, the worse the downfall when it finally comes. In a society where everything is set up by technical means (by wires, machines, mechanized forms of travel, electronics and computers), we will find a total and complete confusion once this system cannot be kept going in case of some material supply difficulty or general breakdown. Many companies have experienced a state of total chaos when their computerized system broke down or did not work properly; this is why I said that the more complicated your lifestyle gets, the more vulnerable you become and the more aggravation you will have. No wonder we have so many mentally ill people in the land! Everything is geared to a fast pace in an artificial environment. As a result, the family life has vanished, divorces have increased and a general, almost complete, decadence has set in. It has become so bad that a normal, natural life and a sound mind have become nearly ungraspable to the average civilized robots of today. Rather than following the voice of nature and the inner man, they have allowed their masters a free control and reign over them even unto their final destruction. The day and age of individuality is about gone. It has become almost a miracle if one finds an exceptional, interesting and different person. Of course the self-appointed power elite would want to consider such a real and genuine human being as suffering from mental illness in order to do away with him behind the walls of some mental institution, lest his refreshing influence could stimulate some other searching soul in need and lest a snowballing effect could prove disastrous to their long-planned schemes of eventual world dictatorship. If the sole accomplishment of this book were the inspiration of a fair number of individuals to seek such a rich and rewarding life, especially as outlined in the pages herein, I would consider my efforts rewarded. May there be those who take courage and look up to see the dawn of a new day!

Don't Get Into More Things Than You Can Handle

At the outset of this paragraph we have to realize that we are all human beings and that our capabilities, abilities, time, resources, etc. are finite and limited. There is only so much each of us can do. There is a certain portion of work, mental and physical stress which we can properly execute. As soon as we involve ourselves above those capabilities, especially if it is not just a temporary situation, we will find that we are not able to perform properly as we will become nervous, aggravated, fatigued, irritable and finally sick. Any reasonable person will understand that we cannot possibly be of much profit when we undertake a multitude of tasks needing our leadership and then in the middle of it all we have a nervous, mental or physical breakdown. The funds and energies which have been spent in those projects could easily be wasted if they cannot be carried on satisfactorily by someone else when their initiator fades from the scene. I have known a fair number of people who had good intentions but who in their overzealousness got so deeply entangled with various projects that soon they could not carry on any longer and the whole undertaking ended in failure.

At this point I would like to recommend very strongly that anyone making plans for the days and weeks ahead leave ample open time on his schedule for unforeseen emergencies and work loads which might quickly arise and have to be taken care of immediately. I should especially stress that anyone who is involved in beneficial projects which are not necessarily in keeping with the general tide should allow even more open time on his agenda because he almost always will run into mild-to-fierce opposition brought upon him by the various agencies of malevolence which will consume an even greater amount of time plus a greater amount of emotional energies. In fact, the more difficulty a person becomes involved in along this line, the more time he will need to devise a continually new strategy to counteract those attacks, and he should spend sufficient time balancing the turmoil in which he finds himself by tranquilizing experiences. I have known of many people who have utterly collapsed when they were faced with extremely adverse circumstances. Napoleon Bonaparte, when spending the evening of his days as a broken man on St. Helena, is reported to have confessed, "There is not a man who would lay down his life for me." His renown and magnificence dwindled into miserable failure. Voltaire, who evidently discovered at the end of his days that infidelity is destructive and not constructive, cried out, "I wish I had never been born." Byron, who lived a life of pleasure if anyone ever did, wrote, "The worm, the canker and the grief are mine alone." Gould, the American millionaire, is reported to have said when dying, "I suppose I am the most miserable devil on earth."

From the above we can see the tremendous importance of a person's having deeper convictions and motivations in which he has been thoroughly grounded during those times of reflection and motivation so that when trouble comes he will be able to keep afloat. It was because of being rooted in such a way that my father, when being asked by his various friends if he did not feel sad about having lost his many millions overnight, could smile without a tear in his eye. As we look around us in the world today with national tensions, pollution, inflation, overcrowded cities and nuclear threats, the above takes on a meaning of special importance. In this great age of escape, jam-packed giant stadiums with performances of rough sport, gambling, horse racing, violence and perversion in theatres and on television screens, we especially need to be solidly anchored.

Time Wasters and the 48-hour Day

There is a good technique you can follow when being plagued by long, drawn-out visits of people who do little but consume your valuable time. Here are some suggestions—pick the situation which applies to you. You could tell them that you are under quite some pressure and that there is certain work which needs to be done immediately. Let them know how much you would appreciate it if they would help you along and don't leave it at that, but put them to work right then. Most of the time they will leave very quickly, uttering some polite excuses. However, if they do stay and help you, they will be a valuable enough asset to you to put up with them.

As "preventative medicine," let your visitors know when they telephone to announce their arrival that you are able to give them perhaps two hours or a certain portion of the day as you are rather pressed for time right then. They will then know that you have no more time available and plan accordingly.

If you do enjoy their visit and if their children behave well, you might consider inviting them to stay for the night. In the past I have had bad experiences by being too generous with my invitations.

When deciding not to keep the visitors for the night and the time you have given them is drawing to an end, keep looking at your watch. Then you could tell them, "It was nice having you, but we have to leave now." If they say they will wait, tell them that you don't know just when you will be back. Also let them know that there is no sense to wait until tomorrow because you already have delayed today's work until the next day and will need to press harder the following day. If they then offer to help but you figure that their capabilities would not be helpful to your type of work, inform them that it would take more time to explain than it would be worth.

At one time I had a supposedly good-mannered and educated family visit me with two or three children. In the early stages of that visit I was hiding out in the daylight basement getting some work done while my wife visited with them. It was not very long before I wondered whether I was hearing things, for it sounded as though an entire army was marching upstairs. Not being willing to spend a week of valuable time fixing broken things, I immediately rushed upstairs. Upon arriving on the scene I saw two or three naughty children marching in a circle: from the hallway to the kitchen, to the dining room, into the living room; round again the same circle they went, tearing things along as they ran, such as tablecloths, smashing on the radio and banging the doors. Believing in disciplining children, I had little understanding for such bad behavior. I immediately made it clear to the people that there were three choices at their disposal: (1) they could restrain their children right away and tell them to behave, (2) give me permission to do so, or (3) leave. They left shortly thereafter, realizing they were not able to restrain their children and not wanting to impose their child training upon me. They were courteous enough to excuse themselves for the bad behavior of their children.

Unfortunately, the bad behavior pattern is not just restricted to children.

Another way to cut down on time waste is to practice speed reading. If you are not able to accomplish this yourself, you might want to attend a course offering it. My personal reading index was boosted from 233 to 4,050 by attending such a course. That raised my reading rate 1,700%! This certainly is of tremendous value to my work as an author and lecturer, which requires an enormous amount of reading, research and study. Just to go through the correspondence is a big task.

Another good exercise is to strengthen your memory or brain power. Books have been written about people who were able to memorize whole magazines and telephone books within very short periods of time—even hours. In many cases it requires a photographic mind, but it is a proven fact that our brain does not deteriorate if it is being used a lot, but on the contrary it improves with use just as the muscles of the body improve when used. Instead of wasting your time looking up telephone numbers over and over, trying to remember the names of people and using further time to look through records trying to find certain information, you can strengthen your memory sufficiently in order to avoid such time-consuming tasks. There are many ways of accomplishing this. Rather than deviating from the main subject in this book, I advise that you consult specific books for details. When acquiring this talent, you will find it much easier to let go of all unnecessary paperwork. Then you will be free to think in a bold, daring manner which will result in thoughts and actions with split-second timing.

Other Time-Saving Tips

Utilize your time whenever there are empty periods such as waiting in dentists' offices or waiting for a bus by using that time to memorize things from a small leaflet or book in your pocket, or by figuring things out in your mind.

If there is a knotty problem which clutters up your mind, get to it right away and see that it is taken care of; then you can erase it from your mind. Many people keep pushing matters like this off until they become more complicated and mess up a person's life.

Things which are difficult for you to master should be taken care of in the mornings.

Use the morning hours of the day for learning and the afternoons for taking care of your paperwork.

Put your most important and most difficult work load into time periods when you have your particular peak time of productivity and are most alert.

While studying things do not feel that you have to do it, but do it for the fun of it and it will become easy for you; utilize available time in ways which will bring you closer to your goals.

Busy yourself in things which give you joy, for then you will be able to accomplish more. Make a list of things you would like to accomplish and read it every so often.

Don't waste your time with petty things and dickerings—just stay where the sun shines and shadows flee.

Get Out of Debt

Try to avoid anything and everything which could entangle you or which could keep you in the spiderweb of bondage as under such conditions you will not be able to move as freely and quickly as our present unstable system necessitates. One such entanglement which is enormously represented in the United States is the great debt and resultant large interest payments the Americans are laboring under. You cannot keep the upper hand and have a free mind if you forever face the repossession of some of your assets. You will not be able freely to change or quit your job to move into different areas in your life because in that case you might not be able to keep up your regular monthly payments. Also, you will not be able to go on extensive land search trips as you are bogged down with much paperwork in connection with the regular monthly payments. It reminds me of a fellow who told me, "I enjoy receiving pleasant mail—but all I get are bills!" Therefore, I advise you to get out of debt as soon as you possibly can. There are various ways of achieving this:

1. You can lower your standard of living to an absolute minimum in every area of life such as housing, cars, food, clothing, etc., and in this way save up funds until you are able to complete payment of your contracts. You may be able to pay off the mortgage on your present, more expensive dwelling by selling it and moving into a smaller home. You will be better off if you can combine this with a move into a more remote area—such as an area you choose after considering the suggestions in this book, especially in the LIFESTYLE part.

2. You can quit your present job and get a better one with higher wages.

3. You can add to the income of your present job by taking a second profitable, no-nonsense, non-committal, part-time job, of which there are a good number on the American market as many of the unemployed people would rather draw unemployment checks than have a side income. There is a further loss of labor on the American market through the recently developed attitude of many young people such as hippies, dope addicts, leeches on welfare programs, and others.

4. You can utilize your own initiative and develop a good-paying occupation of your own.

5. Through prudent investment of any available funds on a temporary basis you could multiply your funds in a relatively short period of time while others lose theirs in the inflation.

6. You can cut down on your food budget by supplying most of your food free of charge by picking it yourself after the harvest is over. There is plenty of food going to waste and most farmers and orchardists will be more than happy to give you permission to glean if you leave the area as clean as you

found it. You can meet your clothing needs for just pennies at the Salvation Army, Goodwill or other second-hand stores. I will not mention here the many other ways of making do without much money which are pointed out in other areas of this book.

7. It is much more profitable to buy your food supply in larger quantities or larger containers and, if possible, at wholesale prices. You can buy grain and related products directly at grain elevators. There are a number of buying services available where you can purchase other various supplies for a small percentage over the factory price.

With a bad economic and political outlook ahead of us, it will become progressively harder to stay afloat financially as well as otherwise, and therefore you would have a rough time making ends meet if you are already struggling at this time. Move yourself into a position of having enough leverage that even when things become worse you still have some leeway left.

In complying with a new thought pattern or project remember not to start with a big overhead, but start small and progress gradually as the sound basis for that undertaking permits; then you should not incur any problems in keeping the enterprise flourishing. Remember, a tree starts as a small plant and if the ground is good, fertile and watered, the tree surely will grow unless there are plenty of damaging insects bothering the tree. Make sure that any project you start will be on a solid basis and keep all potential insects away from such an undertaking (great overhead, large debt, unproductive workers, too much paperwork, etc.). If it becomes necessary that you solve problems with some institution or agency, do not waste your time with small and unknowledgeable employees but go to the top or the management direct in order to receive prompt and immediate action.

A further valuable point of consideration is obtaining a job or setting up your own enterprise with the greatest combination of your interests, because if you work on projects you find of interest, you will be able to be more productive and initiatory. For example, if you like people (even people of various nations), languages, different types of food, travelling and continuous changes of life, then get a job with a travel agency or open your own. This way you will be able not only to receive a greater satisfaction in this type of work but at the same time you will learn a greater number of various things than in another job, which would carry only one such asset. In order to fill the above requirements you could also be in the employ of an airline company or travel as a steward or stewardess. Remember that in order to keep and increase your knowledge—in other words, to receive more knowledge and ideas—you must apply what you have received so far; otherwise, your knowledge will be of no profit to you.

Stepping Stones to Success

1. Try to understand the present and get a clear understanding of the future through a study of the past.

2. Ascertain your personal inclinations as expressed by your interests; develop your abilities and put them to work for you in a profitable way. Start out easy as you field test your knowledge in certain areas and increase your activities in those you are best suited for and find yourself most successful in. It should lead you into an occupation which gives you a chance to use all your faculties: mental, physical and emotional.

3. Concentrate in these areas. Read and study books, particularly biographies and autobiographies of people who had great success in fields that really excite you. This information will not only increase your knowledge and understanding, but inspire you as well. You can always discover a love and enthusiasm for a certain thing which moves through lives of successful men like a red thread. Strong motivation energizes your life, overcomes troubles and obstacles in the way and carries you through into a profitable business founded on ability and understanding of that matter.

4. Do not occupationally entangle yourself too much on a permanent basis in whatever you undertake in today's fast-changing world so you do not leave yourself vulnerable to just one particular trend of the free market system. Most people come to moments in life when they will have to take on a different job as economic circumstances have been very changeable in recent years. If you are trained in different occupations, you will be able to stand secure when others are failing.

5. Try to make money with the least involvement of time, work and expense. You can combine a profitable job with your hobbies such as: adventure, expeditions, music, winter sports, deep sea diving, friendships, ranching, nature study, reading, flying, swimming, horseback riding, tennis, sailing, singing and travelling. You will find that the more fascinating hobbies and jobs on a higher level will also give you a more interesting circle of friends.

6. While you have exciting discussions with your friends and you are mentally very active, many good ideas will come to you. Write down the most valuable ones before they are forgotten. However, it is more important to have one good thought and act upon it than have many and act upon none.

7. Use your own ingenuity. Every invention, every artistic accomplishment is based upon a creative thought which also gives incentive. Then you will receive financial returns as you offer your knowledge and services in a way that is saleable on the general market. It is never too late for splendid business opportunities. New possibilities open up daily. Don't be a pessimist—one of those who thinks that all the great opportunities have passed and have been utilized by someone else who is smarter than you. You are only limiting yourself. Don't be afraid to try something new if it seems feasible.

8. Never make spontaneous decisions when under the influence of some person or your own emotions. Wait several days or as long as is necessary for you to come to a true factual assessment of the matter under consideration.

9. Do not fritter away your time in useless work or unimportant detail, but live by inspiration instead of perspiration. Explore new ways of doing tasks more economically and more accurately. This will also help when you do the same or similar things again. Get a quick understanding of big possibilities and intriguing propositions which offer themselves. Why boondoggle, when you can pick up the whole bunch of nails with a magnet instead of picking up one at a time? Use your intelligence to discern between the most important and unimportant. As you progress, a multitude of most interesting things will automatically come your way which otherwise you would have missed. At the same time, you will provide leadership and direction for others to follow, just as a river attracts and draws smaller, slower tributaries with it.

10. Get rid of all time wasters, such as frequent visits of boring friends and relatives (don't feel "obligated" just because they are related to you). Stay away from clubs which are full of narrow-minded people who will always feel slighted if your ability exceeds theirs. People who only want to impress others will be quickly forgotten because they only touch one on the surface; on the other hand, emotionally sympathetic people will be remembered since they have an appeal to the inner man. If you are truly an interesting person, you do not have to throw yourself upon other people, but rather they will seek you out if you represent something in life.

11. Try to arrange your periods of heaviest concentration in the morning hours or whenever you are the most alert and the least likely to be disturbed by noise and people. A well-spent morning hour will give you bouyancy and a head start. The evening hours should be devoted to leisure and reflection. As the old saying goes: "Early to bed and early to rise makes a man healthy, wealthy and wise."

12. Do things which will put you into a pleasant mood, such as listening to good music. When you are in such a mood, you will also accomplish other things better.

13. Turn all difficulties into opportunities! Tackle the most arduous problems as soon as possible; procrastination only makes them worse. As you take on things which you dread, fear will vanish while you work on them.

14. Evaluate yourself and your actions with a view of creating a more pleasant future, realizing that you can only be genuinely happy if you aim at the highest objectives. The Greek definition of happiness is: "Happiness is the full use of your powers along lines of excellence in a life affording scope." Therefore, put all your energies to work toward your ultimate ideals or goals in life. Plan and work to achieve them, judging your progress occasionally. Eliminate short-lived pleasures if they need to be paid as a price for long-term future happiness.

Look to this day for it is life; yesterday is only a dream; tomorrow is only a vision. Today well lived makes every yesterday a dream of happiness and every tomorrow a vision of hope. Look well, therefore, to this day.

PART III

PROFITABLE

ECONOMIC

SURVIVAL

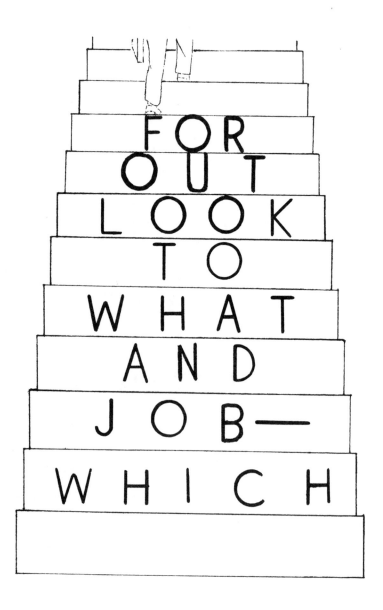

Chapter 8

Which Job—And What To Watch Out For

Trans-Atlantic Ventures

For an adventurous, flexible person there are many interesting jobs available. Some years ago a friend and I were embarking upon a very profitable and extremely interesting undertaking. He purchased an airplane in the United States, which at that time had to be flown across the Atlantic from Canada as laws had just been passed against such flights leaving the United States. My friend had informed the German television of the arrival of his single-engine plane and the television had promised him an award of DM 5,000 for that broadcast.

At that time there was practically no airplane industry at all in Germany as it was only a few years after the war and as there were restrictions imposed upon Germany as far as motor flying was concerned. In those early years people could fly only gliders and motor flying had just started. Therefore we could buy airplanes in America much cheaper than they could be bought on the European market. Then by flying them to Europe ourselves, we could eliminate the high shipping expenses beside having an interesting time ferrying those planes and adding to our flight experience.

In order to utilize both trips across the Atlantic, we were in the process of making contacts in Germany for obtaining good sailing yachts which then in turn would find a ready market this side of the ocean, especially if we sailed them across the Atlantic ourselves. The boats were fabricated in a much better way in Germany at that time than they were in the United States and the price was much lower for those boats in Germany than what they could be obtained for in America. Especially good markets were the Caribbean areas with a lot of United States tourists and Florida.

We could easily realize a $10,000 gain on that venture on a boat transaction alone, not even figuring on the profit from the plane sale, television program and other profitable sidelines connected with this undertaking.

If you run across the very unlikely difficulty of not being able to sell your sailing yacht right then, you can always utilize this boat in the meantime by using it to conduct sailing schools for young people. You can also offer nice sailing cruises and instruct people in deep-sea diving by taking them to some reefs on deep-sea diving trips. All of these would be interesting jobs.

Mail Order Business

For those who are interested in mail order business, here are a few items of interest. Most of the mail order businesses in the United States are family enterprises without employees being done on a part-time basis. They often handle just one to three different articles. By doing this, you have low overhead, no trouble with employees and no red tape. By handling only very few articles you avoid much paperwork and headaches while getting a higher discount from the factories because of larger orders. There are a multitude of items offered by various manufacturers. Some are very good but do not sell very well. For various reasons, some of the manufacturers have too low a profit margin to make it worth your effort. Try to stick with items which have a general appeal and are definitely needed; in other words, for which there are ready markets and not too much competition. Also, they should be economical and reasonably priced.

A few reasons why many mail order houses are going out of business are: insufficient knowledge of advertising and organization, under-estimation of competition and poor quality merchandise. Here are a few characteristics of some giant mail order businesses which blossomed up overnight like mushrooms after a summer rain:

1. All sell specialties.
2. All advertise extensively.
3. All started with a minimum of capital.
4. All extend over-average credit.

Miscellaneous Job Ideas

Importing antique items especially from Europe for resale in stores, auctions or otherwise in the United States is a very lucrative business. If a person is familiar with any of the European languages and has many acquaintances in Europe, he will be able to pick up many items which would otherwise be thrown away by people who have no use for them. Many of those items are being sold in the United States for fortunes. It behooves the buyer in Europe to watch out, however, because there have been numerous enterprises which will age new products by digging them into the ground, leaving them there for a period of time and then selling them as antiques.

There has traditionally been a good profit on products which are used once or twice and then thrown away, such as Kleenex, Q-Tips and disposable diapers. There will be a continuous market on account of the never-ceasing demand for such products. Furthermore, there has been a good profit on well-advertised and established items like Vicks VapoRub and Vaseline.

Also you can acquire land that has some mineable mineral on it; mine the mineral and then resell the land. Be sure that the papers do not contain wording that would exclude mineral rights.

If you are planning to go into big business, you might consider having your company address in a tax-free country, such as Lichtenstein. Extremely low income and business taxes cause thousands of international companies to register there. You can transfer the merchandise at cost to this firm and then add on the profit, arriving at your selling price at time of resale. Import duties in case of re-import to the United States would, however, have to be considered. There are other variations in this procedure.

Many people have become very wealthy by buying up cheap Army, Navy and Air Force surplus items and then reselling them again on the general market with a tremendous mark-up.

Get jobs which have a great educational value for you. Obtain work where you will have a need to study and learn things which you are interested in. If you are interested in working in foreign countries but do not have funds for travelling, you can work for an American company with branch offices in foreign countries. After having worked with them for a while in a leading capacity, they often will be happy to pay your travel expenses when they transfer you to one of their branches in another country. If this company has many branches worldwide, you might be able to pick a country you like if they have openings.

While travelling, keep your eyes open and see possibilities in other countries and reflect upon them during calm periods on those trips. Get acquainted with influential people. On those trips you will also learn languages and geography. Travel into countries during your vacation trips whose languages you would like to learn or which you need in your occupation.

Your possibilities as an entrepreneur are unlimited. For instance, you could charter vessels and have an Austrian yodeling group on board, accompanied by such instruments as a zither, musical saw, violin, bells, accordion and xylophone. Have those ships sail in tourist areas such as along the shoreline of Florida and because of the specialty you offer, you should not have any problem being booked out night after night. If you get enough ideas going for you, you might have to spend most of your time in travelling and negotiations while others do the humdrum work!

Those who are pilots could fly material and supplies for oil drilling operations and oil wells in desert and ocean territories; they could fly on fish-sighting missions, in search of uranium and on research expeditions. You can be an inventor, scientist or explorer. Even in today's sophisticated world there are unlimited fields for exploring expeditions and knowledge to be discovered.

See and utilize future business opportunities.

You can go on expeditions catching animals and deep-sea expeditions making movies of marine life, etc., and then you can present them in lectures.

If you are in the business of producing things, produce things which everyone will need.

It is more fun to build up your own enterprise than to work in one which already has been established where you have to go through much old paperwork in order to inform yourself and keep going.

Take plenty of time to ascertain your hopes and dreams while young and then see how you can use them in a productive way, offering them on the general market.

Rapidly Changing Times Require Versatility

Don't get yourself into a dilemma where you cannot move from one field into the next when opportunities in one field become limited. For instance, my father was involved in the linen business as well as others. As man-made fibers began conquering more and more of the market, the demand for flax products continued to wane because they were more expensive due to the more individual manufacturing process required in the case of natural fibers. That would leave two choices: to live and die with the business or to move out of the field with the capital still available and into another field with a promising future.

Therefore, I say, don't waste your time in a dying field—go only into businesses or jobs which could make a changeover into something else easily, not consuming too much time in needed disentanglements from the old business. Some jobs require almost lifelong training, like the engineering and medical fields. There are constant changes which require continuous study and upkeep on new developments.

While the trend in the United States in recent years has changed from a strongly industrial and technical society into a more ecological society, many engineers, for instance, have been laid off and unable to find work elsewhere. In the case of Seattle, Washington, there were probably more engineers and mechanics without work than any other job group when Boeing started to lay off by the thousands. In such vulnerable jobs, you will find yourself without one when the trend changes, after the majority of your life's time and energy has been invested in it. Just as you distribute your risk in investments, don't tie your life up in one job. Be flexible, anticipate changes, look into the future.

Your interests might change and you might get bored with an activity you liked very well when on a lower plane in life. Try to stay clear of job and financial investments which have a continually fluctuating trend because of being tied to a base of rapidly changing and temporary economics. You might encounter a great waste of effort, money and time in the course of it. Since you spend most of your time with your job, you might as well take one which widens your outlook and mind. Seek one which gives you the greatest combination of your hobbies.

Let me, therefore, stress the following points again.

When you go into business, try to pick one with the least amount of paperwork and one with flexibility, which you can run or leave any time you choose to do so. Time is very uncertain and changing; you put yourself into too vulnerable a position if you go into long-range set-ups. You might end up paying a lot of money getting set up while not having enough time left making enough money to justify the effort and expense. While you went through all kinds of agonies setting yourself up in business, complying with the various government rules and regulations, the same and various other conditions might have changed or most likely will change—so you find yourself in the unenviable position of starting all over again! A number of people have invested a lot of funds advertising certain products only to find out shortly afterward that they became illegal. Beware of advice from people who have self interest in the matter you are concerned with.

Some people spend an enormous amount of time shopping around to save pennies. Years ago while doing the same, I lost a small fortune in paper investments; while saving pennies on one side, I lost a fortune on the other side. Had I utilized the time which I spent saving pennies in properly informing myself of the true trend of the economy, I could have saved a lot of time and a lot of money, too. My gain, therefore, could have been a threefold gain: I not only would have eliminated the loss, but would have added gain on top of that and would have saved the time I spent hunting around saving pennies. However, time was not too late for a future protection of the assets I had left; I then spent my time reading sensible investment books and getting vital information on how to protect and increase my remaining assets. This way I could make my time count along lines of excellence. This I should have done at first.

Job Traps

Once I tackled Telescope Peak; it was a long climb, and not an easy one. At first, the going was easy, but the further I climbed, the steeper it got. I found that the path narrowed and became rockier. Sometimes I wondered if the ascent to the top was worth all the effort and energy I was expending. As I looked around every so often, I could see only trees and the face of the mountain. Occasionally I would get a glimpse of the magnificent scenery from the height I had attained, though, and that would spur me on. At last I reached the summit and found the splendor, freedom, liberty and sunshine up there that I had been seeking. The view from that height was breathtaking everywhere I looked. Once a person has known such a mountain-top experience, he will never forget it and can never be completely satisfied with humdrum, lower-level experiences.

This also applies to a person's business life. He starts off in a little job, stuck away in some dark, airless corner. The hours are long and tiring and he can hardly wait for the end of the working day. Year after year he toils, perhaps getting a fancier job title and an improvement in working conditions, but still confined to the same long, tiring, boring routine, day after day, year after year. Once in a while he glimpses freedom when he goes on his two-week vacation, but the rest of the year he has his nose to the grindstone, working that someone else might profit. If he had a business or undertaking of his own, he could ascend his mountain bit by bit. He might not make giant strides, but go at his own pace and take time off occasionally so he could see the view. As he climbed he would be free—not confined to the humdrum routine any longer! He would not be slaving away for someone else but rather be building something for himself and take pride and pleasure in surmounting whatever problems might arise along the way. He would be filled with enthusiasm as he got nearer his goal. Eventually the day would come when he would reach the summit he has been looking for and have the magnificent view and breathe the clear, fresh air of freedom and liberty which he had been seeking in greater measure.

Be careful of job traps. Don't entangle yourself with long-range programs which get you stuck for years or the rest of your working life. Be especially careful about jobs that offer long-range rewards or bonuses, such as retirement programs, longer vacations and pins, because they can get you permanently entangled. This is the purpose of such machinations. There are fast-money makers available which give you immediate funds you need for getting yourself set up for better things and the days ahead, including survival.

Beware of Shady Business Practices

Here might be a word to the wise: We have had a lot of shady business in our day and age, especially in America. There are many enterprises—so-called "hole-in-the-wall" outfits—which will offer shoddy, overpriced merchandise with phony warranties in big cities such as New York that have a tremendous turnover of people. They will be in business for a while because there are new people constantly moving in, and people leaving, and therefore they will be able to exist for a period of time which would be impossible in areas where they have a steady group of customers. There are manufacturing companies which open up for business, putting out a lot of advertisements offering long-term warranties for their products. However, people later have learned to their dismay when trying to collect on some of the warranties that some of those companies have closed their doors for business and have transferred their funds by opening up under a new and different name. This way all their former obligations such as warranties automatically are cancelled.

This type of enterprise does not pay off in the long run nor does it pay off in the short run if a person has any moral or ethical inclinations at all. It is this type of business which a cautious investor should watch out for when reinvesting his assets in those stormy days we are presently living in, as no doubt they have and will flock into the present gold and silver markets as well to make a "fast buck" no matter how many investors might lose their money by their criminal schemes.

Even if you are reasonably sure that you are investing your funds in a safe asset, you must not forget to make very sure also that the business presenting this safe asset is as secure, or otherwise your investment endeavors for such assets can turn into a nightmare.

The idea of positive thinking (that you can do it if you just think so) applied to commercial things is a gimmick of manufacturers and their high-pressure sales training force in order to dispose of items they cannot otherwise get rid of. The idea comes out of the spiritual realm, and most of those which commercially advocate it are strangely devoid of any spirituality.

Do not get "hooked" by large initial purchases in order to obtain expensive franchises; this is another gimmick used by many manufacturers who cannot dispose of their items in any other way and your funds will be tied up in products you cannot sell. Beware of expensive franchises as you may find out at a later time that the franchise will do you no good as the products of that company might be unmarketable.

Many years ago I had an unpleasant experience along that line. I was contacted by a representative of a Chicago firm which was supposed to be in the business of manufacturing swimming pools and fallout shelters. I was offered an exclusive franchise to market their products and to appoint sub-distributors upon the payment of a $3,000 fee. I was promised a free demonstration swimming pool which was to be installed at the expense of the factory at any place within my territory I desired. I was also told that the company was worth approximately $1,000,000.

Soon I found out that I had been "taken for a ride." The promised demonstration swimming pool finally arrived in the form of a small package and consisted of an imitation leather suitcase which indeed contained a little plastic pool when opened. After further research, I discovered that instead of being worth $1,000,000 the factory was worth only one tenth of that. I also found out that other "exclusive" distributors had been appointed for the same area. While consulting with them, I learned that this factory's products were unmarketable. After figuring together all the expenses, such as freight for getting the material to your location, the costs of the various materials themselves, the hiring of a contractor to install the pool, etc., we arrived at a market price much higher than competitors were offering.

I spent about half a year consulting the various government agencies such as the FBI, Postal Inspector, Federal Trade Commission, Better Business Bureau and the Attorney General in an endeavor to recover my down payment of $500 on that contract. I wound up with much loss of time in addition to the $500 I had already lost, as practically no help was given me by all those government agencies set up through the payment of your taxes for the proposed purpose of protecting the consumer. After finally consulting a lawyer, I realized that in order to recover my $500 it would cost me an equal amount in legal fees, so I would only break even. Unwilling to lose any more time or money on that project, I dumped it at that point.

If you consider representing a certain merchandise for a manufacturer, be sure you are not taken by such fraud. A reputable company has no need of making money by selling you franchises or saddling you with large stores of unmarketable merchandise. They know their products will sell and they are willing to get you started with a small initial purchase. They will offer you full return privileges on those products for a period of thirty to sixty days as an added incentive in case you should not be able to sell them. Be sure you deal only with such reputable businesses. You have no risk because even your investment for a small initial purchase is returnable if you cannot sell. Be sure that you always test the market with such purchases before you tie up your funds in a greater way. Even though a product might sell very well in certain areas, this does not automatically prove that the same product will also sell well in your particular area. The needs and customs of people vary from location to location.

Be sure you do not waste your time with obvious "junk" items, especially in a flagging economy when people are concentrating on necessities rather than on unneeded items; you will find no market for them. Here are a few ways of identifying phony outfits offering "junk" items:

1. They want to sell you a catalog or success booklet or some kind of a course before sending you any merchandise.

2. No return privileges.
3. No free or distributor-priced samples.
4. Extremely high-sounding promises.
5. High-pressure marketing practices.

There are quite a number of persons who offer success books. They usually claim that they have made millions easily themselves by using the method described in their book and promise you also can make a fortune when using their method. It does not take much brain power to assume that if those people had such an excellent recipe of making such easy fortunes then they would have no need of making their money by selling their book. We would have to assume that they need to make their money with an unworkable book because they were not able to obtain funds otherwise on the general market.

Woes of a Small Businessman

Depending a little upon the area where you live, you will quickly find out how much the government will tie you into knots whenever you try to make a little money by using your own incentive. As long as you draw upon some government programs or government payments the legalities will be kept to a minimum; but try and look out for yourself, and you run into all kinds of trouble.

A friend of mine recently decided to have a little side business of his own and ordered some timely merchandise from a factory for resale. While making the rounds in nearby towns, he ran into the arms of an off-duty policeman (as he later learned), who questioned him as to whether he had all sorts of licenses for being allowed to sell his merchandise from house to house. Merciless and unkind, he threatened to call the police!

Later, upon inquiry, my friend learned that one or more licenses would be necessary for every city or town in which he planned to sell and that the fees were exorbitant. One city required that an applicant for a license to sell be fingerprinted, investigated, have a medical certificate from a doctor (within the past ten days) and have a "mug shot" made!

Even before that, while visiting various homes, he was informed by a number of frightened people that the very useable item he was handling was about to be outlawed by the government!

He had the ingenuity to put the word "Enterprises" after his surname, having had a little rubber stamp made with that wording. The second day, while trying to cash a check made to that designation, he had trouble at his bank and was informed by one of the officers that he was not supposed to carry the word "Enterprises" behind his name unless he had filed various forms with the state government which, of course, required further fees. In addition to that, a fee had to be paid for every single county in the state within which he wanted to conduct business!

Many people left Europe in order to free themselves from "red tape" no worse than this!

If the government took from the people in one tax payment, such as one yearly tax, all the funds which it requires for its defunct bureaucracies, then the amount would be so high that obviously the citizenry would rebel. Therefore, those taxes are divided among a thousand different things, making many of them in effect "hidden" taxes. Needless to say, this causes a further tremendous waste of finances because of all the unnecessary paperwork involved.

"TAX, TAX, TAX

Now he's a common, common man.
Tax him! Tax him all you can.

Tax his house and tax his bed,
Tax the bald spot on his head.

Tax his bread and tax his meat,
Tax his shoes clear off his feet.

Tax his 'Henry' and tax his gas,
Tax the road that he must pass.

Tax the farmer, tax his fowl,
Tax the dog and tax his howl.

Tax his plow and tax his clothes,
Tax the rags that wipe his nose.

Tax his pig and tax his squeal,
Tax his boots run down at the heel.

Tax his cow and tax his calf,
Tax him if he dares to laugh.

Tax his barns and tax his lands,
Tax the blisters on his hands.

Tax the water and tax the air,
Tax the sunshine, if you dare.

Tax the living, tax the dead,
Tax the unborn before they're fed.

Tax them all and tax them well,
And do your best to make life Hell!"

by Fred Foster of Silver City, Idaho.

"Sometimes I get the creeps"

Bimrose, *The Portland Oregonian*

Chapter 9

The Present State
of the Economy

America's real debt—government, private and business debt—now totals over one and one-half trillion dollars. That's more than $1,500,000,000,000. This represents more than 65% of present United States wealth in current (inflated) dollars. But computing the national wealth in terms of constant (1947-1949) dollars, our debts now equal 98% of the total wealth.

According to the government's own records, the dollar has lost 3/4 of its purchasing power during the last 41 years since Franklin Roosevelt came into office. Nearly 2/3 was lost in the nineteen years following World War II. It finally lost 1/3 of its purchasing power in the six years after the time when Nixon took over.

With a skyrocketing government budget and increasing illiquidity of business and the general public, coupled with high unemployment, it will be necessary to conduct the sale of government securities through monetization as little money is available elsewhere. This, in combination with a possible fast harvest of approximately ninety billion Euro-dollars by the United States, can really shake things badly. More than 80% of the dollar's world gold market value has been lost since the abolishment of the two-tier system. On an average, this nation has borrowed approximately $200 million per day since the end of World War II.

The fact that price controls were first imposed on August 15, 1971, almost simultaneously with the breaking of the dollar's last ties to gold, illustrates gold's power and restraining influence on inflation. Several devaluations followed suit.

In past recessions and depressions producers' prices have fallen in relation to consumers', but this time we have seen the strange phenomena that while some producer prices such as industrial commodities have fallen, consumer goods' prices generally continued to rise! We are suffering at the same time from the worst features of both boom and bust—an inflationary recession or depression with the threat of sudden contraction bringing on a crash.

In fact, there are definite signs that we are moving and for some time have moved between an inflationary recession and a deflationary depression, eventually leading to a crash or a "major war (probably world war)". The more important *Dow Jones Spot Commodity Index* had declined during some of the recent years. Another main indicator, copper, had fallen considerably. Unemployment worldwide, even in such countries as West Germany is rapidly rising.

There is the great chance of net debt liquidation (deflation) instead of net debt expansion (inflation) as there are so very many more paper debts in this country. The number of illiquid debtors in this country are rapidly on the rise. Watch out for a chain reaction with devastating results!

As the government sees in that eventuality that a deflationary depression is in full gear, it will be too late to curb it with further monetary and debt expansion, as by that time private debt will shrink faster and there will be those who, because of bad experiences, do not want to make further loans and others who will want to get liquid at any price. When bank failures become widespread, there is no way for the Federal Deposit Insurance Corporation to obtain unlimited funds from the Treasury without a further inflationary run of the money printing presses, which will cause yet more illiquid debtors and also make the Treasury go back on the Federal Reserve, which has been directly involved to some extent with bank failure already.

The United States Constitution gave Congress the authority to *coin* money (not paper, but silver and gold coins), and it is through the central banks' underwriting of tremendous paper expansion that we have moved into final monetary chaos. Since gold never fails, it is still *the* investment even in a deflationary depression as many paper assets (even though rising in value) will actually lose value with illiquid debtors running rampant.

Most of the foreign countries, however, might continue their inflationary recession. We have had further warnings in the case of Penn Central, Lockheed and Franklin National Bank. It took the combined help of the Federal Government, the Federal Reserve System and the FDIC in some cases to contain failure and in others temporarily to bridge over the troubles. Another very explosive field is the Euro-dollar area. Nearly all those funds are at banks on a 24-hour to 30-day deposit term, yet much of it is on a long-term loan by the deposit institutions.

Below are some vital sample statistics of what happened during part of our past 1974-75 economic fiasco. They clearly show how close we came to a major depression already at that time.

There were signs that we had been heading into a deflationary depression. The United States money supply had been growing during much of that time at an annual rate of only around 3%, well under the Federal Reserve short-term target, which is thought to be as high as 7% or more. In late 1974 Albert T. Sommers, Chief Economist for the Conference Board, stated that the industrial wholesale price, which ran at an annual rate of 34% from May to July 1974, would stop rising completely in March 1975. He said, *"It's a temporary victory over inflation, however, won by an insupportable degree of recession."* From the foregoing, the big question was whether the second "round of inflation" which the government then again set into motion would take effect soon enough and with enough momentum in order to avert a crash through an increased stimulation of the economy by the inflowing of more funds. It almost looked as though the retarding economic measures had been too strong and too long, and that the return to the overly inflationary policy might have come too late.

Short-term interest rates had declined sharply since July of 1974. The yield on prime four- to six-month commercial papers fell from an average of 11.88% in the first two weeks of July to an average of 6.67% in the last two weeks of January 1975. Yields on ninety-day CD's fell from 12.18% to 7.05%, the Federal funds rate fell from 13.45% to 7.08% and the prime bank loan rate decreased from 12% to 9.5% over the same period. In spite of all this, all major reserve aggregates had grown at considerably slower rates since July 1974 than in the previous five months when interest rates rose rapidly.

". . . For example, the source base, which consists of member bank deposits at Federal Reserve banks and currency in circulation, had increased only at a 4.7 percent rate since July (1974), compared to a 15.4 percent rate over the previous five months. Even the monetary base and adjusted Federal Reserve credit, which included the effects of several reductions in reserve requirements, had grown at slower rates over the last six months.

"Therefore, the growth rate of all those aggregates which act to increase the supply of bank credit had shown noticeable decelerations in the last six months. Hence, it appeared that the fall in interest rates over the last six months reflected a decrease in the demand for credit rather than the effects of easier monetary actions.

"Growth Rates of Reserve Aggregates
(Annual Rates of Change)

	2/74 - 7/74	7/74 - 1/75
Member Bank Reserves	16.3%	-2.5%
Federal Reserve Credit	8.9	5.7
Source Base	15.4	4.7
Monetary Base	7.6	6.9
Money Stock (MI)	6.6	1.2"

(Monetary Trends, Federal Reserve Bank of St. Louis, February 27, 1975).

This significant slowing down of aggregate demand since the summer of 1974 had added a new dimension to the current contraction of economic activity. It was compounding the problems which arose from constraints on production through the recent years. Total production declined sharply in the fourth quarter of 1974.

The output of the nation's factories, mines and utilities in 1974's final quarter dropped at a 12.1% annual rate, the sharpest decline since World War II. Factory activity slowed the fifth quarter in a row.

"The sharp decline in production since late 1974 had resulted in an equally large decrease in employment, at a 6.3 percent annual rate from September to January. The rate of unemployment, which had held steady at slightly more than 5 percent of the labor force from January to August, had since risen sharply and reached 8.2 percent in January of 1975.

"The average level of prices in the economy, as measured by the GNP deflator, rose rapidly in the fourth quarter of 1974 to a level 12 percent higher than a year earlier. The rate of increase of prices had moderated in the beginning of 1975, however, as the adjustment to the special factors ran its course. The consumer price index, for example, had increased at an 8 percent annual rate in the first two months of 1975, compared to a 12 percent rise over the prior year." (National Economic Trends, Federal Reserve Bank of St. Louis, February 26, 1975.)

Residential construction continued to slide throughout 1974. New housing starts in 1974 fell to 1.34 million units, the lowest since 1967 and 35% below the 1973 level. Housing starts for December 1974 were down 12% from November. Even domestic silver consumption during the third quarter of 1974 was 15.7% down from the same period in 1973. But also the domestic mine production of silver went down 11% according to estimates. The Silver Institute reported that 16.4 million ounces of .999-fine silver were refined from coins in 1974, up from 3.2 million ounces in 1973. United States gold consumption during 1974 was down 37% from 1973, according to preliminary estimates from the Bureau of Mines.

"In January, 1975, the Commerce Department revised its index of leading economic indicators for November (1974) to show a 3.5% drop. It was the worst monthly decline on record, surpassing a 3.3% drop in September (1974). The Department said the index declined an additional 2.4% in December (1974). The index had

now fallen for five straight months for a total decline of 11%—the worst sustained decline in the index since the Department began compiling it in 1948, according to **The New York Times.**

"*. . . New orders for durable goods fell 11.1% in December (1974), the steepest drop in 20 years. Since June's peak of $49.06 billion, orders had fallen 22%, says* **The Wall Street Journal.**

"*Auto sales in 1974 were down 23% from 1973. Imported car sales declined 20% over the same period. Auto sales fell 30% in the last quarter of 1974, says* **The New York Times.** *Even with U.S. auto makers' rebate programs for new car buyers, mid-January sales still fell 15.4% from 1974's low levels at the height of the fuel crisis.*

"*Loan losses in the banking industry in 1974 were the highest since the 1930s. However, they amounted only to 0.33% of total loans outstanding, in contrast to 3.4% outstanding in 1934 says John McGillicuddy, President of Manufacturers Hanover Trust Co.*

"*The unemployment rate rose from 5.5% in the third quarter of 1974 to 6.5% in the fourth and then 'threatened to average 7.5% in the first quarter of 1975—with worse to come' warned an editorial in* **The New York Times.** *Approximately 300,000 of 700,000 automobile production workers in January 1975 were either on temporary or indefinite layoff status, in addition to some 25,000 supervisory personnel in the auto industry.*

"*The Labor Department reported 813,600 initial unemployment claims in the week ending December 28 (1974), the highest since the program started paying benefits in 1937. 4.6 million people were receiving unemployment insurance benefits for the first week of January (1975), a record level. Economist Walter Heller saw 'no marked turnaround in the economy in the second half of 1975. As a result, unemployment would rise to a peak of about 8.25% and average 8% for the year.' It actually rose to 9.2%.*

"*The Administrative Office of the United States Courts reported that bankruptcy petitions filed in the beginning of fiscal 1975, were running 29% above last year. If the present rate continues, the report said, the total for the year would reach 231,660, highest ever. Close to 90% were filed by individuals. Commercial and industrial business failures were at their highest level for any period since May 1967,* **The Wall Street Journal** *reported.*

"*The dollar reached a 14-month low against the French franc and was near its record low against the West German mark and the Swiss Franc in mid-January 1975. In a few months alone, reported* The Wall Street Journal, *the U.S. dollar had slipped in value by around 15% in relationship to such strong currencies as the Swiss franc.*

"*Consumer prices in 1974 rose 12.2%, the highest annual increase since 1946, the Labor Department reported. In 1974, food rose 12.2%, housing 13.7%, transportation 13.3%, health and recreation 10.9% over 1973. Wholesale prices climbed 20.9% compared with a 13.1% rise in 1973. The Gross National Product price index, the broadest gauge of inflation, rose at a 13.7% annual rate in the December quarter of 1974, exceeding the previous record of 13% in the 1951 first quarter. During 1974 prices of processed foods and feeds rose 20.9%. Industrial commodities rose 25.6%.*

"*Federal spending will have risen by an average of 11% a year from fiscal 1970 through fiscal 1975, compared with the growth rate in the nation's real output of some 3.5% to 4% a year. For the first 5 months of fiscal 1975, the federal budget was in deficit by $11.01 billion, compared with a deficit of $8.42 billion in the same period a year before.*

"*The Treasury estimated that it would have to borrow a record $28 billion in the first half of 1975 to finance rapidly rising budget deficits. Treasury Secretary William Simon had asked Congress for a record $109 billion boost in the federal debt ceiling to help cover $65 billion in new Treasury borrowing in 1975. For fiscal 1976, beginning July 1, Mr. Simon estimated the deficit at $50 billion.*

"*In December (1974), Congress approved a $5.5 billion program to aid unemployed workers, including $2.5 billion for local governments to hire some 330,000 jobless workers in 1975; $500 million for public works projects; plus funds for extension of unemployment benefits and for unemployment compensation for workers who were not then covered. The Labor Department was preparing proposals to bring nearly 7 million more workers under the nation's unemployment insurance system at an added cost of $3.5 billion.*" (Gold & Silver Newsletter, Monex International, Ltd., March 1975).

The Money System

Inflation has been made mysterious and complicated, and for nearly two hundred years the people of this country generally have not understood it. Some simple arithmetical computations should make it clear:

Say I am the banker and you are the borrower. Because I am a banker I have the right to manufacture all money—a "right" given to me by your corrupt public "servants" in 1790. This so-called "reason" (or should we call it by its right name—lie) given to the people at that time was that the money of the bank had a 10% backing—actually 10% gold and 90% faith—called the Gold Standard. The people did not realize then the tiny difference between 90% and 100% faith and did not understand how they were being tricked.

All the money in circulation is manufactured by me and borrowed by you at my interest rates as all the money in a given country is put into circulation through loans and is based on and backed by debt—on which "interest" must be paid which amounts to mere bookkeeping magic (hocus-pocus financing). If you don't want to pay the interest I charge, I won't let you use my money and you will have to resort to the barter system.

You decide to use my money and ask to borrow $3,000 for business purposes. Since I monopolize the entire money system, I decide to charge you 15% interest. At the end of the year you will owe me $3,000 plus $450 interest. Where will you get the money to pay the interest, since I have all the money? I am generous and allow you to borrow the $450 interest. At the end of next year you will owe me $3,450 plus interest for a total of $3967.50. I am very kind hearted and will offer to allow you to continue this snowballing process as part of your doing business. It will be necessary, however, for you to raise the prices of your merchandise, creating inflation. I am, in effect, a silent partner in your business and take a portion not only of your earnings but those of your customers as well.

The result of this will be the eventual total enslavement of you and your customers. Communism was invented by the bankers to complete this process. The Bank of England began it and the Federal Reserve System and the United Nations World Bank (the two United Nations agencies—the International Monetary Fund and the International Bank for Reconstruction and Development or World Bank—drawn up at the Bretton Woods International Monetary Conference in July 1944 by 44 participating countries) will finish it.

Quotations from famous sources:

JOHN ADAMS: *"All the perplexities, confusion and distress in America arises, not from the defects of the Constitution or Confederation—not from want of honor or virtue so much as from downright ignorance of the nature of coin, credit and circulation."*

THOMAS JEFFERSON: *"I believe that banking institutions are more dangerous to our liberties than standing armies. Already they have raised a money aristocracy that has set the Government at defiance. The issuing power should be taken from the banks and restored to the people to whom it properly belongs."*

ANDREW JACKSON: *"If Congress has a right under the Constitution to issue paper money, it was given them to be used by themselves, not to be delegated to individuals or corporations."*

Speaking directly to the bankers, President Andrew Jackson said: *"You are a den of vipers and thieves. I intend to rout you out, and by the Eternal God, I will rout you out."* This he did, but it was only temporary.

JAMES MADISON: *"History records that the money changers have used every form of abuse, intrigue, deceit and violent means possible to maintain their control over Governments by controlling the money and its issuance."*

SALMON P. CHASE, Secretary of Treasury, 1861-1864: *"My Agency, in promoting the passage of the National Banking Act (1863) was the greatest financial mistake of my life. It has built up a monopoly which affects every interest in the Country. It should be repealed, but before that can be accomplished, the People will be arrayed on one side and the Banks on the other, in a contest such as we have never seen before in this Country."*

JOHN C. CALHOUN: *"Place the money power in the hands of a combination of a few individuals, and they, by expanding or contracting the currency, may raise or sink prices at pleasure, and by purchasing when at the greatest depression, and selling when at the greatest elevation, may command the whole property and industry of the Community. The Banking system concentrates and places this power in the hands of those who control it. Never was an engine invented better calculated to place the destinies of the many in the hands of the few."*

ABRAHAM LINCOLN:*"The money power preys upon the Nation in times of peace, and conspires against it in times of adversity. It is more despotic than monarchy, more insolent than autocracy, more selfish than bureaucracy. It denounces, as public enemies, all who question its methods or throw light upon its crimes."*

"The Government should create, issue and circulate all the money and currency needed to satisfy the spending power of the Government and the buying power of the Consumers."

(Shortly before his assassination): *"I see in the near future a crisis approaching that unnerves me and causes me to tremble for the safety of my Country; corporations have been enthroned, an era of corruption in high places will follow, and the money power of the Country will endeavor to prolong its reign by working upon the prejudices of the People, until the wealth is aggregated in a few hands, and the Republic is destroyed."*

JAMES A. GARFIELD:*"Whoever controls the volume of money in any country is absolute master of all industry and commerce."*

HORACE GREELEY: *"While boasting of our noble deeds, we are careful to conceal the ugly fact that by iniquitous money system we have nationalized a system of oppression which, though more refined, is not less cruel than the old system of chattel slavery."*

JUDGE P. E. GARDNER (In his book OUR MONEY SYSTEM): *"The money trust knows no God but Mammon. It declares allegiance to no country. It cares not who are elevated to office so long as it creates the money are regulates the value thereof."*

SENATOR CHARLES A. LINDBERGH (Father of Colonel Lindbergh):*"Under the Federal Reserve Act panics are scientifically created; the present (1920) panic is . . . worked out as we figure a mathematical problem."*

THOMAS A. EDISON:*"People who will not turn a shovel full of dirt on the project (Muscle Shoals Dam) nor contribute a pound of material, will collect more money from the United States than will the People who supply all the material and do all the work. This is the terrible thing about interest . . . But here is the point: If the Nation can issue a dollar bond it can issue a dollar bill. The element that makes the bond good makes the bill good also. The difference between the bond and the bill is that the bond lets the money broker collect twice the amount of the bond and an additional 20%. Whereas the currency, the honest sort provided by the Constitution, pays nobody but those who contribute in some useful way. It is absurd to say our Country can issue bonds and cannot issue currency. Both are promises to pay, but one fattens the usurer and the other helps the People. If the currency issued by the People were no good, then the bonds would be no good, either. It is a terrible situation when the Government, to insure the National Wealth, must go in debt and submit to the ruinous interest charges at the hands of men who control the fictitious value of gold. Interest is the invention of Satan."*

WOODROW WILSON: *"A great industrial Nation is controlled by its system of credit. Our system of credit is concentrated. The growth of the Nation and all our activites are in the hands of a few men. We have come to be one of the worst ruled, one of the most completely controlled and dominated Governments in the world—no longer a Government of free opinion, no longer a Government by conviction and vote of the majority, but a Government by the opinion and duress of small groups of dominant men."* (Just before he died, Wilson is reported to have stated to friends that he had been *"deceived"* and that *"I have betrayed my Country."* He referred to the Federal Reserve Act passed during his presidency.)

SIR JOSIAH STAMP: (President of the Bank of England in the 1920's, the second richest man in Britain): *"Banking was conceived in iniquity and was born in sin. The Bankers own the earth. Take it away from them, but leave them the power to create deposits, and with a flick of a pen they will create enough deposits to buy it back again. However, take it away from them, and all the great fortunes like mine will disappear, and they ought to disappear, for this would be a happier and better world to live in. But, if you wish to remain the slaves of Bankers and pay the cost of your own slavery, let them continue to create deposits."*

JOHN F. HYLAND (Mayor of New York City, 1922): *"The real menace of our Republic is the invisible Government which, like a giant octopus, sprawls its slimy lengths over our City, State and Nation. At the head is a small group of Banking houses—generally referred to as 'International Bankers.' This little coterie of powerful International Bankers virtually run our Government for their own selfish ends."*

HENRY FORD, SR.: *"It is well enough that the People of the Nation do not understand our banking and monetary system, for if they did, I believe there would be a revolution before tomorrow morning."*

MAJOR L. L. B. ANGAS: *"The modern Banking system manufactures money out of nothing. The process is perhaps the most astounding piece of sleight of hand that was ever invented. Banks can in fact inflate, mint and unmint the modern ledger-entry currency."*

RALPH M. HAWTREY (Former Secretary of the British Treasury): *"Banks lend by creating credit. They create the means of payment out of nothing."*

ROBERT H. HEMPHILL (Credit Manager of Federal Reserve Bank, Atlanta, Georgia): *"This is a staggering thought. We are completely dependent on the commercial Banks. Someone has to borrow every dollar we have in circulation, cash or credit. If the Banks create ample synthetic money we are prosperous; if not, we starve. We are absolutely without a permanent money system. When one gets a complete grasp of the picture, the tragic absurdity of our hopeless position is almost incredible, but there it is. It is the most important subject intelligent persons can investigate and reflect upon. It is so important that our present civilization may collapse unless it becomes widely understood and the defects remedied very soon."*

CONGRESSMAN LOUIS T. McFADDEN: *"The Federal Reserve (Banks) are one of the most corrupt institutions the world has ever seen. There is not a man within the sound of my voice who does not know that this Nation is run by the International Bankers."*

MARRINER ECCLES (Chairman of the Federal Reserve Bank, 1935): *"The Banks can create or destroy money—bank credit money. It is the money we do most of our business with, not with that currency which we usually think of as money."*

Mr. Eccles verified the fact that the Bankers get the Government bonds at no cost, while being questioned by

Representative Wright Patman on September 30, 1941, before the House Banking & Currency Committee:

Patman: *Mr. Eccles, how did you get the money to buy those two billions of Government securities?*

Eccles: *We created it.*

Patman: *Out of what?*

Eccles: *Out of the right to issue credit money.*

GENERAL P. A. DEL VALLE, U.S.M.C.: *"Twice this Country has been led into wars of no concern to us, and from which we derived only loss of precious blood and enormous treasure. And who, if not the International Bankers, gain from the transactions inevitable in War?"*

REPRESENTATIVE WRIGHT PATMAN (D., Texas): *"The People do not understand that the Banks manufacture money. They are the manufacturers creating money. The Federal Reserve Banks create dollars out of the Government's credit when they issue Federal Reserve Notes . . . the Federal Reserve ought to be impeached . . . it's a disgrace to let a few fellows representing Wall Street absolutely run this Country and have more power than Congress does."*

WICKLIFFE B. VENNARD, Sr.: *"It is important to understand that this same type of control exists in all 'banker' Nations. In the United States 200 families control two-thirds of the property . . . and they are dominated by a small group of International Banker families. In England, one-half of the Island's property is in the hands of 12 families. . . In France half the property is in the hands of 20 families, dominated by Banker families. It is more important to understand that in the 'Banker Nations' the Governments themselves are indebted to—and therefore dominated by—the International Bankers. It is even more important to understand that the desired synthesis is 'Socialism', wherein the Government owns everything and the International Bankers own the Government."*   (Vennard is the author of *The Federal Reserve Hoax.*)

The above quotations bring to mind the following statement from the Book of books: "For the love of money is the root of all evil."

Have Control and Liquidity

As this country's worsening economic fiasco develops, we can expect all kinds of controls and licensing requirements unheard of for a long time, such as various bank regulations, foreign account regulations, regulations on ownership of various strategic items, ad infinitum. Therefore, I would like to stress once more that your most important assets in such a vulnerable time are flexibility and mobility. Stay away from long-term investments which are illiquid and maneuver your funds out of investments which require a large share of your time watching and observing—they would be very bad for your nerves. In a fast-changing economy you just might be too late for remedial actions no matter how much you watch.

Try to be very cautious and, if possible, pull out of paper investments or assets such as bank notes, stocks, bonds, insurance or large savings accounts.

Rather than studying many of the distorted or meaningless statistics issued by the government pretending to reflect the economy, you should get your understanding from more reliable sources than that, such as the Dow Jones Spot Commodity Index, which drastically started to move upward somewhere during 1972, after many decades of little movement. There has, however, been a downward movement on this index recently. An upward move on the Dow Jones Spot Commodity Index, in combination with a landslide in Democratic election outcomes, would indicate that we are heading fast for runaway inflation within the next few years, if we last through the aftermath of the monetary and credit contraction which had been in process for some time because of past intermediate deflationary measures. The Democratic Party policy has a long-lasting and outstanding record on fighting economic slowdowns through inflationary spending programs. Through inflation the individual is being robbed in many ways. Another means of hidden theft through inflation is demonstrated by the fact that as a person earns more of the less valuable currency, he moves into higher tax brackets and finds himself in the position of ending up with less net purchasing power.

> Shortly after President Ford came into power, "a Paris banker, interviewed by *The New York Times,* said that currency dealers now recognize that President Ford's economic program is 'highly inflationary.' Dealers in several money centers, the *Times* report, (sic) said that the large budget deficits that were foreseen were setting the stage

for a new wave of inflation." (Gold & Silver Newsletter,
Monex International, Ltd., March 1975).

As you sell your holdings, such as real estate, stay away
from long-term payment contracts like the plague. What good
will it do you if you continue to receive money years from
now, on an 8½% contract, for example, when inflation even
now takes a toll of between 10% to 20% (pick whichever
statistic you believe the most), and if the dollar in a few years
might only be worth one tenth of what it is today or even less,
and when you face the additional definite risk of seeing your
debtor become insolvent in the failing economy? By all means,
consider rather to discount your contract—even considerably
if you have to—in order to obtain cash! Stay away from
holdings which are reconvertible into dollars at a stated
amount or on a fixed schedule and which are restricted to set
interest rates. In a period of increasing inflation it will ruin
you in no time!

Be sure that beside the various other items we recommended
to you as safe investments you also have a good store of barter
items on hand which you can trade with your neighbors or
other people in times of need. During and after the last World
War in Europe we found that such items as coffee, sugar,
wool, clothing, shoes, and tools were very good items to have
for barter. Use your brain to think of other items for which a
need would arise in case of a complete breakdown. Even in the
unlikely case that a breakdown will not occur in the not-too-
distant future, you will still have wound up with a good
investment of your capital as you will find that the prices for
those products will continue to jump in the years ahead.
There might be shortages arising for many of those items,
which would accelerate such price jumps even further and
make some items worth small fortunes. Naturally, you should
avoid items which normally would be required but because of
the circumstances involved will not be needed, such as
automobiles, car tires, art items and other luxury goods. What
good will cars and car tires be if there is gas rationing? What
good will art items be if people are struggling to keep alive?

Speculation and "Hot Inside Information"

Many people are relying upon "hot inside information" and on
the advice given by the various financial newletters. Many of the

financial newsletters seem to stay in business by complicating matters and by keeping their clients busy with unnecessary juggling around of funds. If this were not so, they soon would run out of material. Basically, the main points of a sound and permanent investment strategy could be summed up in very little space and, beside this, the importance to a person of having a sound understanding of the overall functioning of the general market system and through this understanding to arrive at his own conclusions seems to be more valuable. This way he does not have to worry about daily fluctuations and trends and he will be unconcerned about many rumors, as his personal in-depth understanding of what is sure to come will leave him in the satisfied state of mind of knowing that he has done the best he could. His decisions are based on a true understanding of the economic system and not on the multitude of opposing opinions floating around on the general market. He knows the vulnerability of market-bottom-step-in and market-top-step-out investments. To him it does not make any difference whether he purchases at the absolute bottom if he knows that in the long term the small points he might have lost would be insignificant as compared to the tremendous gains he has achieved over the longer time period. There is no way of knowing at what time the market for any item will bottom out and at what time it will top out. Waiting for such time periods catches most investors in the opposite trend from what they were waiting for and, instead of saving, they find that they have lost money in addition to all the time and nerve power that they have expended in the endeavor. Most speculators will in the long run lose at least as much as they have gained for various reasons. If they have made spectacular profit, they will become careless, and, thinking that their past luck will stay with them, they continue in their speculations until they find themselves on the losing side. The quick attainment of wind-falls makes most people careless about them and spend them in the way they receive them.

Be especially watchful of hocus pocus types of individuals who have all types of spectacular charts and sketches with which to impress you. They usually have their own interests involved and charts can be made to read in many ways. They can be started when an item was at a bottom period and can be discontinued immediately after a spectacular rise. If you were to take the long-term performance of such an item under consideration, it might show that over the long run it would actually have produced a considerable loss. Many years ago I was tricked into investing with mutual funds by similar gimmicks and lost as least one half of the investment.

As I look back, it seems to me that most of the advice I have received from various individuals has backfired on me soon after I started following it. No two individuals are alike, and investment strategy which would give perfect satisfaction to one might give nightmares to another. Some individuals crave a nerve-racking life; they seek investments with miraculous short-term potentials, great margins and risks. Any other way for them would be boring. Some use the approach of "all or nothing." Others would have trouble sleeping a single night in such a program. They are looking for conservative investments with safe long-term potentials and if there is an extreme ascending potential and a small down risk in their investments they will mostly fare well in the long run as there is plenty of margin to cover them. Make sure you only use funds for speculation which you can afford to lose and try to stay away from investments which have to pay off within a short period of time because the market could just turn the other way.

If you stay with the sound advice given above and if you make sure that no fast talking, so-called "insider" gets a hold of you, you can sit back and relax and have the noise and loud confusion pass you by. You won't have to read dozens of papers and investment advisory circulars, sweat it out some more on the hot line and burn up the telephone wires. If you invest wisely, you will be far ahead of the others running off their heels in a round-the-clock vigil. I am staying away from speculative and more volatile investments such as margins accounts and futures contracts in the framework of this book, since in such cases you should be more immediately available by living in town with constant access to the telephone. This book does not major in speculative investment strategies but deals mostly with a conservative approach and retreat type of a set-up.

One more point of advice. If the market turns sour on you, don't wait to pull out of it until it begins to turn back. Cash out and invest some other place where you can quickly regain what you have lost on the previous investment, which might not have turned upward for the next ten years. If you want to be successful, recognize when you make a mistake and quickly take your consequences. Don't remain on a sinking boat!

Take full account of your own individual personality.

The Real State of the Union

At various places in this book I have mentioned the need of an enlarged understanding in respect to the underlying and all-around tendencies of the economy. In order to give you such a summary and provide you with a base for sound judgment in your future investment strategies, I now bring you "The Real State of the Union," a message by E. C. Harwood, published by the American Institute for Economic Research, Great Barrington, Massachusetts 01230, in their *"Economic Education Bulletin,"* Vol. XV, No. 1, January 1975:

"Based on the research conducted by American Institute for Economic Research during the past four decades, I have become convinced that the United States confronts threats to its future more dangerous than any ever encountered before including the major wars. The general nature of these theatening developments already is becoming clear in the form of initial stages of a breakdown in money-credit arrangements and probably the beginning of a major depression. That worse developments are ahead has hardly been mentioned by anyone but is evident from recent trends and their actuarially calculable inevitable consequences. Unless the citizens are informed about these dangers, I do not see how appropriate action can be taken to lessen the adverse consequences and safeguard the future of the United States.

"For nearly 40 years a great experiment has been underway. For the most part it has been guided by men of good intentions in an effort to achieve perpetual prosperity and banish fear of depressions. The means chosen has been perpetual inflating of the money supply, a panacea derived from the secular revelations of Lord Keynes, which have become the dominant dogma among the economists of Western civilization. For obvious reasons, this dogma won the enthusiastic support of politicians thereby enabled to enlarge spending without correspondingly increasing taxes and of bankers whose profits were swollen about in proportion to the excessive issues of purchasing media.

"The consequences of this great experiment and other unwise policies now confront us.

"DEPRECIATION OF THE DOLLAR

"In only four decades the buying power of the dollar has decreased nearly 75 percent. From the savings, life insurance assets, and pension funds of Americans more than $1.1 trillion has been subtly embezzled by the inflating process. Real things produced thus have been diverted from the accumulation of capital equipment needed for providing future benefits to current spending including that for the Vietnam War, grandiose welfare programs, foreign aid, the support of Socialist, even Communist governments abroad, and other purposes. That wealth is gone, irretrievably lost, and cannot safeguard the future of those from whom it was taken.

"EFFECTS ON WAGE EARNERS

"Some statisticians argue that the average wages of weekly wage earners have kept up with and at times exceeded the rise in the cost of living reflected in the U.S. Bureau of Labor's Index of Consumer Prices. As a mathematical conclusion this has been true except in recent years, but concealed behind the figures are the disastrous facts for a majority of wage earners.

"First, the average wage is much higher, statistically, than the wages of a majority of wage earners because of extraordinarily high wages for many construction workers and others. Therefore, the average wage of the great majority has lagged far behind the rise in consumer prices.

"Second, a third or more of all wage earners receive only enough to buy the necessities of life: food, clothing, and shelter. Extensive studies made by American Institute for Economic Research show that the cost of necessities has risen much more rapidly than has the Consumer Price Index during recent decades. Therefore, for many millions of families, continued inflating has meant a lower and lower standard of living so that millions are desperately trying to make ends meet.

"EXCESSIVE PUBLIC AND PRIVATE DEBT

"Many people apparently believe that monetizing Federal deficits has been the sole means of inflating the money supply.

This was true during World War II, but most of the increase then was hoarded in the form of currency or was inactive in idle demand deposits until after the war. These purchasing media gradually were used to buy things not available during the war, thereby tending to minimize each post war recession until 1963.

"However, shortly after World War II excessive monetizing of private debt began. This was encouraged by the seeming immunity of the economy to serious recessions and by increasing corporate profits attributable in part to the inflating that resulted from the gradual activation of monetized Government debt. By late 1974, the overexpansion of private debt had reached huge proportions that dwarfed, by comparison, the overexpansion of private debt in the 1920's prior to the Great Depression. Recently, about half of the $200 billion of inflationary purchasing media in use was derived from monetized Government debt and about half from excessive expansion of private debt. Therefore, the problem of restoring economic order is far more complex than simply balancing the Federal budget.

"The foregoing observations reflect the data that are presented in the chart on page 135.

"EFFECTS ON CORPORATE PROFITS

"During the prolonged inflating, corporate profits have been swollen by a combination of inadequate depreciation charges for replacing machinery and equipment at higher and higher prices plus inventory profits year after year. Taxes on these fictitious profits have drained cash from nearly all business corporations with the result that the net quick-asset ratios of businesses generally are at all-time lows. Consequently, bankruptcies are occurring on an increasingly ominous scale.

"Another consequence of the prolonged inflating is found in the unfortunate condition of corporate pension funds. Investment 'experts' in leading banks have had custody of nearly $200 billion of such funds. Deluded by the stock market performance during the first two decades of inflating, nearly all such fund managers invested heavily in common stocks expecting growth to provide about 10 percent annually hoping thus to enable corporations eventually to meet their funding obligations. Many such pension funds, which never did become adequate, now have lost half or more of their value. Few corporations have fully funded their pension liabilities.   Some of the Nation's largest corporations today are not earning enough to put aside their pension-fund obligations, and cannot in a short time make up recent losses. (Recently, the Congress has voted to have the U.S. Government underwrite the railroads' pension fund.) For corporations generally, such obligations have become, in effect, a first mortgage on earnings that will be burdensome on the corporations and will substantially reduce Government income from corporate taxes for years to come.

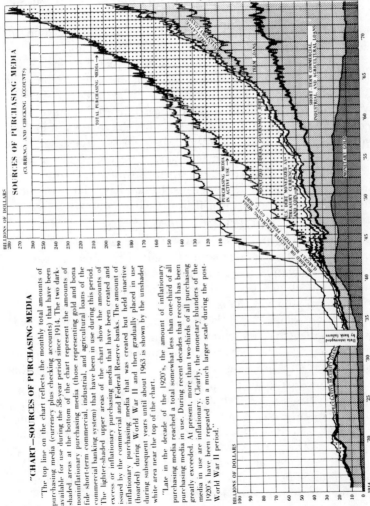

"CHART—SOURCES OF PURCHASING MEDIA

"The top line on the chart reflects the monthly total amounts of purchasing media (currency plus checking accounts) that have been available for use during the 58-year period since 1914. The two dark-shaded areas at the bottom of the chart represent the amounts of noninflationary purchasing media (those representing gold and bona fide short-term commercial, industrial, and agricultural loans of the commercial banking system) that have been in use during this period. The lighter-shaded upper areas of the chart show the amounts of excess or inflationary purchasing media that have been created and issued by the commercial and Federal Reserve banks. The amount of inflationary purchasing media that was created but held inactive (hoarded) during World War II and then gradually placed in use during subsequent years until about 1963 is shown by the unshaded white area near the top of the chart.

"Late in the decade of the 1920's, the amount of inflationary purchasing media reached a total somewhat less than one-third of all purchasing media in use. During recent decades that record has been greatly exceeded. At present, more than two-thirds of all purchasing media in use are inflationary. Clearly, the monetary blunders of the 1920's have been repeated on a much larger scale during the post-World War II period."

"SLUMS AND OVERBUILDING

"Entire sections of major cities, square miles in some instances, have become blighted slum areas, the combined consequences of inflating and rent controls. Individual owners of two and three family housing have been unable to increase rents as rapidly as costs of maintenance and repairs have spiralled upward. Moreover, the owners must eat, and rising prices have forced them to use the depreciation portion of rent receipts as well as funds that might otherwise have been used for maintenance in order to keep alive. Properties have become run down, and many such areas now are slums.

"At the same time, money rates for many years held artificially low and Government subsidies have encouraged overbuilding such as the excessive supply of new office buildings in New York and in many other cities. Also overbuilt have been condominiums in Florida and elsewhere, often with Federal subsidies of one kind or another. Many years will elapse before the construction labor thus employed during recent decades will find similar opportunities. In the meantime, creditors will lose large sums, and numerous banks have far too many nonliquid assets, which jeopardizes their solvency.

"POLITICAL PANACEAS

"Beginning in the 1930's, several experiments with Government intervention via regulatory commissions and boards as well as other legislation were initiated. Most of these experiments were political panaceas, i.e., politically popular attempts to remedy symptoms of the maladjustments that accounted for the Great Depression. The inflating during and after World War II was so great that its stimulating influence for many years overshadowed any adverse consequences of the political panaceas. Now, inflating no longer creates the euphoria that accompanies synthetic prosperity but rather increases fears of an obvious consequence, rapidly rising prices. Thus the adverse influences of many political panaceas no longer are counter balanced. All should be re-examined, because neither agricultural nor urban problems have been solved; rather, they have been exacerbated. The serious economic distortions that have resulted in many instances can be remedied only by repeal or other drastic alteration of the political panaceas.

"FOREIGN AID

"Among the programs initiated after World War II and continued on a lavish scale was foreign aid. As tax collections were swollen by the levies on partly fictitious business profits and as monetizing deficits made still more funds available, the U.S. Treasury seemed to be a magic cornucopia that could spew out real wealth to all the world at no real cost to anyone. Now the costs are becoming evident.

"Billions in foreign aid to India have facilitated the efforts of a ruling group to force that unhappy nation into a Socialist straight jacket and may ultimately incarcerate its citizens in a Communist madhouse. Instead of using funds given by the United States for encouraging agriculture in a land where about 20 percent of the potential crop land is not farmed and primitive methods are applied, grandiose heavy industry projects were undertaken. Even the 'food for peace' program made it easier for the government of India to ignore the plight of starving millions and develop nuclear bombing capability. These developments raise serious questions:

"a. Is government-to-government aid a practicable means of advancing the interests of the American people, except perhaps in time of war or when war is threatened, and then only to allies?

"b. Would private charity through such agencies as the International Red Cross, Care, and others be far more effective in alleviating the sufferings of the terribly underprivileged of this world?

"c. When taxes for the lower third or more of American families have become so great a burden as to force them into poverty, have a majority of the citizens (or possibly merely a vocal minority) the right under our Constitution to insist that the poor contribute even more to sustain Socialist governments anywhere? Ever since the days of the Plymouth Colony, when starvation nearly destroyed it during the early years of its Socialistic organization, no Socialist government anywhere, even when all-powerful as in Russia, has been able to provide for its people freedom from the threat of mass starvation.

"The problems already outlined are so serious that coping with them would require great fortitude during the years of readjustment, of restoring economic order. However, un-mistakable evidence of an even more sinister aspect of the situation now is clear.

"THE SUICIDE OF WESTERN CIVILIZATION

"In recent years much has been written about the population explosion. Many of our fellow citizens are greatly concerned about the adequacy of food and of living space for all even here in the United States.

"I have startling news for you. Western civilization is committing suicide. We should be worrying *not* about the population *ex*plosion but the population *im*plosion. The number of children born has been decreasing year after year since 1960, and that is true in Western Europe as well as here. Now the number of new births is not sufficient to maintain population growth much beyond the end of this century. This startling change has occurred as the post World War II baby boom reached the child-bearing age. In spite of a great increase in those ages, which in the past have provided most of the new born, births have decreased 30 percent.

"Already, the elementary schools report decreasing enrollments. No more schools will be needed for 30 to 40 years at least, and many will be closed. In several years, college enrollments, already decreasing, will shrink to disastrously low levels for many colleges. In New York State, for example, the vast empire known as The University of the State of New York, expanded at a cost of multiple millions in several areas of that great State, will be partially occupied 'white elephants,' overstaffed and underutilized.

"What accounts for this great change?

"During the Great Depression, the birth rate decreased markedly. Clearly, couples responded to adverse economic influences by having fewer children.

"In the past few decades two marked influences have created depression-like circumstances for many families.

"1. Inflating the Nation's money supply has driven up prices. As was pointed out earlier, the incomes of a majority of those employed have *not* kept up with the rise in the so-called cost of living. Moreover, those families, being among the lower wage groups, are able to buy little more than the necessities of life: food, clothing, and shelter, the prices of which have risen much more rapidly than has the official Government index for these and other things usually purchased by moderate income families. For millions, this squeeze has forced postponement or even abandonment of plans for children.

"2. Also important has been the increase in Social Security taxes to nearly 12 percent of payrolls, 6 percent from the employer, whose costs necessarily are reflected in higher prices. This increasing burden bears heavily on those families able to buy only the necessities in any event. Already there have been protests that such taxes are too high. For millions Social Security taxes already exceed their income taxes.

"The outlook is worse, far worse. Clearly a recession has begun, and it may become a great depression with all that alone would imply for the birth rate.

"If recent trends were to continue, the taxes for old-age pensions would increase greatly, in only a few decades to 60 percent of payroll incomes (including the employer's share), and to 100 percent a decade or two later. Such a situation is impossible, of course, because changes will have to be made before long or none but the aged, retired on Social Security, would be able to eat and there would be no funds for national defense or other needs of government at all levels.

"During the next several years, the financial pinch reducing the birth rate will become catastrophic. This is not an academic theory that may or may not be valid. It is an occurrence already under way in trends clearly apparent.

"Our Nation is confronted with a disaster that almost no one has ever imagined. Somehow, the citizens must be told the truth. Perhaps, if the problems are sufficiently understood by enough people ways can be found to avoid a decline of Western civilization unprecedented in speed and magnitude during the long history of mankind.

"The facts that have been described including trends already apparent, which may be accentuated by a prolonged depression, demonstrate that the threat to the future of the United States is no passing nightmare. A breakdown of organized society already is beginning, and it will accelerate unless the problems can be solved.

"WHAT CAN YOU DO ?

"Everyone who has benefited from the opportunities provided in the United States has an inescapable obligation to do what he can to preserve the best we have inherited from the past.

"Many readers, especially those of middle age or younger, must remain in the United States in order to support their families. Moreover, most older readers have descendants for whom restoration of the basic principles of the Constitution of the United States is vitally important. Therefore, we urge that every effort be made to communicate to others the full nature and extent of the problems confronting our Nation.

"Readers who have been following our work for decades know that present developments were foreseen as a result of long-continued research. Even in the early 1960's we were raising the question, 'Can Our Republic Survive?'

"Many supporters have told us of difficulties encountered in trying to interest friends, even family members, in these problems. That was not surprising at a time when inflationary prosperity was pervasive. Today, the situation is markedly different, and it is getting worse, much worse. We confidently predict that you will find more willing listeners now than you did several years ago.

"We invite your participation in the great educational program that will be required to save our Nation. We suggest that you begin at home with children and close relatives. Put in their hands the material that you have found most useful for your own guidance, then extend your efforts to business associates and others.

"American Institute for Economic Research has worked in this field of economic education for more than four decades. The Institute staff, are well aware that educating a majority of the public in these matters probably is a hopeless task. However, the important fact to remember is that *not* a majority but an independent balance-of-power minority decides elections in the United States. Such a minority, even if relatively small in numbers, can remove from office politicians who fail to learn and apply the lessons that should be learned from the disastrous experience of the past half century.

"Even if you knew that halting and reversing the decline of a civilization would be impossible, can you do otherwise than put your shoulder to the wheel and do what you can? After all, you are a human being, not a lemming; you have an internal guiding star, a best aspect of your personality that must be satisfied if you are to live in harmony with your inner self. That the chances of failure may be great should only stimulate the best efforts of which you are capable. We urge only that you fully satisfy your inner self, and we here pledge to do likewise.

"SUPPLEMENTARY NOTE:

"Some readers may believe that the so-called energy crisis should have been included among the serious problems. However, if the United States had avoided inflating and thus had retained a sound currency rather than one rapidly depreciating, the Arabs would not have been forced to form a cartel in order to protect their rights. They would have been pleased to accumulate assets denominated in a sound dollar. If the United States considered reliance on external sources of energy inadvisable in the event of war, internal energy sources could have been developed on a stand-by basis for use in the event of war. Moreover, as is now widely recognized, unsound regulatory policies have restricted exploration and hindered new discoveries within the United States and its coastal waters. In short, the energy crisis is only one more symptom of maladjustments attributable to unwise policies discussed in the summary above."

United States Economy and Its International Influence

Forget about the Federal Deposit Insurance Corporation, or the Federal Savings and Loan Insurance Corporation as their coverage of the deposits is infinitesimal and would only protect you in the case of a few small bank failures. If there should be a nationwide stampede on banks, the whole system would collapse like a house of cards. Dumping investments by financial houses to pay withdrawing depositors in inflationary times could expose some bank skeletons as they will have to sell at discount many low-interest-bearing papers in a time of high interest, thus reducing their book net worth.

Any sound long-term investment should be fail-proof against all imaginable market influences, including the various forms of breakdown.

When we consider the fine line that divides the United States' shaky economy from complete collapse, including a stock market crash and a banking panic, and considering further danger signals such as the ones we have seen in the case of the automobile industry, Franklin National Bank and the financial woes of New York City (the major banking center of the nation), to mention only a few, then we know that we are in the terminal stage. Furthermore, with a shaky Social Security System (whose rapidly increasing budget now constitutes the biggest single payable on the Federal books) heading for failure, one can imagine what the results will be on the economy when these vast amounts of money will no longer be spent on the American market by the Social Security recipients. This in itself will spell catastrophe. It does not even include other long-term obligations such as to veterans, military and civil service totalling $299 billion. A drastic revision of the course from inflation would bring us to an abrupt deflationary recession, probably ending in a sudden crash. A renewed play with inflation, however, is the course the government has taken again and it will eventually lead us to a runaway inflation and complete collapse of our currency. This is, if we survive the latest monetary and paper contraction.

At one time toward the end of World War II, the United States dollar was one of the most stable and favored currencies in the world. At that time we had overwhelming gold reserves which caused various other nations to base their monetary systems on the dollar. When visiting Haiti, I found it interesting that they were preferring the use of the United States dollar as their medium of exchange over their own native currency.

Some years ago when travelling the world, I never encountered problems obtaining foreign currencies as long as I had United States dollars. It seemed that the United States dollar had a magnetic attraction for men everywhere around the globe. It was no problem for people to exchange dollars (often on black markets) for very favorable exchange rates. However, this situation has drastically changed in the recent years.

This situation made many of the foreign nations vulnerable to the United States economy and financial system. In the first stages of a dollar flagging, many foreign governments supported the United States dollar by buying up large amounts of that currency through their central banks. This, however, could not be done indefinitely as it would bring their own economies to a quick collision course with inflation as they do not have the broad economic and population bases to support such programs as the United States utilizes through its taxation measures. We are facing the peculiar fact that "Uncle Sam" had also been weakened through many of the giveaways to other nations and now that he has become very sick, he has been a catastrophe for a number of strong nations. From this we conclude that there are no absolutely safe currencies found any longer. The measure of safeness will, to a large extent, depend upon how much the individual governments detach themselves from the influence and stranglehold of the United States dollar and nefarious organizations such as the International Monetary Fund.

We have seen what monopolistic monetary manipulations and organizations can do in the backfire the Federal Reserve brought in the 1929 crash. The Federal Reserve System was only in operation for fifteen years prior to the 1929 crash. A similar "enterprise", the International Monetary Fund, has been in existence since 1944-45 and has brought enormous distortions and definite signals of financial decay and ruin worldwide. It had about twice as long as the Federal Reserve to cause proportionately much more disaster. Switzerland, never having been part of the International Monetary Fund nor even of the United Nations, naturally has definite added advantages.

As a result, our nation has found itself in a suicidal two-figure inflation rate, an extremely high interest rate and a dilemma in the stock market arriving at grossly unreliable statistics, since we have to look at our economy after we subtract the inflation which is taking such a large toll today. There has been shown a 4.5% increase in the Gross National Product in the beginning of 1974, for instance. However, after adjusting that figure with the inflation then in actual process (11.5%), we find that the GNP actually fell 7%, which was the greatest drop in fifteen years. At that time there was a large corporate profit shown for the first three months of 1974 amounting to 12.5 billion. After considering the inventory markups, their profit actually fell 3 billion. This has brought confiscatory taxation on such fictitious profits which has drained cash from nearly all business corporations, resulting in many bankruptcies across the land. I could go on and on, relating such obviously phony figures to the right figures. Many programs, such as research developments which were under a 7% rise proposal, are actually going to end up with a negative figure because of rising costs. The real spendable earnings of the worker were down when you consider the net buying power of the earned dollar. When economic experts are questioned as to what happened, they often say they don't know. Some private economists conclude there was a recession, but White House spokesmen declare there was no recession. When asked about predictions for the future, many experts simply do not know what to say.

This, of course, beautifully suits the international monopoly capitalists (Communists) when we consider the importance the Communists place on the economy as seen in the following law called "Economic Determinism":

". . . Reduced to its essence, it states that the character, personality and ideas of a mature individual are created by the experiences provided by the environment particularly the environment of infancy and childhood. These experiences are stored up within the brain structure and determine brain function. Brain function in its turn determines personality,

character, and thoughts. Since the environment is created by the relationship to the productive forces which provide food, clothing, shelter and transportation for mankind, it is essentially economic. Therefore, the economic environment determines what a person feels, thinks, and does. Man and society are economically determined." (C.A.C.C., April 1, 1974).

Price Freezes

Here are some of the results of anti-inflation price freezing as we already have experienced them in the United States in our immediate past:

1. At a time when there has been demand for goods and services, the ability to contract for new business has been almost completely paralyzed.
2. Importers of raw materials have been faced with a shutdown of their plants because of uncontrolled foreign prices which would make their product a loss item with a domestic price ceiling.
3. There have been whispers of black markets.
4. Government red tape on firms has increased.
5. Increasing unemployment is plugging up the economy.
6. Many manufacturers, especially of heavy machinery, are contracting six months to two years ahead. At a time when there was a great backlog of orders, companies were unable to contract for more deliveries at agreed-upon and set prices because of continuously rising costs.
7. It also caused companies to stockpile rather than sell, adding to their storage expense. Some industries such as the machine tool industry have been hit with a near economic disaster.
8. It has especially hit companies which have been heavily involved in projects because they then are not able to keep up their liquidity on account of a holding back of some of their merchandise.

What government regulations can do in the instance of price freezes has been especially apparent in the case of the silver industry. When a lid was put on silver prices, we arrived at the curious situation of silver price controls in the United States but no controls on silver in foreign countries. That caused a great havoc with some of the major silver and chemical processing companies such as Englehard Minerals and Handy and Harman, which were about to be confronted with the option of selling at a loss or closing down their plants. Silver is greatly needed by large companies such as General Motors and International Business Machines, which manufacture electronic equipment, and Eastman Kodak, which produces films. Manufacturers of those products were just about forced to buy their own silver at inflated world prices. Under such circumstances it would be well understood that other silver hoarders within the United States would be unwilling to sell their silver for such an artificially low price. This just is one more example of how ineffective such a government program is in generating a genuine price on a product under its intervention; but instead, it causes a great havoc on the general market. This price control dilemma has especially also affected importers in disastrous proportions.

Chapter 10

Investment Suggestions

There is a great need for people to come to an overall understanding of the economy rather than relying upon conventional investment advisors who have been proven wrong so many times in the past. Especially in the confused mess we find ourselves in today with the perverted economies, politics and everything else putting their spider webs around the individual, we need this definite comprehension more than ever. This is why I again want to underline the necessity for the individual to get some factual material and study it in an endeavor to gain a clear-cut perception of the main issues at stake and of the hidden tendencies and motivations which brought about our present dilemma. If you have come to a firm understanding of the underlying causes of today's economic situation, and I hope that the preceding chapter has contributed in this to a great extent, you will be able to ascertain the future trend, judge other people's advice and chart your own course.

When tackling the subject in such a way, you will find that economics can be much more exciting than dry, boring college professors make it out to be. Your knowledge will become alive to you as you assemble the economic jigsaw puzzle yourself. From this perspective, things which were puzzling to you before will not any longer be a mystery. Also, you will see no need to get your opinions from the press, which is proven wrong most of the time, anyway.

Cash and General Investment Information

In your investment be careful not to "put all your eggs into one basket" but rather divide your risk by investing in various fields. First make sure that you have a one- to two-month money supply on hand in cash. In the case of sudden bank closures this would tide you over for some time and also enable you to pick up good bargains in times of extreme cash shortage. You can have that money stuck away in some secret place.

Depending upon your financial situation, I would recommend that you have savings in an amount (according to your need) between $2,000 to $10,000 on deposit for emergencies in large banks with a low loan-to-deposit ratio and a very broad base of domestic depositors. After this you could invest your funds approximately in the following manner: five to ten per cent silver coins, twenty to forty per cent gold coins, twenty per cent in such investments as gold stocks and/or silver stocks of either the high-income group or long-term prospect group, Swiss annuities or other investments with good companies and countries with a strong economy, or other recommended investments available in Switzerland or other countries with a sound monetary and economic system. The remainder of your assets will probably be tied up in such essentials as your home and property, cars and other such items of daily living. At the slightest sign of a crisis with global repercussions I would definitely liquidate all remaining paper assets entirely and invest the funds in assets with intrinsic value such as precious metals; in fact, some might prefer to do this now as there might not be time later. We face the increasing risk of major recessions and depressions, even though we may not be able to predict the exact time on a scientific basis. Certainly the economic blunders of the 1920's have been continued on a larger scale. Ever since the gold reserve requirement for Federal Reserve notes was removed in March 1968 and since the dollar/gold fiasco in 1971, the last barriers of continuously inflating the dollar have been eliminated. The nation's monetary managers were under certain restraining influences while substantial gold reserves were required by law, which is not the case any longer. The question is how long will it be before the dollar will be practically worthless, as it appears doomed by losing more buying power continuously.

Since our currency as well as that of the world is becoming more and more debased as time goes on, people everywhere are looking for other ways of investment. Any student of finances of course knows that our entire national income is being eaten up by the interest we are paying on our debt. There are many books on the market which show the unredeemable shape of the dollar and make plain that the situation we are in today is worse than the conditions that existed before the 1929 crash. For the greater part of 1975 we did not have more serious inflation in the short term since we were experiencing the ultimate result of inflation: a recession.

Unfortunately, however, if the traditional solution to a recession is used (increased government expenditures to reduce unemployment), the basis will be established for another round of even greater inflation.

Consider that the 495.2 billion dollar United States government debt alone will cost the American worker and taxpayer 30.5 billion dollars in tax payments during the next fiscal year. That is about triple what it was just about ten years ago. The interest paid for 1973 and 1974, for instance, is actually more than the entire national budget for 1941! If this sounds complicated, think of it in terms of a smart young fellow in a leaky rowboat who drilled a hole through the bottom to let the water out. The boat may be likened to "principal" and the inrushing water to "interest" that eventually sank the boat.

Looking down the corridors of history and studying the various books on sound investment strategy for a crash time, we find that the following investments are outstanding:

Diamonds

It seems that the diamond market which has been coming more into the picture lately would be of appeal mainly to those people who are very wealthy and are looking for investments which they can store very compactly. Diamonds would offer great mobility as a person could grab them and run in case of evacuation needs. I am rather doubtful that diamonds will hold their value in a major global economic upheaval, however.

This market has never been popular enough to guarantee immediate liquidity.

The most recent years have proven to us the reality of an inflationary recession. However, we are continuing to teeter on the brink of disaster because once an inflation has reached a certain point even a small reduction of the inflationary trend necessary to keep the economy rolling can bring on a sudden crash; in other words, without even any deflationary measures. Therefore, let us look further at other investments.

Gold

As crises continue to occur in foreign-exchange markets for currencies, it will be increasingly harder to retain paper profits and the purchasing power of such profits will vanish like smoke unless they are invested in assets with intrinsic value or otherwise not subject to manipulation by monetary managers. Throughout history gold has proved to be the best medium of exchange that is of easily measurable value, convenient to store and a safe means of holding wealth. The desire of private citizens to hold gold increases in proportion to the efforts of monetary managers to manipulate the currency of a country and extort wealth from the citizens. Efforts to demonetize gold will only backfire, as intelligent citizens will become educated as to the true value of that precious metal. Such persons will seek to safeguard their present and future financial security by leaving in savings accounts only sufficient funds to cover emergencies and investing excess funds wisely in gold, silver and other items of intrinsic value.

Gold is mentioned in the oldest historical records, including the Bible. I know of a person who bought a whole restaurant for a DM 5.00 gold piece during the bad time in Germany.

There are many positive and few negative points with regard to gold. Let me issue a warning first. When obtaining this precious metal in the form of coins or bars, it would behoove a person to be very cautious. There are certain gold coin dealers who will promise to send the coins to you soon after receipt of your funds. If they are located any distance from where you live, you might run into trouble. There are those who will keep the money for a number of months, getting interest on that money all the while without ever sending the coins to you. Then if the price goes down for gold, they will cover your order with them through a lower purchase price and eventually send the coins to you. In this case, you will wind up with a loss of interest for the entire period on the entire amount of your funds and also with a further great loss as you could have covered this purchase of coins for a much lower price since the value per ounce went down.

On the other hand, if the price for gold goes up they finally might send you your money back, saying that they have not been able to obtain the coins to cover your purchase. In this case you wind up with a loss of interest for that period of time, including all the trouble you had corresponding back and forth (and possible legal fees), not to mention the aggravation of your mind at the very least. A number of those coin dealers went into bankruptcy and receivership. In that event the person having his funds held with them is in very bad shape. These individuals can quickly lose their entire investment and some evidently have. This presents a further danger for margin accounts. Only after you take delivery can you be one hundred per cent sure that you won't wind up with a loss of your investment.

There are a few other points to consider when investing in gold and which might have adverse effects:

1. Some believe that money should be used rather than invested in metals and stored. However, this point could only be validated if a person had a possibility of using his money in a way that would bring more profit than it does in the rising gold market. Those with strong patriotic or other ideals might prefer to keep their funds in the form of money so they can put and keep them in immediate active investments for their cause.

2. Those who go on record in their gold purchases can face the future possibility that the precious metal might once more be outlawed in this country and be called upon to turn it over to the government.

3. In spite of some great rises in gold prices, there had been a number of other items which had risen yet more spectacularly, such as anise oil, certain vitamins, certain chemicals and sugar. The future record can easily change and certainly

gold as a whole seems to be headed for a spectacular future.

Let us now move on to the many positive points.

The gold coins with the greatest intrinsic value rather than the ones with numismatic value form one of the better gold investments in the market. In times of need they would be easier to redeem and handle than gold bars because of their small size and because of the greater difficulty in imitating gold coins than gold bars. Also, they seem to be internationally more favored. It would be possible to file shavings from a gold bar and repolish it afterward, but this would be practically impossible in the case of a coin because filing marks would immediately appear since the engravings on the coin would be diminished or defaced. Coins as a whole are a more-sought-after gold trade item than bars. The reason I advise staying away from gold coins with numismatic value is that as the international financial climate deteriorates there will be fewer and fewer people who will have sufficient funds to maintain their collection hobbies. They will have enough of a struggle to stay alive in the oncoming disaster, let alone pursue such a time-consuming hobby.

Some of the coins which give you better intrinsic value are the Mexican 50 pesos and, to a slightly lesser degree, the smaller denominations of that peso line: the 20, 10, 5, 2½ and 2 gold pesos. Better yet are the Austrian 100 corona, the South African krueger-rand and the Hungarian 100 korona, which is a very beautiful and polished coin.

Since ownership of gold in any form by the citizens has been legalized in the United States, we have seen how quite some effort has been put forth by the government as well as the publication media to belittle gold as an investment.

The Treasury's anti-gold talk also found expression in the implication that only a small minority of Americans are interested in gold because the gold price did not soar into the high heavens the very day gold (in all forms) generally was legalized for the first time after forty-one years at the very beginning of 1975.

I don't suppose that this silly supposition was swallowed by many Americans.

1. First of all, the legalization came at the time of the year when people were busy jumping from one festival to the next.

They were drained of immediate cash, just having passed the major gift-giving festival of the year (and the uncertainty whether legalization would be activated in time kept people from saving funds generally).

2. We had just gone through a year of extreme inflationary recession, leaving a large percentage of the people extremely illiquid.

3. Gold coins could be owned for many years before 1975 and the regulations for that market had even been eased more, so coins with hardly any mark-up over the bullion price could be bought. This enabled those who really wanted to invest in the yellow metal (and had money) to do so, and the funds of the most important buyers had already been committed.

4. The gold price at the time of general legalization (which included bullion) was extremely high for that particular time (at $190 to $200 per ounce), considering gold had been at $129 on July 4, 1974. There had been a number of great swings in the gold market. Just a little over two years ago the price was $60 an ounce. In July of 1973 it had climbed to $127 an ounce, but in November 1973 it had moved back down to $90. April 1974 saw a gold price of $180 and about three months later it was back down to $129. The majority of people did not want abruptly to commit themselves lock, stock and barrel to a thin and volatile market experiencing some heavy shock waves mostly on account of some big-time speculators. They had no need to rush into a market which had just topped out at a price level never experienced before on the American scene. What happened at the dawn of the new general American gold market compliments the American public.

5. There have been so many warnings issued by the various government agencies and publication media which have had a further temporary restraining influence. Now that the general United States citizen has become aware of the gold market and its prices, he will step into that market with accelerating force as he sees its long-term price level continuously rising, under a renewed economic slump and a coming monetary chaos.

There will be up and down movements for sure, as we have seen again also in 1975, but we will see a further persisting expansion of paper money on a world-wide scale—which, of course, was also tremendously bolstered in the United States by the fact that Nixon closed the gold window on August 15, 1971. This completely removed the restraining influence on the dollar by means of a fixed-price relationship between gold and the dollar. As soon as the administration got rid of another restraining influence (its hobby), it could print paper bills galore. This simply means that in the future, the gold price will rise (in the long term) in relation to increasing paper money flowing into the market especially because of the floating exchange rates. Keep the *long-term* gold price potential in mind. The lower gold price ranges in the recent years (the ones we have seen after gold had already been much higher) have nearly always been shortlived and shortly the price climbed back toward the more realistic level as compared to the value of paper currencies.

At the very time when there has been a world-wide move to discredit gold through the SDR (Special Drawing Rights) of the International Monetary Fund and other interest groups, we see the curious phenomenon of gold being looked upon with increasing interest by many foreign central banks, which see a great strengthening of their liquidity by the raising of the gold price. Due to the recently increasing chaos in the world's economy, their liquidity has been continually worsening. There probably will be more and more pressure on the United States government by some of the foreign central banks not to sell any more gold in order to drive the price down. Further, the United States places itself in a very vulnerable position by selling off more of its gold as paper bills might not be very acceptable media of exchange in the future, especially on an international scale, and in times of war it could spell near disaster. Already the Arabians have been getting weary of the continuously depreciating dollar which increasingly is flowing into their treasuries. An oil shortage would be a catastrophe for America in case of war.

The official anti-gold attitude is not any longer limited to one or a few nations as was the case in the past, but now is worldwide. The production of new paper money flowing into the market is by far outrunning the production of gold and that would spell a very lucrative market to the gold investor. Rarity and desirability of gold will give people a greater incentive to work for it rather than rapidly depreciating paper money. In many countries of the world we already have seen a decreasing willingness to work for quickly inflating currencies. Since about half of the gold in the world is owned by the central banks, it would seem that the abolishment of the two-tier system in November 1973 would be of utmost importance in relation to a further upward move in gold prices. We have seen signs for that in the French Central Bank's raising of the gold price on their books after President Giscard d'Estaing met with President Ford on that issue. Earlier we had the $2 billion Italian loan from the German Bundesbank secured by roughly one fifth of their gold at a $120 price. As economics worsen on a global scale, we find central banks ogling gold with increased fervency. I deem it very fortunate that, due to greater demand from the public reflected in increasing pressure by the Congress and also a worldwide gold legalization move, the United States government finally had to legalize gold. Both Congress and the Senate had already passed several bills in that regard. The Treasury found itself in the dilemma of not being able to come up with excuses not to allow the American public to own gold after it had demonetized the same. The Federal Reserve System's rampage against gold and for the United States dollar has only resulted in more worldwide distrust of the once mighty dollar.

There are a number of rumors concerning new money having been printed and ready to be used. There are other rumors concerning the eventual elimination of money, just using credit cards in combination with computer systems. Whatever the case, you are largely unaffected by such manipulations when you are holding exchange media with intrinsic value in your hands. A new monetary set-up or a totalitarian computerized credit number system will not be able to condition the mind of every individual concerning the merit of accepting the age-old exchange media such as gold and silver coins for barter.

The facts are that gold has been a medium of exchange for many thousands of years. In the case of barter it is not always possible for a person to make a direct exchange of his merchandise for other merchandise needed. Gold became a very helpful medium of exchange to bridge the gap because it is of definite intrinsic value, compact, durable and easily dividable. It is in extensive use for dental work, plating of certain industrial parts, art work, jewelry and many religious items. In the very unlikely event of gold being discontinued worldwide as a monetary metal, it would still have its value for the other reasons stated above. It has been for those reasons that governments have issued gold-backed currencies down through the centuries. Deviation from this policy has usually met with fatal consequences. There have been government sales of gold in the free market to lower the prices temporarily. Many potential investors in this yellow metal have been frightened off by such manipulations; however, any sensible person would realize that the more gold the government sells, the more it will open itself up to the risk of runaway inflation. That, of course, will eventually make the price of gold rise even more.

Also, you can buy old gold mountings quite cheaply from some jewelry shops. You may keep them as an investment or you might utilize them by inserting into them your own stones if you are interested in cutting and polishing of stones.

Jewelry can be bought for about one third of the retail price through membership buying services as previously mentioned.

You might not want to keep your valuables in a safety deposit box as banks could be closed down again and you might have no access to those valuables for a long period of time, if ever. If purchasing such items as gold and silver, try to obtain quick delivery because some companies will run out of supplies and not be able to fulfil their obligations. For added privacy, some people conduct their coin purchases over the counter on a cash basis without using a check or a name. Then be sure you keep those valuable items in a safe place under your own control; that is, that you can have access to them at any time without being dependent upon a third party, a breakdown or changing conditions.

Gold was a very practical asset to us under Communism. Currencies were then practically valueless and my father's earnings were negligible, but we were able at intervals to sell some gold rings or gold watches which we had been able to bring through the fiasco, and the funds from those sales would carry us over for a number of months at a time to secure some of the items which we could not otherwise obtain or produce ourselves.

In times of inflation or political showdowns, the fact that you can produce much of what you need, in addition to what you already have provided for yourself and your family, will be very important. Any surplus can be traded for other items, or you can purchase needed items for inflation-proof gold or silver.

Here are some gold statistics:

In the second half of 1975, manipulations such as the IMF announcement to sell gold put further temporary downward pressure on the gold prices which made the acquisition of gold a bargain throughout the latter part of 1975.

"The United States and French governments agreed on December 16 (1974) that nations could use current market prices to revalue their gold reserves, thus ending U. S. insistence that national gold holdings be valued at the 'official' rate of $42.22 an ounce. In January (1975) France revalued its official gold reserves from $42.22 an ounce to $170.40 an ounce, increasing the value of French gold from $4.4 billion to more than $17 billion. French finance minister Jean-Pierre Fourcade says higher prices for official gold reserves will be 'widely accepted' by central banks within a couple of years. While the U. S. has said it doesn't plan any immediate revaluation of its gold, it has indicated that it may ask Congress to abolish the $42.22 an ounce price in order to permit revaluation, according to *The Wall Street Journal*." (Gold & Silver Newsletter, Monex International, Ltd., March 1975).

In 1957 the U. S. currency had a backing of approximately sixteen per cent gold. By 1972 all legislation requiring minimum gold reserves was repealed. By 1973 U. S. currency was backed by only three per cent gold. The situation is continually worsening, so I will refrain from any further statistics because they would be outdated by the time this book reaches the market.

Silver

The upward potential of silver is extremely good because of the continually increasing differential between supply and demand. For many decades the silver market has been strongly influenced by the government which still had a stockpile of two billion ounces of silver by 1950. However, in the 1960's the U. S. government sold most of this stockpile in an effort to keep the price down. The supply of silver is lower than the demand by approximately 100 million ounces. In 1958 we started using more silver than we produce. Today the United States only produces about fourteen per cent of the world's silver but consumes about forty per cent. Speculation in silver will increase as the stockpile gets continuously smaller and the government probably will blame the general public's hoarding for the subsequent price rise. As the stockpile continues to dwindle and the price of silver continues to soar upward, more and more of the weaker companies using silver as one of their components will fizzle out of the market. Eventually only the stronger companies which use only a small percentage of silver in their products and therefore can afford a great price increase in silver will dominate that market and run silver prices to a maximum. This game will continue until the silver demand and supply will become equal. Don't believe that the silver price is leveling off when you read that silver consumption is going down (which it will have to), nor when you read that production will go up (which it might); but rather when the condition mentioned previously has been met. May I point out that those potential predictions can be disturbed by various abrupt influences such as government intervention and wars. Still, silver should do very well in the long term.

I do not recommend specially minted silver coins because of their high mark-up. You can find a better value in silver bullion bars and United States silver coins.

There has been a very lively market in silver investments, especially the American silver coins minted until the end of 1964. Silver coins seem to be a better investment than silver bars because of their familiarity, ease of handling and small denomination. There is less of a risk because even if silver prices should plummet the coins will always keep their face value as long as the government backs up its present currency. In addition, there is the appeal of a certain collector value as they become more rare in the future.

You can buy your silver and store it yourself or you can have it stored, preferably at a Swiss bank if being bought through a Swiss bank.

I don't recommend silver dollars because of their high premium. Stick with ten- and twenty-five-cent pieces and half-dollar pieces. Silver coins usually sell per bag with a face value of $1,000 (ten thousand dimes, four thousand quarters or two thousand half dollars), which contains roughly a net total of 720 troy ounces of pure silver. Each bag weighs approximately 800 troy ounces (55 pounds) in unrefined silver. If you take the silver bullion price at any given time and multiply this per-ounce price by 720, you will arrive at the value of the silver per bag.

Do not be disturbed by news you might hear about potential silver substitutes that have been found. Occasionally you hear much noise about such inventions, but soon no more is heard of them.

Some feel that since silver is in great industrial demand there will be a decline in silver prices in an inflation, depression or collapse because many of the factories at that time become nonfunctioning and their demand will leave the market, creating a greater supply and a smaller demand on the silver market with dropping prices. This argument, however, does not seem to be valid because if the factories are forced to shut down under such declining conditions, there will certainly also be a shutdown as far as the silver mines are concerned; therefore, the decline in supply should more than equal the decline in demand as there will still be investment activities aside from some other demands in that market.

In II Kings 6:25 we find for one reason or another that silver had become of relatively small value during those disastrous times mentioned there. This, of course, would depend upon the amount of merchandise as related to the amount of silver on the market, and there seemed to be quite a lot of silver available then. Today's situation is quite different.

Also, silver has a greater weight by far than gold and in case of needed mobility it will be nearly impossible to carry along large amounts. However, it is recommendable to have some of both metals—gold for larger transactions and silver for smaller transactions—during times of complete monetary chaos when paper currencies become valueless.

Temporary Investments In More Stable Foreign Currencies

There are many strong voices recommending an investment of funds in so-called "foreign money havens", such as the

Swiss franc, the Dutch guilder, the Austrian shilling, the Belgian franc and the German mark. Even though the Lebanese pound and the Portuguese escudo have one of the highest gold backings of any currency, they would be the ones I would desire least because of the unfavorable governmental change in Portugal and because of the highly explosive situation in the Middle East in the case of Lebanon.

The Dutch guilder has had a very good potential which ranks right behind the Swiss franc. However, it is not traded as universally and has a much shorter history than the Swiss franc. There has been a total oil embargo against the Netherlands and the extent to which such a potential future embargo could damage that currency will have to be seen. In addition to this, Holland is an extremely flat country which easily could be wiped out in the case of big tidal waves caused by earthquakes or nuclear blasts.

Depending on the strength and weakness of the dollar, foreign currencies and other factors, the Lebanese pounds, Dutch guilders, Swiss francs, silver coins, silver bullion, gold coins, gold bullion, speculative gold stocks and futures contracts can give you a maximum short-term profit potential.

I would definitely consider the foreign currency investments less recommendable than the two previously mentioned (silver and gold). The reason for this is as follows: Swiss banks, for instance, charge for nearly all of the services they perform. It is expected that more restrictions will be placed on foreign investments as more foreign money keeps flowing into their countries. There have been some restrictions added recently. Switzerland is high on the list because of its past magnificent performance for foreign investors. However, this time I feel there is eventually going to be a universal crash, which will affect every country on this globe because we are so much involved in international trades and exchanges and many international monetary systems, such as the International Monetary Fund. When the bottom drops out from the economy in the United States, the shock wave will be felt in disastrous proportions around the world. Even Switzerland has already felt the adverse effects on its economy and currency.

We have seen what the past monetary devaluations of the United States dollar have done to the economies in such countries as Japan and West Germany. Japan is very much inter-dependent upon the United States market and has had 25% inflation already per year and many bankruptcies. West Germany's momentarily strong economy has felt the reverberation as there has been increasing inflation, some bank failures, other bankruptcies and increasing unemployment. Deutsche mark investments might be more risky in the future since the German economy is too much dependent upon the United States economy. The Volkswagen factory alone lost approximately 30% of its United States market in 1974. A country such as Germany is very much inter-dependent upon its import-export markets, and major economic and financial changes such as the fluctuation of the dollar/Deutsche mark exchange rates will necessarily have an adverse effect on the German economy.

If and when that international shock wave encircles the globe, it will not be possible for Switzerland to remain an isolated island amid a raging and wild sea. The Swiss economy is not any longer that self-sufficient. Being an autarky would be a prerequisite.

As mentioned, there probably will be sudden showdowns on international money transactions such as restriction of currency transferrals. If and when this happens, then the investor in foreign currencies could find himself easily caught with just paper again. This could be as bad as a completely devalued dollar bill in his hands. Also, bank holidays would make access to Swiss holdings impossible as the funds then could not be redeemed.

The way to future foreign bank account restrictions had been paved by the United States government through the foreign account reporting provision on income tax returns and through regulations which force the banks to report transmissions of funds in the excess of $10,000 and individuals to report funds in the excess of $5,000 carried abroad with them.

Once foreign account restrictions have been initiated, some persons will no doubt still transfer funds by taking them to nations across the border, transferring them from there if laws affecting a general transferral of funds into foreign countries from these nations have not been passed simultaneously.

It might be advisable to have limited funds in foreign countries for the purpose of merely keeping some cash funds available for unseen, sudden emergency situations a person might find himself in, which could be recalled any time. He could keep his funds in a currency which has less inflation and at the same time would have the funds available if a sudden need for cash arises. It remains to be seen how soon, however, this strategy will become more valuable once again, for as long as things move in a recessionary trend in the United States we might not have this encouragement. Except for temporary small adjustments, the dollar had generally declined against the strong foreign currencies such as the Swiss franc and German mark in the past, even though there was a slight reversal throughout much of 1975, for instance.

A further upward move on the part of the European currencies is dependent upon how much these countries decide to support the dollar in the future. When they discontinued such support in early 1973, the dollar dropped dramatically against theirs. While a strong foreign currency account would be a good bet for short-term investments which will give you immediate funds when needed, gold and silver would be the better long-term investment by far. In the long range gold and silver has a great upward potential, but for the short term it might show a considerable temporary drop while any short-term drop of the Swiss franc would be very minimal. Also, there is the added security of a safer currency while facing the possible collapse of another currency. However, as I have said, I feel that investment in objects with definite intrinsic values which a person can have right close by is a better one by far, and gold and silver should definitely be one of the best investments if taken as a long-range investment. As previously mentioned, it can also bring a loss as a short-term investment as this market is in some ways volatile on account of big up-and-down moves due to strong domination by many investment speculators and financially powerful individual speculators.

Benefits of Swiss Bank Accounts

1. Probable tax benefits.
2. You can utilize the account for investments all over.

3. Strict privacy.
4. Safety of funds in case of a breakdown or confiscation in your home country.
5. More banking freedom.

Withdrawal restrictions are enforced except when certain investments are being made through the same bank. A very important rule is to have your liabilities in weak and your assets always in strong currencies. Be sure the bank has a high position of secured loans and large reserves.The possibility of the Swiss government freezing accounts of foreigners is small and since governments are usually glad for sound entries, it would seem that it would always be possible to bring the funds back into the United States. This does not apply the other way around.

Through a past effort of Switzerland to support the dollar and increasing social programs, the Swiss franc has been in a slowly weakening position even though still favorable in comparison to other countries' currencies.

Another point in favor of Switzerland is that it has not been dependent upon American economic aid and therefore less inter-dependent upon the United States. Swiss mountaineers, shepherds and farmers which form the backbone of the country are hardy, independent and resourceful. The country has a strong form of self-government by the people which dates back to the 1200's. When legislature does not approve a law at times, it is voted on by the people *by initiative*. This is what we need in America—that people will take the initiative instead of letting the one-eyed monster deteriorate their brains. Back in 1291 men from Schwyz, Uri and Unterwalden determined that they were free men in the face of a strong threatening power— the Hapsburgs. One time the Swiss mountaineers trapped and totally defeated an Austrian army ten times stronger. Swiss neutrality has never been broken since 1815. Switzerland has been untouched by most of the major troubles of the last century such as invasions, dictatorships and famines. Two world wars swept around rather than through that little republic which is one of the oldest in the world and whose hard-working people are united by a strong love of liberty. Their favorite sport is target shooting as a result of the tremendous national defense system which teaches nearly all men in Switzerland to handle firearms. This is interesting as we are about to be disarmed in this country—it seems to follow right along with a disarming of the currency and economy in general. Switzerland has been a refuge to many foreigners as it has rested like an island amidst the many neighboring wars. Rather than having police, increasingly controlled by the Federal government, (most of the police forces throughout history have been nothing more than paid mercenaries defending the powers that be) run your life, I believe that the above can teach Americans some very valuable lessons as to how this country should also be run (according to the Constitution).

Here is some information from the Swiss Credit Bank at Paradeplatz 8, in Zurich, Switzerland. Its various accounts are as follows:

1. Current Account (Kontokorrent) (in Swiss francs). No interest, withdrawals can be made in any amount and at any time. The same applies for current accounts in foreign currencies.

2. Private Account (Privatkonto) (in Swiss francs). Interest 3% with 35% tax on the interest. Up to 10,000 francs can be withdrawn per month without withdrawal notice. For larger amounts, three-month notification of withdrawal. No such withdrawal notice needed if you buy commercial papers through that bank. A fee of 1.50 francs per month is charged for a service charge.

3. Savings Booklet (Sparheft) (in Swiss francs). 4¾% minus 35% tax. Up to 5,000 francs can be withdrawn per month without notification. Larger amounts need six-month notification of withdrawal.

4. Investment Booklet (Anlageheft) (in Swiss francs). 5½% interest minus 35% tax. Up to 10,000 francs can be withdrawn per year without advance notice. For larger amounts, six-month advance notice is required. For persons above sixty years, same notification requirements as with Savings Booklet (see paragraph 3).

Even though I am still holding funds only in Germany (funds which, by the way, originate in Germany because of my having come from that country), I would not recommend Deutsche mark investments any longer very highly because of the vulnerable base of the German economy and the increasing rate of unemployment. This is rather a sudden change in a country which not long ago employed 5 million guest workers (foreigners working in Germany on a temporary basis as there was not enough working force available in Germany itself).

In this book I am trying to stay away from citing a lot of regulations or a lot of other information which can much better be obtained at the time they are needed. In our day they are changing so fast that by the time this book will reach the market many of them no doubt would already be outdated so it would serve no useful purpose in quoting them.

Further points of importance are: If you desire a deposit of Swiss francs on your account, your money will be exchanged for the rate effective that day. There is no minimum amount required for opening such an account; however, it is expected that you do so with at least 3,000 francs.

If you want to use your funds from an account for the purchase of commercial papers, gold, silver or coins, you have to have a Current Account. Those transactions can only be done via the Current Account or the Private Account.

Savings and Investment booklets can be held at the bank without any fee.

At the end of each year you receive a statement.

The bank reserves the right to change the interest rates at any time.

The bank reserves the right to discontinue any existing business connections at any time, especially also to annul loans and recall any outstanding monies of the bank without prior notice.

The Current Account can be opened in Swiss francs or in foreign funds. The other accounts mentioned in points numbered 2, 3 and 4 above require Swiss francs for all transactions. The accounts in points 3 and 4 can only be opened under one name. Provision is made for the naming of a beneficiary on the accounts.

Correspondence can be conducted in German, English, French or Italian. Any correspondence can be kept at the bank and only be mailed out on special request.

There are three banks which carry the label "the big banks"; Swiss Credit Bank is one of them and has 112 branch offices throughout Switzerland. Because of instability on the international exchange market, the Swiss government has put in effect certain restrictive measures. This means that since October 31, 1974 Swiss franc amounts on an interest-bearing account will only receive interest up to and including 50,000 francs for depositors not residing in Switzerland. Amounts which are being credited to a Swiss franc account are charged a 3% commission only on a deposit above 100,000 francs; in other words, there is no commission up to 100,000 francs. Deposits on foreign currencies do not carry such a commission charge. Furthermore, there are no restrictive regulations concerning the acquisition of commercial papers and precious metals. The bank offers its own bank bonds for a term of seven to eight years with 7¾% interest, for a term of five to six years with 7½% interest or for three to four years with 7¼% interest.

Tax Treaty USA—Switzerland

Claims to refunds of Swiss tax are deducted at the source.

Under the terms of the convention between the United States and Switzerland for the avoidance of double taxation with respect to taxes on income, individuals resident in the United States (other than Swiss citizens who are not also citizens of the United States), as well as partnerships, corporations and other entities created or organized under the laws of the United States, *may claim refund of tax withheld in Switzerland as follows:*

	(% of gross amount of income)	
	Total Tax Withheld	*Refund*
Dividends	*35%*	*20%*
Bond interest and interest on cash deposits and savings accounts (interest on savings accounts not exceeding Fr. 50.—a year are tax free)	*35%*	*30%*

Refunds as listed above may be claimed by filing Form R-82 in duplicate with the Federal Tax Administration of Switzerland, Bundesgasse 32, CH-3003 Berne, Switzerland. Forms R-82 will be supplied upon request by Administrative Office of International Operations, Internal Revenue Service, Washington, D. C. 20225.

Form R-82 should contain a list of all securities and all income therefrom for which a tax refund is claimed, and it should be accompanied by suitable evidence of deduction of the Swiss tax, such as our credit advices or statements of savings accounts showing the amount of dividends or interest collected.

The claimant's signature on the original and duplicate of Form R-82 is to be legalized by a notary public. Upon receipt of the claim, the Federal Tax Administration in Berne will send the duplicate to the United States Tax authorities who then may verify whether the respective income from Swiss sources has been properly reported in the beneficiary's United States income tax return.

The foregoing does not apply to Swiss citizens resident in the United States who are not also citizens of the United States. Instead, these persons are entitled to apply against their United States income tax liability a tax credit for the Swiss tax withheld on their income from sources within Switzerland. If the amount of tax so withheld is not fully allowable as a tax credit, a claim to refund for the difference between the tax credit allowed and 25% of the gross income being subject to Swiss withholding tax will be accepted on special Form R-82 A. Such forms must be completed and filed in the same way as Forms R-82 described above. You pay tax in the country you are a citizen of for assets you hold in that country and you can apply this tax withheld against your United States income tax liability.

Currency Futures and Long-Term Investments

Large futuristic dollar payments to be made to you can be protected in value through currency futures. They will protect you against a further dollar decline until you receive your money and redeem the contract.

If you are interested, you might add Swiss francs, long-term futures contracts and gold bullion margin accounts to your long-term growth potential in addition to the other long-term investments I have already mentioned.

Even though time is running out fast, you still have time to do a lot of maneuvering and can utilize many of the techniques recommended to you in this book unless there has been a complete breakdown by the time this book reaches the market. Even in that case, there will still be a number of things you can do if you use your imagination.

Stocks and Other Paper Assets

There had been some voices heard from the circles of informed investment advisors recommending a reacquisition of shares toward the very end of 1974 with the intent of selling them after a short intermediate climb in the Dow Jones index. They felt that as we move from an inflation to an apparently brief monetary and paper contraction with further recession people will temporarily gain a certain amount of confidence when noticing a short halt or slowing down of inflation and some declining prices. We now know that people assumed things were taking a better turn and indeed there was a remarkable and temporary boost for the stock market. I, however, would strongly recommend the readers of this book definitely to get out of the general American stock market. Temporary and intermediate tendencies on the stock market are very difficult to assess properly and even though you might find yourself with a small increase of funds, it might not be worth it on account of your vexation of mind. There are many better ways to invest your funds than to play with such "maybe" profit possibilities unless you are an expert. If you have to hold paper, consider investments in gold stocks as well as investments in countries with a stable economy and a lower rate of inflation such as is the case in Switzerland, for instance.

As I mentioned elsewhere in this book, extreme caution is recommended in regard to nearly all other paper assets.

Real Estate Investment

Real estate has been a classic investment in times past; even during wars, devaluations and destructions by bombing the land always has stayed there and kept value. However, the many changes of recent times have not even left that classic investment untouched. Real estate values with some exceptions have no longer increased in value but instead have decreased considerably in value, especially in certain areas of big cities where people practically had to abandon their holdings because they were unable to sell them and unwilling to keep paying high taxes to support government programs which they did not favor. Some owners abandoned apartment buildings since they were unable to sell them and did not wish to rent them to people who could not or would not make payments.

For all practical purposes no private persons own any land in the United States but are just renting it from the government for a regular payment called taxes. If you were to forfeit those payments, you would lose your property. As the national government and the state governments get deeper into debt all the time, they will keep raising taxes until it might finally be impossible for some people to continue holding on to their land as they will find that the taxes are eating up their last savings. It seems that the property tax racket has become nothing but a legal theft of the governments to support social and other programs which the people otherwise would not be willing to underwrite. Some people have moved in great numbers from their properties into other areas because living conditions had become too unfavorable. Then they discovered that the governments in the new localities were raising their taxes and using the tax money to support the very programs the people were fed up with.

Legislative Dangers

Another danger lurks on the horizon in the form of legislation introduced in state governments as well as in the national government to disinherit the people from their properties through various ways and means. As America has become nearly bankrupt in its gold holdings and as tax and other payments are not any longer taking care of the rising national debt, the land grab might be designed as the last-ditch effort of the national government to "bankroll" its sky-rocketing financial obligations. This, however, would seem to me as one of the last death cries of this fair land.

Beware of Phony Land Promotion Schemes

A word of caution should be issued here about the dubious methods some land promoters use. I had contact with one such land-promoting outfit that advertised lake front property in Arizona. When I visually inspected the properties, I saw that they had dug a little pond, simply throwing the soil around the pond in such a high wall that even the houses to be built adjoining that little pond would not have a view of the water. There were only some dirt roads through the property and the primitively built entrances to the land were already falling apart. At a later time that company went bankrupt (intentionally or unintentionally) and the people lost their investment.

Some of the outfits will pay transportation expenses to inspect the land and while the people are there, they will cater to them in various ways just to make the sales. I met a farmer from the

Midwest in another such development who was sitting before his house, one of the few houses around there. I looked at the dust around him and the dirt roads as he told me how they had flown him to the development and driven him around for an entire week on little sightseeing tours in the area until he had bought. That man still thought he had a bargain. After questioning him to find out how much he had invested for the small lot and the tiny house he owned there, I found out that the development company had made an enormous profit on the poor man after they had spent a very small percentage of that profit on him.

Further examinations revealed that this type of land developer will put up a few very poorly built improvements on the development such as a swimming pool, community building, etc. Other cheap improvements may be thrown together for a quick and immediate appeal to the prospective customers who are being shown around the area under much bombardment by high-pressure sales talk. After the lots of the development have been sold by very fraudulent methods and false promises, the developer will cash out the contracts at a substantial discount with some bank. The funds which have been spent by well-believing people with the understanding that they will be used for the development of the property have then to a great extent been wasted on the discounting and people are stuck with long-term payments to some bank. I cannot warn people strongly enough to watch out for such gimmicks.

I was able to purchase ten acres of land across from such a development from a private party and paid less for the entire ten acres than the people paid for a small lot in the development which folded up a short time later. When I finally sold my ten acres, I just barely broke even; you can imagine what happened to the investment the people made with the development!

I have even run across a real estate outfit promoting land in Florida on an international scale. When wanting to visit the property, I was not able to do so for it was situated about twenty miles away from the Tamiami Trail (the next street) out in the swamp and a person would have had to take a boat out there and then stand knee-deep in the water!

When looking for real estate or jobs, try to stay away from areas with extensive government jobs or where large civilian companies which are dependent upon large government defense and other contracts are located. We have had some classic examples in the Seattle, Washington, area when Boeing laid off many thousands of people. Whole neighborhoods became vacated and houses were impossible to sell—what a change in government policy can do! Those areas are by far too much dependent upon vulnerable industries.

Barter Items—A Wise Investment For Chaotic Times

A very important investment in these times is in items you can use for barter when the monetary system becomes nonfunctioning. You should stick with items which will have a broad appeal to many people and will be definitely needed and utilized in chaotic times ahead. Such items would be coffee, sugar, honey, vegetable seeds, various types of tools and many of the items I mention on the stockpile list.

Stay away from luxury items that people would have no need for when times get bad, but rather look for items of barter as mentioned.

These items should keep their value for an extended period of time and they will be readily exchangeable.

You will find that garage sales and flea markets, for instance, are very good places to pick up barter items (many of these you will want to use yourself) for an extremely low price. Old, used items are literally thrown at you in this country price-wise (beware of "antique" pricing) and, in addition, they will have been produced out of much better material than the junk you buy today. In fact, some of the very practical items especially good for a simpler way of life and which cannot be purchased new any longer can be found at such places.

Move Into Assets You Control

Any assets you have which are not under your complete control, sell and liquidate them and move them into assets under your control. Store up a food supply for at least one to two years and save about twenty-five per cent by buying it wholesale, if possible. If you have a lot of equity in your property, try to pay it off as quickly as possible because almost-paid-for properties will likely be the first to be seized by foreclosure. All throughout history such practices were used by financiers to enrich themselves and the more equity you have, the more enrichment themselves and the more equity you have, the more enrichment it will bring those who foreclose on you. If you only have a very small equity in your home, you might consider either one of the two following procedures:

1. Do not pay off your mortgage or contract at this time as you will be able to do so at a later time for cheaper money after inflation has taken its toll. You can invest your funds meanwhile in a more profitable way as long as it is easily reconvertible and then pay off your mortgage or contract whenever your equity is large enough to be seized. As long as you have a very small equity, you would not lose much even in a foreclosure and your profits in other investments probably will more than pay for what little you might lose.

2. You might consider selling the property in order to relocate yourself in a place which will better suit the present and coming economic dilemma.

PART IV
LIFESTYLES

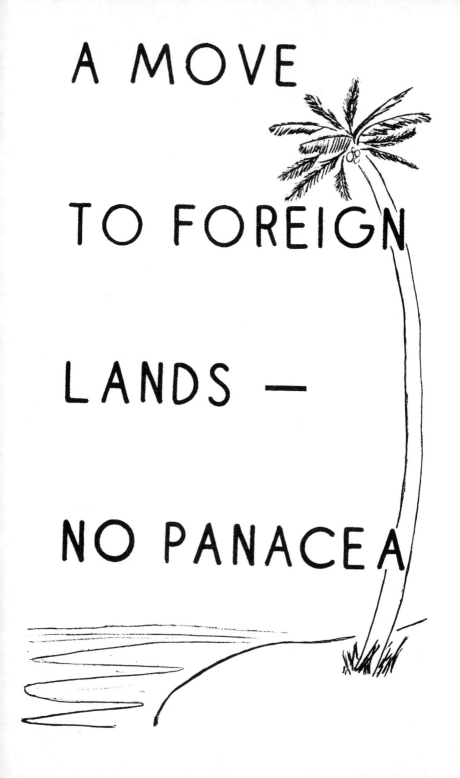

A MOVE

TO FOREIGN

LANDS —

NO PANACEA

Chapter 11

A Move To Foreign Lands—No Panacea

Some people are playing with the idea of moving into foreign countries as they see the continual erosion of freedom and economic prosperity in the United States. However, they do not realize that in our day nearly all the countries are strongly interdependent internationally. Foreign countries are just as vulnerable as the United States, and some even more so, in the increasing onslaught against its economy. So we find erosion of freedom not only in America but overseas as well. Things are changing quickly everywhere and you will find that conditions overseas are not the same as you might have found them when visiting there many years ago, just as a traveller revisiting America many years later would not find it at all the same as it was earlier. In the event that a crash does not come within the next few years, you want to be very sure that the foreign so-called "haven" you are picking will suit you for that extended period of time. There will be many inconveniences, especially if you left properties and gadgets behind in the United States which would need your administration.

Many Americans have looked upon Canada as one of their foreign havens. Canada has never been attractive to me on account of the extremely cold weather, with the exception of British Columbia. A further distinct disadvantage, as far as I am concerned, is the fact that it is even more socialistic than the United States.

New Zealand, which is a beautiful country, has a poor currency with only a negligible backing of gold (less than one tenth of one per cent). It is far down the list among the various better-known currencies. The extreme geographical isolation of that country and its underpopulation have made it a definite attraction for a long time to totalitarian governments such as Red China contemplating a take over in order to obtain more land to help solve its overpopulation problems.

The Japanese economy has an extremely vulnerable base because of its complete dependency on foreign oil and other import as well as export markets.

In Europe we have too many small nations too close together, each fighting for elbow room, with too many people in them.

Many of the South Sea islands, long looked upon by some as a potential hideout in hectic times, could be wiped out by huge tidal waves caused by earthquakes or nuclear blasts as many of them are extremely flat. If they were occupied by unfriendly forces, you would have a rough time to find a place to hide out if they are small islands.

Jungle areas such as the Amazon territory or the Matto Grosso in Brazil are hard to live in on account of the mosquitoes, poisonous snakes, poisonous plants, extreme heat as well as high humidity, which is a breeding ground for sickness.

Furthermore, if the showdown you are awaiting is not immediately forthcoming, you might be stuck for a long time under rather hostile conditions.

For those who consider a move to South Africa, it might be of interest to know that the South African government has far-reaching and intricate agreements with the International Monetary Fund regarding the distribution of its gold to the general market and to various governments. When the free market price of gold was above the $100 range, the South African government sold much of its gold to various central banks at—believe it or not—$42.22! Here is a better one yet: a country which is the main producer of gold in the world does not even allow its own citizens to own the main commodity, gold!

Chapter 12

Try Yachting!

Living on a yacht seems to be the answer to the growing complexity of modern living. Although it is a good life for people of all ages, it also has a special appeal for still-active retired couples on smaller retirement incomes as your money goes much further than in living ashore. It also is a fine alternative to stagnating there. You are with congenial, like-minded folks with a youthful outlook. There is just enough to do and enough that is new to see to keep you active.

When buying a boat have the boat independently surveyed as to condition before closing the deal. There could be quite a number of things wrong with it. As for expenses, obviously some major shore expenditures will be eliminated if you live permanently aboard: rent or the cost of maintaining a home, heating and utility bills, cost and upkeep of a car, expensive clothing. The tax situation is far more favorable. Seafood is cheap in season and it can be had for the catching. The modern marina provides restrooms with showers, lounge and watchman service.

Many persons reduce their fees for dockage by frequently anchoring out, especially in summer. Movements are far less regulated. The modern boat marina's services and charges are comparable to those of today's trailer camps. You are not compelled to use such places, however; you can still anchor almost anywhere. Moreover, you can choose your spot for its isolation or to be in the company of other boats. Water travel is still far from congested; instead of being bothered by traffic you look forward to seeing other boats. Boat travellers are hardly at the mercy of the other fellow. At the speeds boats travel—five to fifteen miles per hour to make their fifty- to one hundred-mile daily runs—water traffic accidents are almost a rarity.

You will not only learn different languages while you communicate with interesting people as you sail the world, but also have a quiet time to read and study things which interest you greatly.

Points to Consider
Before Buying a Sailing Yacht

1. Points in favor of living on board:
   a. Mobility
   b. Excitement of new things (no dull routine)
   c. Inexpensive way to travel around the world
   d. Can haul bigger loads
   e. Family close together
   f. No public school
   g. Can see many countries easily
   h. All children can be actively engaged in tasks on the boat (fishing, sails, motor, cleaning, navigation, studying, etc.)
   i. Quiet means of travel
2. Points against living on board:
   a. Would probably have to sell home
   b. No United States mailing address
   c. Would have to get rid of many things
   d. Very little fresh produce
   e. High dockage (at some areas when not using boat)
   f. High purchase price
   g. No family doctor, dentist, handy when needed
   h. Would have to re-establish contacts for supplies, insurance, etc.
   i. Much paperwork (during changeover from conventional life)
   j. Would have to check around for reasonable and competent repair facilities, docking, etc.
   k. Slow means of travel (this to some is an advantage)

     l. Hard to get place for moorage sometimes

     m.Sometimes only moorage available is
        undesirable

     n. People could break in and steal while
        family is ashore

     o. Boat could easily be damaged by
        careless persons docking alongside.

3. Additional negative points (part-time residence
    on board):

     a. More insurance if you have home, yacht
        and car

     b. More maintenance worries

     c. More likelihood of burglary,
        vandalism, etc.

   Some of you might want to decide between buying a sailing yacht or a small plane (for travel). The purchase of a plane has the following points to consider:

1. Points in favor of having a plane:

     a. Low tie-down fee

     b. Can look over possible survival land from
        the air carefully

     c. Speedy travel

     d. Airports are scattered throughout
        country; plane is more accessible,
        suitable for overland travel

2. Points against having a plane:

     a. Longer, more expensive training to become
        a pilot

     b. More dependent upon weather conditions

     c. Much paperwork (to acquire and keep
        a plane)

     d. Increasing requirements: bi-annual pilot
        checks, medical, plane annual, electronic
        equipment requirements always increasing,
        continuously more government rules and
        fees, etc.

     e. Expensive maintenance and repair

Armchair Sampling of Global Living Conditions

   As a person lives on board a yacht, circling the globe, *he will at the same time have a wonderful opportunity to sample living conditions in the various parts of the world for as extended a period of time as he likes in each area.* He might decide at a later time to divorce himself from living on a boat entirely and become a permanent settler in some other country or some romantic, idyllic island in the Southern Hemisphere. There are today, more than ever before, strong advantages for moving into the Southern Hemisphere.

Advantages of the Southern Hemisphere

All of the atomic powers, including India, Israel and maybe in the future also Egypt, are located in the Northern Hemisphere. The power-hungry war nations are also located in the Northern Hemisphere. Should it come to a global atomic war, practically all of the radioactive fallout will be scattered over the Northern Hemisphere. As there is an effective separation between the two main air circulation systems at the equator (the hottest geographical area), the Northern Hemispheric air movements coming down into equatorial territories are heated as they move over hotter territories until they are driven up into the higher altitudes (hot air rises) and then they turn back northwards. In the Southern Hemisphere this system works the other way around. In the case of an atomic war, therefore, most of the radioactive fallout will concentrate in the Northern Hemisphere and the Southern Hemisphere will be in a much better condition.

For those who consider settling in the South Pacific we might mention that New Zealand is a much nicer area (friendly people, more attractive scenery) to settle down in than Australia. There have been numerous immigrants to Australia who finally discovered that and moved on to New Zealand. This advice is for those who still take either one of those two areas into consideration.

A movable set-up, such as living on a sailing yacht, would enable a person to be at liberty to move on to a new and better location whenever that becomes desirable. (I favor sailing yachts rather than motor-powered yachts because they are not dependent upon a fuel supply.)

I realize that the decisions for such major steps in life, with a rather considerable outlay of funds and great change in lifestyle, are not always so easy to come by. There are many points a person might want to consider before going ahead on

any such undertaking. In order to make things easier for you
along this line, I am bringing you the next topic.

When a Choice Becomes Difficult
First Approach

We have found a good way of resolving difficulties such as
not being able to make a decision between two very appealing
choices by the following method: We take a sheet of paper,
draw a line down the middle and have a heading on the left
side such as "Favorable Points" and a heading on the right side
such as "Unfavorable Points". Then we fill out the sheet. We
might keep expanding this list for several days or even weeks
and then if in the final analysis we find that the positive points
far outweigh the negative points, we know that this is a choice
which we would further consider. If the negative points far
outweigh the positive points, we might decide to dump that
project altogether. In comparing two choices and therefore two
such charts, we could find whether one chart contains less
negative points and more positive points than the other chart;
therefore one choice might single out itself more than the
other one. Through such an elimination process we will be able
to come to a faster conclusion by having substantiated our
weak ideas by projecting them solidly on a piece of paper.

Second Approach

Another good approach of handling difficult projects or
decisions is to get your mind working on that matter as you lie
down in the evening for a night's rest. Then during your sleep
your subconscious mind will continue to work for you, sorting
out essentials from non-essentials and you might find that the
answer to your problem comes more easily the following day.
You can repeat this approach for over a period of several days,
if necessary. This system has worked for me, many times
unintentionally.

Practical Application and Further Meditation

While deciding between a move into the wild, open country
from a city life or a move onto a yacht, we followed just such
a procedure. There were a number of negative points for both
choices and many favorable points for both. We could picture
ourselves sailing the calm or stormy sea, letting down the
anchor in some peaceful harbor of some far-away romantic

island, lying down for another night's sleep while listening to the gentle breezes sweep through the rigging of the boat and the waves gently splashing onto the hull. We knew that we would be able to obtain food for less money because we would be able to buy in "free ports" where there would have been no duty added onto the products, or have a trustworthy native purchase fresh food for us. Then we could not only avoid hotel food and being charged expensive tourist prices, but enjoy the pleasures of sampling local products in their natural state. We knew that much nourishment could be obtained from the ocean and we strongly favored the aspect of mobility. We could just stay at an area as long or as short as we desired and when becoming tired of that particular surrounding or when finding out negative aspects at that locality we could just set the sail, haul in the lines and sail off for another beautiful place more suitable and more appealing to our individual lifestyle and interest. These aspects we could not find in a permanent set-up someplace on the land.

Much Research Needed

We had made an extensive search of the best boats on the international market with regard to seaworthiness and price. We were studying boat literature from various nations such as England, Norway, Canada, Germany, Taiwan and the United States. We had our need narrowed down to the minimum of a forty-foot-long sailing yacht. After much research we finally pinpointed our choice to a beautiful forty-foot sailing yacht built in Taiwan. Portions of the mahogany interior were artistically hand carved. The yacht was outfitted with a chartroom, various sleeping quarters, attractive and efficient galley, auxiliary engine, inside and outside steering, a shower room, polished teak deck areas and many other desirable items. We would have been able to obtain this yacht for less than half the price we would have had to pay for a comparable boat on the American market. We had the contracts in our hands ready to be signed.

This was prior to the second devaluation of the United States dollar, and today we wonder whether it would not have been a good investment for us to have purchased that yacht anyway as we could have sold it on the present market at good profit after the dollar devaluation.

Making Our Choice

We finally made up our minds that our particular situation was in favor of finding a suitable place somewhere out in the mountains rather than living on a yacht. Some points under consideration were a relatively large family, which might have been somewhat crowded on board a ship for any period of time; furthermore, the need of fresh homemade and homegrown food products for the family as well as some small children in the family who could easily fall overboard.

Life Can and Should Be Interesting

The experience of living on a boat would have been very appealing to me as an individual or with maybe just one more person. This type of life would not have been a novelty to me because while still in Germany I attended the Nautical Academy in Bremen, studying the extensive curriculum which included astronomical navigation, ocean and river marking systems, and other practical aspects of high sea sailing. In times past I have enjoyed sailing yachts on some of the ocean areas of this world with many unforgettable memories which will stay with me the rest of my life.

There are so many exciting and wonderful experiences available in this world which bring a broadening and uplifting effect upon the individual that it is difficult to understand how so many people can satisfy themselves with the daily rut of getting up, eating some chemicalized, pre-manufactured breakfast, going to a monotonous job which they have held for perhaps the greater portion of their lives, coming home, eating another meal and then being bombarded by some prefabricated pap on television—rather than living their own lives which would give them fulfillment, happiness and better suit their abilities and dreams.

I have found much joy and excitement on a higher plane in life by doing such beautiful things as listening to opera and other classical music, sailing the high seas, flying small planes, travelling, roaming the wilderness and visiting and studying nearly all major archeological sites of the world. It has always been a puzzle to me how people—nowadays particularly young people—try to find fulfillment for their lives in such things as watching television, taking dope, smoking, drinking, vandalizing and stealing, when it is very obvious that the perverted thrills they get from such activities will not last very long and, even worse, will prove a price too heavy to pay for the rest of their lives by permanently wrecked health, brain deterioration and many other damaging effects.

When I think back to some of the wonderful uplifts I got when I sat on the deck of a sailing yacht looking at an undulating blue or green ocean, waves gently splashing along, fish playing in the water and seagulls overhead fading into an evening sky beautifully colored with shades of pink, red and lilac by the setting sun; or when I compare the thrill I received when I climbed into my private plane, flying it over magnificent scenery below, I feel sorry for the many young people who have fallen short of finding fulfillment in life with truly worthwhile endeavors.

Chapter 13

The Land Beckons

This chapter will probably be the most important in the LIFESTYLE part. The reason for this obviously is that most of you will probably prefer this particular type of life since it will be more closely related to your present mode of living than any of the other lifestyles mentioned. It will also take less adjustment on your part. Because of this, it will naturally be very appropriate for me to go into more detail here.

Many of the books written on crashes, dictatorships and monetary chaos have had amazingly little to say about this particular subject. This is all the more astonishing as personal survival with its needs for food, clothing and shelter is much more important than merely protecting one's financial holdings. What good is money if you cannot sustain your life because of the lack of essentials (food, clothing and shelter)?

However, we know of some people who panicked into unsuitable retreats many years ago and then did not endure very long when the crash did not come. Be sure you will set yourself up in such a way that you will adequately last for a long time just in case the breakdown is delayed; this is for your own protection. I believe always in presenting both sides of the story.

How to find Information on Potential Living Areas

One good way you can gather information ahead of time when you wish to choose a remote area to move into is to write to the

Chamber of Commerce of the states that interest you and request material for newcomers. Seek especially the following: the temperature variations, rainfall averages, frost records, fish and game laws, population distribution, wildlife surveys and contour maps. By studying this and other data, you can figure out the most likely areas according to your needs and likes. This will form a basis from which you can work, concentrating then in those most likely areas and checking them out until you find what you want.

Location and Climate

Some favor moves to Alaska and similar regions, but if it is too cold or especially rainy it takes that much more time to maintain yourself under survival conditions, not to mention the added misery! Such conditions would tend to make a person locality-trapped as he would have a difficult time trying to survive if he had to leave his house (which provides a shelter from the fierce elements), his winter wood and food supply and the many other items of need. Under adverse weather conditions not only would it be much harder to survive after being forced to leave behind an established homestead, but it also would be much more difficult to set up new living quarters and take much more time to do so. In more favorable weather areas these things should be much easier.

An Excellent Way of Examining a Place and Its Environment (Three ''Acid'' Tests)

Air Inspection

We have always made it a definite rule to fly over any piece of real estate with our private plane before buying such for the purpose of living there. Once we found a beautiful piece of land on top of a small mountain with a beautiful view over a lovely valley with a romantic river winding its way through. However, while flying over that area, we discovered a big stone quarry very close to that property just on the other side of that small mountain. We could see that there would be plenty of truck traffic and noise in the area.

Another time we found one piece of property that seemed ideal. The house was spacious and lovely; the living room was especially large and featured a cathedral ceiling. Outside there were beautifully landscaped gardens and majestic oak trees and the entire property was surrounded by forest. Upon checking further, however, we discovered there was a gravel pit nearby which would create daily noise and dust.

From the air a person is much better able to see the lay of the land and get a bird's-eye view which enables him to ascertain exactly the advantages and disadvantages of the property in question. If you do not have your own plane, contact a few airports in the immediate area for price comparison and find out how much they would charge to take you on an inspection flight over that particular area with their smallest plane. A smaller plane is cheaper and will give you a much better view of the land. It would be preferable to use a high-wing plane for this purpose as your view will be unobstructed. Ask the pilot to circle around the property in all directions and in different altitudes for different or changing perspectives.

Actual Living Conditions Simulated

Another very good manner of checking out a prospective property is for you to return to the same on your own—that is, without the real estate agent or the owner. You should obtain permission first. Then, when you return, bring your camper or your tent along and set up quarters right on the land you consider buying, preferably at the very location where you would set up your buildings or where they are already set up. Spend at least a few days living there and you will be surprised how many details come to your mind in regard to this land, how many things you find out about the land and how much better you will be able to assess the situation thereafter. While having followed this practice in the past myself, I have come to notice that certain places were perfectly quiet during some periods of the day but excessively noisy during other periods. Sometimes they would be situated in the flight pattern of arriving or departing planes with the traffic being concentrated only at certain times of the day. Also keep in mind that the flight patterns change with the prevailing winds. While your place might be nice and peaceful during some days, there might be excessive noise on other days.

You might find that you would have to contend with the noise of stone quarries or other intermittent noise sources, including barking dogs and hollering children. There might be other distracting things, such as frequent strong winds, rattlesnakes, unpleasant neighbors, etc. While some of these points might seem negligible to you, which indeed they may be if you only acquire the property for investment purposes, you will find that they take on a very important meaning once you plan to spend a major part of your life in such an area.

Get the Score From the Old Timers

Give the property a third "acid" test. Visit all or several of the old timers in the area. Try to make friends with them first. Then inquire about the property you are interested in and get all information you possibly can from them about that land, including all problems relating to it such as you find listed in this chapter. Make sure the old timers do not give you an intentionally gloomy rundown in answer to your questions in an effort to keep out newcomers. This is why I said to make friends with them first.

Environment Potential (Future Trends)

Conditions in today's world change so much that if a person finds a good place somewhere and spends a lot of time and money on improvements, he might later find that the environment has changed unfavorably because some undesirable elements have entered the area or factories have been built close enough to contaminate the air and create noise.

When you relocate, make sure you are far enough away from cities so that there will be no problem along this line. It will be unlikely that factories will locate near you as there would be no working force quickly available. Beside this, you have the added bonus of being less vulnerable in the case of war when cities are being bombed. Also, your real estate tax structure should be lower. You at the same time enjoy much cleaner and fresher air when there is enough of a distance between you and the cities.

A friend of ours living in the mountains has found an additional advantage environment-wise by living right on the boundary line of two states. He has no trouble when hunting season comes around as the hunters avoid that borderline area, not knowing what state they are in. That eliminates further trouble, especially for his livestock.

Resources of the Land

A very valuable asset for your place will be forests surrounding the same and assurance that there is sufficient wildlife in the area which you can utilize for additional food supply when needed. You might look for an area with a satisfactory population of deer, rabbits, squirrels and fish.

It would also be wise to consider the proximity of a connecting mountain chain so you could move under cover in case of needed mobility. If possible, try to combine a type of scenery which suits your liking with nearby mountains and water.

Elimination Process

Floods and Avalanches

You should also make sure that you are not locating in an area which could be flooded especially during the winter or spring. We experienced very great flooding in the Pacific Northwest in December of 1964. It happened after extensive snow deposits in the mountains and the lower elevations as well were quickly melted by a sudden warming trend accompanied by heavy rains. During this great flood entire villages were torn away and bridges, streets and many other installations were washed out. Much further damage was caused as the fast-melting snow cover mixed with the heavy rains and turned into avalanches and mud slides as the soil became extremely soft, losing its binding consistency. Whole mountainsides broke off, carrying along rocks, logs and other heavy objects, all of which went thundering down into the valleys. For this reason it might be advisable not to locate on a steep mountainside nor in valleys closely bordered by precipitous mountains.

I remember one experience I had while searching for land in the northeastern corner of Oregon. After I found a beautiful place in the wilderness I took my plane and flew over the area before proceeding any further. While flying over the property, which was bordered by steep, high mountains, I could see a giant ravine which ran from the very top of one of the highest mountains bordering this place all the way to the bottom in such a way that any avalanche coming down that ravine would completely wipe out everything there. It was remarkable that I was not able to see this from the ground, but had a perfect view of that potential danger from the plane. Needless to say, that ended my consideration of that place.

Earthquake Zones

Another important research you should do before moving to a different area is to check whether that area is located close to a fault line or in an earthquake territory. Late research has proven that all various fault lines which are scattered throughout the globe are interconnected. For instance, such a system rings the Pacific Ocean, following the Pacific "Circle of Fire". It runs along the West Coast of South America, through Central America, up the West Coast of the United States, through western Canada, up into Alaska and then on down through Japan, the Philippines and Indonesia. Any of the volcanoes located along that Pacific "Circle of Fire" could become active, especially during or after extensive earthquake activities. The crust of the earth is relatively thinner than the shell of an egg and any violent shaking could produce a chain reaction. Atomic warfare might initiate strong earth-moving forces which could release further natural disasters through earthquakes, tidal waves, volcanic eruptions, floods, etc.

It would be wise to keep in mind the areas of the United States that are in zones of relatively high seismic activity and strong intensity of earthquakes. When choosing land, these areas should be avoided:

1. From the Canadian border near Kalispell, Montana, almost due south, through Salt Lake City, Utah, all the way to the Mexican border near Tucson, Arizona.
2. The western portion of California, especially from San Francisco south to the Mexican border.
3. From Sault Ste Marie, Michigan, to Buffalo, New York, then northeasterly, roughly following the Canadian border.
4. The strip of land from the Ozarks to the coast of North and South Carolina.
5. Northwestern Nevada.
6. A triangular area southerly from a point at about Santa Fe, New Mexico, broadening to a base roughly from El Paso, Texas, to Del Rio, Texas.
7. Southwestern Alaska.

A European newspaper brought the following report with the headlines "Giant Earthquake Predicted". The article states that the authors of a book, entitled *The Jupiter Effect*, predicted a giant earthquake catastrophe on the Pacific Coast of the United States for the year 1982. The mathematician, an astronomer of NASA, Stephen Plagemann, and the astronomer and reporter of the scientific magazine *Nature*, John Gribben, reported in their book (published in London) that this earthquake will be the result of an unusual constellation of planets. In 1982 all the planets of the solar system will be lined up on the same side of the sun. Their combined gravitational force can cause solar storms and earthquakes of catastrophic extents. Especially endangered, according to their opinion, is the San Andreas Fault located on the West Coast of America, which is known for its earthquake activities. The two astronomers consider this fault the most dangerous break in the earth's crust. Other scientists have agreed that the computations of the rare future constellation of the planets are correct.

How To Buy Land

When looking for land, you would do well to contact an old, established, dependable real estate agency or, better yet, that you get in contact with some decent, reliable old timer living in that area who might be willing to sell you some of his land or be able to recommend some good buys. You could receive a comparison of prices by spending weekends or vacations in your area of choice, watching newspaper advertisements, and you should then be able to look around more extensively in that area. Try to stay away from high tax zones such as expensive school districts as most of your taxes are allotted to the school districts. Move into an area where there are not a lot of schools presently in existence, being built or planned and a lot of social programs in operation or contemplated.

What To Look For

Once, while looking around in the northeastern part of Oregon in the Eagle Cap wilderness area, we ran across a fantastic wilderness camp set-up with numerous sturdy log cabins furnished with good wood stoves and integrated water heating systems. It was located in a beautiful setting completely surrounded by wilderness and national forest area and had many of the aspects we were looking for.

There are certain criteria we check before we consider buying any land. They are as follows: The land should be on a dead-end road (paved, gravel or dirt), which means there will be no traffic, ensuring complete privacy, or at the end of a short (one-half to one mile) private road off a county-maintained road not heavily travelled. This way the county will maintain the longest stretch to your wilderness home and you will only have to maintain the short stretch of the private road which leads off the county-maintained road to your place. This might include the pruning back of obstructing trees, the occasional build-up of the road with gravel or cinder to keep it firm and the clearing of the road of snow in the winter. To keep the road driveable under snow conditions, you could merely drive over it a few times every few days with your four-wheel-drive vehicle in order to keep the tracks clear rather than plowing the entire road. Some of our friends are located in such a way that their road becomes so extremely soft and muddy in the winter and early spring that if they were to use their car on that road at those times the wheels would disappear. As a result, they have to pack in their supplies the rest of the way. Be sure, therefore, that your road can be driven on all year. Other friends live on a little-travelled county-maintained road but they are occasionally fumigated by clouds of dust and dirt when speeding cars pass their residence which is located right next to the road. Their problems arise because they are not located at the end of a road. The place should be accessible year round at least by four-wheel-drive vehicles. The homestead could be located across a bridge on the other side of a creek.

There must be pure water available for home water supply, either through a year-round, fast-running clear creek or river, or a spring or well, and there should be enough water for irrigating a garden big enough to supply the needs of the inhabitants. The parcel should be surrounded by an area which will be kept in its natural state and not used for developments or for subdivision and sale, such as national forest, Bureau of Land Management and railroad land.

Privacy

Some people prefer to set up their survival quarters at an area or on a piece of land which they do not own themselves, for if

they owned their survival land the government would have a record of their residence through the tax department and would easily know where to find them for such potential futuristic projects as forced labor and resettlement. For this purpose, these people prefer to set up survival quarters in remote wilderness areas where no one is likely to look for them. Such land is still plentiful in the United States. I say this with reservations, as I know about people who have been evicted from such land with considerable expense.

You can also get yourself a little trailer, pull it into some quiet mountain terrain and hide it on the ledge of a shallow canyon or amongst a dense grove of trees. This will better prevent vandalism and will, of course, give you more privacy. You should paint this trailer green. You could stock it with the various items we have discussed elsewhere in this book.

Once, while on a hike, we ran across a very similar type of set-up. As we were walking on an old, abandoned logging trail far from any trace of civilization, we found a small green trailer stuck away on the upper edge of a shallow canyon with just the roof visible from the trail. I sighted that trailer more by accident than by anything else. It was very hard to recognize. We marvelled for the longest time how the people had been able to set that trailer where it was placed—completely blocked in by trees from the front and rear and on both sides by large rocks and the ascending canyon wall. It was furnished with a little wood stove and various other necessities. This would be a very ideal type of set-up for a purpose we are discussing in this chapter.

When Time is Short

If you are in a hurry to move and you do not have enough money to build, then your parcel should have some buildings in good enough condition that they could be made habitable before the first winter. It would also be helpful if the land has a portion of cleared area and the rest in timber. Then you will have pasture for animals, space for garden, timber for possible construction use and sufficient firewood for your winter fuel supply.

If you are not able to obtain a parcel of land with suitable buildings, you can always pull a trailer onto that land after checking the zoning regulations and being sure that the road will allow passage of the size of trailer you desire.

If you are not able to make any retreat preparations, you can at least have a few suitcases packed with the most necessary items needed for short-term survival. They should contain some of the items we have mentioned elsewhere in this book, such as first-aid kits. Then when caught off guard you could just throw them into your camper, or you could have a camper already well provisioned for such a purpose and be on your way on a moment's notice. Be sure, though, that you store a sufficient amount of gas safely to get you to the place you have designated for short-term survival.

Be sure you are independent of electricity, which will most assuredly fail completely when there is a breakdown in this country. Most of the nation's economy is geared to electricity. This, of course, applies to freezers, gas pumps, etc. Therefore, you will not be able to obtain gas from gas stations even though they might have gas. Your food supply stored away in a freezer which is hooked up to public power will soon be worthless.

If you live near a river, ocean or other large bodies of water, you could use a boat to transport you to the area you have chosen for short-term survival.

Finances

Make sure that your financial ability is not overtaxed by the price of the parcel of land you choose. If you are limited in funds, there are areas which have their own scenic beauty which are still very reasonable in price. We have found some areas in the Pacific Northwest where we could have bought larger parcels of land at an average of $40 to $60 per acre. If possible, it would be good if you could pay off your property quickly. If your financial means are very limited, you can find some small parcels of land—a little more or a little less than five acres—which is sufficient to maintain you. Some of those parcels will have a small, inexpensive building on them. Our preferable size is more like twenty-five acres, big enough to give you what you want, but not so large that it becomes a hassle. Also, many farms are deserted, especially in the western United States, as people have migrated to the cities. Often these can be purchased for a low price.

If you have been able to set up a retreat, you could use it as a vacation paradise away from the crowded public places even if you never need it for survival. This would make your investment still very worthwhile.

Additional Points to Watch

You might want to locate in an area with low fallout in case of a future war. There are charts which illustrate fallout conditions during the various seasons of the year from which you can obtain the needed information.

Also we have found that a most ideal altitude would be around 2,000 to 3,000 feet. This way you are above the smog, fog and haze layer created by cities and weather conditions. You are in crisp, clear air and not high enough to have too limited a growing season or excessively cold weather, and yet you will find the summers more pleasant than at sea level. The preferable altitude will vary slightly depending upon the latitude along which you live. In more northern latitudes you might seek out a slightly lower elevation and in southern latitudes you might prefer a slightly higher elevation. To illustrate the point: The City of Ashland in southern Oregon, which is located at an altitude of 1,895 feet, is usually clear of smog and fog while the City of Medford, only twelve miles away at 1,382 feet, is usually blanketed over by those weather conditions.

Non-Necessities

Don't waste your time looking for non-necessities such as electricity and other utilities which you usually find where there are too many people, anyway. We have no electricity, no telephone and not a single utility bill—which we consider a blessing rather than a curse. In spite of our world-wide contacts and outreach, we are doing fine even without a telephone. Just make sure your soil conditions allow you the installment of a septic tank system if your zoning regulations require such a system.

A Word of Caution

I do not want to go on record to press people into forsaking their present employment and going on a panicked stampede into some open country areas only to have problems later making ends meet. A number of people have broken with their old way of life such as city living and city employment and have moved out into the hills and mountains. Then they have not been able to get along under those unusual and difficult living conditions and have had to move back again into the cities.

It would be very good and helpful if a person had the necessary experience, training and determination to endure when such a step is taken. For some it will be helpful if they make the transition in steps, such as from a big city to a small town or community and then into the open country at a later time.

Therefore, while making your initial transition from a city-type life to a wilderness-type life you might have adjustment troubles, but if you have any call of nature within yourself at all it will not take you very long to find out that you will become so accustomed to your new type of life, feel so much at home and be so joyful and happy in it that a return to stereotyped and artificial city life would be nearly unthinkable. At the end of all your resettlement and adjustment problems you will admit and gladly exclaim that it was worth the effort after all, even though you might nearly faint along the wayside in the process.

A move from the city to the open country will be even more appealing after learning the results of tests performed upon rats. The rats were put under the same conditions man is living under in big cities. Those tests have proven that the rats became very ferocious. They would attack and eat each other. They would literally become insane—does this sound familiar?

There is plenty of information in this book which, if observed, should make a transition much easier. I wish I had such a book when I made my moves! *This book incorporates lifetimes of intense research, investigation and, above all, real life-related experiences.* This should make it well worth your investment of a few dollars. Just think of all the money and trouble it can save you! I do not know of any other such unique book on the American market with such a multitude of practical advice and help. It is backed up by an extraordinary life which hardly anyone wants or dares to live. Most books are just on specialized subjects.

Chapter 14

The Refreshing Simple Life

Get Out Of The Rat Race

Pioneers are still part of our culture. Americans long ago conquered the western part of the United States and many are now turning to frontiers in Alaska and Canada. Canadian officials have said that some of Canada's best immigrants come from the western United States. They are pioneer people who are not afraid to leave urban centers and go in and open up remote areas. Some areas are still available for homesteading as long as the requirements are complied with. Be sure you know where these areas are—don't be misled by "fast-buck" real estate agents. Unfortunately, Alaska has recently closed the door for homesteading.

Reducing Life To Its Essentials

Don't waste precious months or years on non-essentials. Take time now to set yourself up in a simple life stripped of all bonds that only drag you down. All you really need are food, clothing and shelter. You could construct a log cabin somewhere in the wilderness using little more than the materials at hand. A garden, some fruit and nut trees, a couple of goats, a few chickens plus some wild game will provide you with the food you need. Clothing needs can be kept to a minimum as you can clothe yourselves and your family for very little cost by shopping at rummage sales, second-hand stores, garage sales and by making your own. If you have one or two sheep you can have wool that can be spun into yarn for knitting socks, mittens and sweaters.

There is work involved in such a life, but it is very enjoyable work and gives you the benefit of being out in the fresh, unpolluted air and sunshine. You can observe the beauties of nature and animal life around you and begin to enjoy living. Don't wait until you retire to do these things—you'll be too old to get established—start now, and make your dreams come true!

Artificial vs. Genuine

There is a great thrill in living a simple life. You will be surrounded by more genuine friends who will be the lasting ones. After the artificial, glimmering and glittering life is left behind, the shamming so-called "friends" will leave also, and you will be surrounded by more genuine companions.

A Visit From Outer Space

It would be interesting to know the thoughts of a being from outer space who should arrive suddenly on this planet in a space vehicle and see a drama of two contrasting individuals.

One is a rough, tough sort of a character with buckskin-type clothing and a coonskin cap on his head. He has a gun slung over his shoulder and a pack of freshly killed venison for his daily ration on his back. He would represent a person with ideas of his own, a life of most interesting experiences and the ability to stay alive any place when lost—of course, he would not get lost except in the civilized man's jungles, the "cities". He would be a man of enough courage to say what he means and to mean what he says and to back it up by fast physical action if necessary. He would have no need to contact the local police which usually arrive when it is too late and even then practically never find the offender; also, he would have no need to find some slick twister of what we call white man's modern law as he would be man enough to be his own law enforcement agency and lawyer. He would be the type of man who has enough sense to know that he fits into the world the way the world was meant.

Next to him stands an altogether different and rather strange individual. He is dressed in some funny-looking garment called a suit with a little string hanging from his throat which looks as though it were torn off from a gallows. That implication would be appropriate, for he is barely escaping slaughter. On his face he wears some peculiar-looking mechanism called "eyeglasses" and in his ear he carries another machine called a "hearing aid". When he smiles you wonder if you are looking at the teeth of a rat or at the teeth of a man because only a few teeth are left. If given X-ray glasses and allowed to look on the inside of that strange-looking creature, you could detect all kinds of horrible sicknesses and diseases such as an ailing heart, growing internal malignant tumors called cancer, nearly strangulated arteries and ulcers. In his mouth he carries an odd white stick from which he sucks a great amount of smoke. Due to the lack of a smokestack on his head, he brings the smoke out the same way he sucks it in. Knowing that babies like objects to suck on, it makes you wonder if he is just a giant baby! Also, his head is rather shiny as all the hair has left him early.

As he speaks in a soft voice with a forked tongue many words of obvious hypocrisy, you can tell there is no genuine meaning behind them whatsoever. If he gets in trouble he rests assured because he can always call upon the local police and consult his lawyer. If he is out of work, "Big Brother" can put him on welfare and give him food stamps to obtain a nauseating diet of white sugar, cake, ice cream, soft drinks, mushy white bread, coffee, and what-have-you. When he goes to bed at night he swallows some chemical poison called "pills" or he needs the noise background emanating from a one-eyed monster called "television" to keep his nerves wound up so he can drowse off. Then in the morning this tragedy continues. He needs some more pills and then coffee to get going on another chaotic day. When he finally gets sick, he can be committed to some hospital or sanitarium where they have many more drugs available to soothe his pain until his natural warning signals, the nerves, are completely gone.

He, in stark opposition to the other individual, has no privacy whatsoever because there are various files regarding him held by the various government agencies with a rather complete dossier. If he continues to dance to the tune of his leaders, he may be allowed to eke out his miserable existence. Should he dare, however, to have a few ideas of his own—even though he would not know what they were and had no opportunity to arrive at them due to the continuous bombardment and brainwashing of various communication media such as radio, television and newspapers—a multitude of various agents sponsored and paid for by his and the other suckers' taxes would immediately swarm all over him, doing their benevolent best to apply to him the great amount of their well-learned and practiced torture techniques. Since this miserable individual is already in poor condition, he could not take this terrible treatment and would collapse, causing him to be committed immediately to the nearest brainwash back-up center called the mental hospital. Unless this unfortunate individual would forget the few thoughts of his own he ever had, it would probably be the last we ever saw of him.

The visitor from outer space would notice that the old timer was a man of few words and meant what he said, while the other funny-looking creature was a man of very many empty words.

Would it be a very difficult matter to decide which of those two individuals would elect the better government? We do not have to spend much time to find out that naturally the old timer was represented by men of his own caliber, such as Abraham Lincoln. When watching our politicians of today perform on television, etc., we find them to be a true representation of the so-called "modern" man. They utter many finely polished words of deceit while the person who believes the opposite of what they say might well be looked upon as an oddball. Today's governments do indeed reflect the earth-based actor of this scene.

Unfortunately, "since days immemorial the craving for power and rulership has been part of the frailties of the human race. Despots, dictators and imposters of all shades and ranks have come and gone. Always those tyrants could count on and, indeed, did find fools and dupes galore who followed their doctrines and creeds lock, stock and barrel. Intellectual dormant partners en masse would join in rank and file to march after the orders of imperious orators who many a time have their vocal chords (sic) in high gear while their minds seem to be idling.

"History in its past applications has taught mankind many disastrous lessons where the swaying of the gang after the notion and tune of a compulsive talker will lead. But it seems that men have not and will not learn. It is a human characteristic to run after those with the biggest slogans of promise and appeal to the gratification of the flesh.

"Nearly always bitter remorse follows an ever-so-quick decision for some kind of a powerful leader. But that remorse almost always comes too late, to the horror of the populace." (MASTERS OF LEGALIZED CONFUSION AND THEIR PUPPETS, by Hans J. Schneider.)

Making Do With Bare Necessities Brings Appreciation And Joy

When you are away from manmade civilization, you can much better appreciate the simple things of life, things like dry firewood for the winter in the woodshed, a supply of stored food, warm winter clothing and just the home itself. No matter how cold it gets outside, it can be made comfortable and snug inside with your wood cookstove and perhaps a wood heater or two.

Extreme cold spells seem to bring with them an aura of excitement, and it is exhilarating to realize that you are able to take the worst winter weather nature imposes and come out the victor!

There is an inherent excitement in battling the elements, quietly strolling through the snow-covered forest after the last winter storm has passed, leaving a scenic grandeur beyond description. Mirific old gnarled and snow-covered tree branches raise toward the sky like a man lifting his arms heavenward. Absolute quiet surrounds the visitor to the winter wonderland, making his heart mirthful. This is life's greatest and most beautiful challenge!

It is this spirit that made the United States, a country which was almost completely unsettled, a great and unique nation. In those days it was usually not possible to purchase what men needed, so they had to make or improvise with what was available. It was this pioneering spirit that led Daniel Boone to say, "If I cannot fell a tree next to my house, it is time to move on."

Henry The Unique Fisherman

Henry the Fisherman was a person I remember from time to time. He supported his family to a great extent with the many fish he caught by means of the large nets he made himself. He was three-fourths Cherokee Indian and one-fourth White. I spent about a week at his cabin. He was very gifted in gathering the net over his arm, holding one portion of it in his mouth and then throwing the net out in such a way that it would be spread open in a big circle. At times there would be people around who had been fishing all day, hardly catching anything. But Henry would observe the wind directions as well as the water currents and he would say, "Just watch me, Hans," and every time he would pull the net in it would be just loaded with fish. Then he would prepare them in a most delicious way, selling the rest.

He was a very kind-hearted man with many talents. Besides fixing some difficult matters on my car, he made me a mosquito-proof screen which fitted into my open car window frame that eliminated further torturous nights sleeping in my car when travelling.

One night I pulled into his automobile wrecking yard after I had been refused permission to park and sleep in my car at any of the few other homesteads along the Tamiami Trail. The Tamiami Trail, having been built right through swamp territory, offered no other parking site. When arriving at his place, I was immediately invited into his small shack, which looked like a storehouse on the inside with petroleum lamps, fishernets and other items scattered all over the floor. When he looked at me, he realized I had ulterior thoughts—after all, not long ago I had come from a well-kept European home. When questioned by me, he indicated that he was only camping there. I immediately asked, "Aren't you living here?" Upon this he repeated, "I am just camping here!" and pointed to the sky. I then understood what he meant.

There were many other unusual experiences of interest with this extraordinary person—too many to relate here.

I enjoyed the *genuine*, life-related atmosphere around him and his family much more than the time I spent at millionaires' mansions with their artificial and false facade.

Why not get out of your environment-created identity trap and reflect your individual creative personality! It will make you a much happier being.

Interesting Old Timers

I am particularly interested in talking with old timers I meet when travelling. One time after we had driven through a seemingly endless long western canyon, we passed an old homestead built on the other side of the river adjoining the road we were driving on. Since I enjoy searching and examining old, abandoned ghost towns and homesteads, I blew the car horn first to see whether any people still resided at that place. The door opened and an old man appeared who, after I motioned to him, walked across a narrow rope footbridge. To our astonishment we found out that he was the person who had at one time engineered the road going through that canyon and he very courteously invited us to come across to his old homestead. Soon we came to find out that he had also been mining for gold in the surrounding hills and he showed us some most interesting samples.

While sitting in his shack on the davenport, my wife asked him if there were any rattlesnakes around there, upon which he answered, "I just shot two the other day under the davenport you are sitting on, and they rattled to beat the band." Needless to say, my wife took a rather abrupt jump!

He related an experience he had. One night he heard a commotion and, realizing that someone was about to break in—which seemed a frequent occurrence there, apparently on account of his stored gold—he very quietly walked from his bedroom into the very room the thief was busily trying to break into. Without any light, with a revolver in his hand, the gold miner quietly stood, motionless, in the center of this room. The window had already been broken at the door and the thief was just about to stick his hand through the hole in order to open the door from the inside. All the while the gold miner was waiting until the thief had his arm stuck far into the hole surrounded by sharp glass splinters. At the very moment he had his arm thrust through the hole and was trying to unlock the door from the inside, the gold miner put on his searchlight, pointed his gun at the thief and hollered loudly, "HOLD IT!" The thief was apprehended and turned over to the authorities.

Another time, while in the State of California, I discovered an old gold mill. The only remaining resident was a man over eighty years old and, as I visited with him, he told me he was about to start running his mill again—singlehandedly.

While sitting there, I questioned the man as to whether he had any problems living there so alone, at which he said, "Open the door." The next thing I knew, he was holding a pistol in his hand, shooting at a small tin can some distance away from him outside! It was "dead center." I did not have to question him on that subject any further; his gun had spoken.

He also told me that if he had an idea that thieves would want to break in, he would not sleep in his house but on the outside, which he did frequently anyway. He stated that prowlers were not going to look for him underneath every tree; they come looking for things in the house, also expecting him in the house. Then he can wait quietly until they enter the building, watching them all the while from a vantage point, and then sneak up and surprise them. Evidently this system had worked for him in times past.

Those old timers had sense enough to know that they had to be armed in order to survive. They considered their guns as part of their most necessary survival equipment. At a time when a lot of anti-gun legislation is being introduced into Congress, it is important to realize that criminals will always be able to obtain guns but that it will be the honest and good people who will suffer because they will be the ones who to a great extent will abide by the law and then be defenseless at the mercy of criminal elements.

Switzerland has been a country where the government has made it a rule that every individual person has a gun (paid for by the government) at his home. The Swiss realize that it is nearly impossible for enemy forces to take over a country with all of its citizens armed. Hitler in the Second World War stayed away from Switzerland. He would have had quite a time to invade that country with Swiss people fanning out everywhere, moving back into caves in the mountains, defending themselves with their guns.

Historically speaking, gun registration has usually preceded gun confiscation in various countries. Government confiscation of the people's guns is the final step to total slavery. This means that then all the power belongs to a few in government—and what such types of governments have imposed upon people is historical fact. It is also implied that people are too dumb to possess their own guns. This is whitewashed by "official sources" citing increasing crime which, in turn, has been created by the very ones who now want to disarm us. It is astounding how many people in the so-called "land of the free" have swallowed that long-planned tactic.

A Spine-chilling Roar and the Startled Bow Hunters

As you can see, the old timers led an exciting life filled with unforeseen events. In the lifestyle we have chosen (as described in the next chapter) we, too, have many thrilling experiences.

One evening we were reading a letter just received from my mother in Germany in which she enclosed some German newspaper articles about signals received from outer space. It was a dark night; a small moon hardly supplied any light.

Suddenly we heard a spine-chilling, high-pitched scream followed by a terrifying roar. Many thoughts came to mind as we wondered what creatures were making that cacaphony. The sounds ceased before I was able to grab a weapon and flashlight to go to see what was going on.

The next day we found a completely mutilated deer on the other side of our creek. Its heart, lungs and other entrails had been ripped out and one side of its body was torn to shreds. The remains were badly mangled and much of the meat had been eaten. Then we knew that a bear had chased the deer across the river and killed it by tearing the entrails from the dying animal until finally it died when its heart was torn out. Apparently we had heard the cries of agony from the deer followed by the fierce, brutal thunders of the bear.

Recently we encountered an incident of a different nature. One morning our young teenage daughter was taking the flock of goats and sheep to pasture, accompanied by our German shepherd dog. Helen was riding on the back of the big sheep, shouting and singing as the sheep scampered across the rocky terrain bouncing her up and down. Rex barked excitedly as he ran alongside. As she approached the little brush shelter she and her brother had made for the animals, Helen was surprised to see two hunters crouching inside.

It was opening day of the bow season and the men had camped nearby the preceding night in order to locate themselves in a choice spot by daybreak. They had seen many tracks and droppings they thought were deer and saw the shelter they assumed was made by previous hunters. A creek flowed by just in front of the shelter and the hunters were waiting expectantly during the bitter cold pre-dawn hours for their quarry to come to drink. Instead, they stared in open-mouthed amazement as only a young girl and her flock clattered toward them across the creek from a different direction!

Our

Preferred

Way of Life—

A Mountain

Retreat

Chapter 15

Our Preferred Way Of Life—A Mountain Retreat

Our choice constitutes a blend of mountain retreat and ranch of small size. It is in a complete wilderness setting; most of it is forested and includes two crystal clear creeks. (Before acquiring this place, we applied all three "acid" tests referred to previously.) Our ranch part consists of a small herd of goats, a few sheep, about five dozen chickens, some ducks, dogs and cats.

Homesteading

A word about homesteading. Even though the homesteading law is still in effect in a few states in the United States, it would be by accident if a person could find sufficiently good land for this type of a set-up. Much of the land is practically useless—too dry and without water, for instance. The improvements which would have to be accomplished in order to satisfy the homesteading requirements would be so costly as to render the whole undertaking worthless. There are territories where homesteading is still very promising, as in Canada, for those who would like to commit their lives to such a long-range program and who do not shy away from living in extremely cold areas.

Building and Maintaining The Homestead

In our move to the open country, few building and construction skills have remained unchallenged. The following work has been done: improving of roads, building of dog compound, roofing of practically all the buildings which were already available, remodelling much of the interior of the buildings, building closets, laying of electric lines (including the deciphering of the lines already laid for the purpose of troubleshooting), building of drainage systems, refurbishing the bridge, workshop, garage buildings and fireplace, putting in a stove and stovepipe into the far end of the house, building a stable for our livestock and a chicken coop for our chickens. We were also busy overhauling the water wheel with the gears, working on the fencing and gardens, setting up the new office, getting firewood and sawing it with the chain saw (enough for three wood stoves), taking care of the livestock, painting, fencing of other areas, building on the guest house, setting up a complete workshop, working on the vehicles, fixing walkways and staircases, doors and storage areas, setting up of two generators and building a woodshed and a root cellar. When being called upon, it is interesting for a person to find out how much he is actually able to do without ever having learned that particular trade.

Investigate the ground (for the foundation), including drainage, direction of the sun, prevailing winds, scenery, accessibility, availability of water and building materials for your particular need before building. For the roof you can use shakes (which you can make yourself). For log cabin construction you can use almost anything suitable to fill the cracks, including moss, sawdust mixed with glue, oakum and potato sacks. Pentachlorophene is good as a log preserver.

A Workshop—A Necessity

As you move out into the open country or wilderness, it will not be possible for you to call a repairman every time something breaks down; rather you will be challenged by the necessity of helping yourself in such situations. For this purpose a workshop with all the needed tools and other related supplies such as nails, screws, bolts, nuts, fence staples, mending plates, rivets, a vise, metal plates, glue, etc. are an immediate necessity. It will be advantageous to have many hand tools rather than power tools in case of a power failure or even when you move to an area where there is no electricity.

You might have a few electric tools such as an electric drill to help you out, circumstances permitting.

Much needed items in that workshop would be equipment for the fixing of shoes or even the making of shoes, such as a last, tacks, certain types of glue, an awl, a leather punch, etc. You can get your own supply of leather from the animal hides which you can tan according to the directions given in various books on the market or in the public library. You will be able to get a cheap supply of rubber in the form of old car inner tubes and even tires for making soles for the shoes which will literally never wear out.

We find our workshop one of the main assets we use continually. It looks just like an old wild-west general store.

Generators And The Main Power Line

Your workshop could be an ideal station for a generator set-up. (Don't store gasoline in your workshop.) This way you have the generator in a dry place away from the house (on account of the noise) and repair is easy with all the tools, oil and supplies at hand. Also, you don't have to worry about getting your house dirty and you have at the same time electricity available for your power tools and other electric needs in the workshop.

For normal needs such as running vacuum cleaners, mixers, blenders, record players, radios, house lights, small electric grain mills (three-fourths to one horse power motor), water pumps (one-third horse power) and tape recorders, you should have at least a 3,000- or 4,000-watt generator. Depending upon your electric needs, you might even consider a more powerful generator. If you are looking for a continuous duty generator, then you will want an 1800 rpm unit. This is heavier than a 3600 rpm unit, mostly for stationary use and for those who run their generator a lot. If you use your generator only once in a while and if you might need to transport it around with you at times, you might want to pick a 3600 rpm unit. This is lighter and therefore easier to move, less expensive and smaller. For units to be operated on LP or natural gas carburetion, an additional twenty per cent load factor should be added to compensate for the lower BTU count in this type of fuel. These keep the motor cleaner and give less polution. You won't have to worry about refuelling a small generator gas tank all the time when it is hooked up to a large (500-gallon) propane tank.

Therefore, when you select a power plant, consider the following points:

1. The power required to handle the job
2. The proper speed required for your power plant
3. The starting method of your plant
4. The fuel being used.

Also observe that electric motors fall into three classifications and, depending upon the type, require higher starting currents than normal running currents. The split-phase motor, which requires approximately three times as much power during its starting load as the ordinary repulsion induction type, is the hardest to start.

You won't have to worry about electric needs for refrigerators or freezers as you will have to set them up someplace else with permanent power supply. You are using your generator only in intervals—maybe a half hour or so every second day to fill your water tank or handle your other electric chores—unless you have your generator hooked up to a water wheel or turbine.

You should use at least a twelve gauge (or better, a ten gauge) properly insulated copper wire as conductor from your generator to your house as long as you don't run the line much longer than about two hundred feet.

Water

Be sure you have a supply of pure water for your use. Well or spring water that cannot easily be contaminated would be best for drinking and cooking purposes. A fast-running, pure mountain stream would be the next best choice for human consumption and is also excellent for livestock, fowl and garden use if the water can be brought to where it is needed by gravity flow, hydraulic ram or other available means.

The Garden

The United States has long been known as "The Land of Plenty" with bountiful crops grown all over the nation. The vast farmlands have been overworked for many years, however, and the soil is worn out. Attempts to rejuvenate it have been made through the use of inorganic fertilizers. These have stimulated plant growth but add only a part of needed nutrients to the soil, leaving a continued imbalance of ingredients vital for fertile soil.

Since fertile topsoil averages only seven or eight inches over the face of the earth, it is readily apparent that we must treat it carefully if we are to survive. Healthy soil contains many living organisms that live almost entirely in only the upper few inches. Approximately ninety-five per cent of the estimated 1,000,000 insect species live in the soil for at least part of their lives. The soil is made up of billions of particles, each covered with a snug film of water, oxides and pieces of organic matter, which provides a home for the thriving soil life. The surface area of these particles is unbelievable: only one ounce of soil can have surfaces totalling 250,000 square feet, which is about six acres!

Humus, created by the action of soil life upon decaying organic matter, is essential to soil. As the organic matter is being broken down, it produces humic acids that make minerals soluble. The blended mixture that results is a true and complete plant food; the greater the humus content of a soil, the healthier it is. Humus soaks up water, supports organisms in the soil, increases permeability and aeration, keeps the soil temperature constant and improves the general physical condition of the soil. If humus is used up due to poor farming methods, the balance of the soil is upset and plants suffer. Production lessens and the crops become increasingly inferior in quality, presenting a definite health hazard to those who eat the nutrition-poor foods.

In nature the condition of the soil is just right when undisturbed by humans. Litter from plants and animals return to the soil to create humus. But man plows up the soil, introducing increased oxygen into it, which breaks down organic matter more rapidly. Then repeated crop plantings deplete the soil of its humus.

Several minerals were discovered to be regularly present in the ashes of burnt plants, especially nitrogen, phosphorus and potash. When these were added to worn-out soil as chemicals that would dissolve in water, production increased markedly. For a time these chemicals were added only as a supplement to organic matter. But with the advent of modern farm machinery, land began to be farmed intensively and chemical fertilizers replaced organic fertilizers entirely. This has resulted in crops damaged by insects and diseases and the increased use of chemicals in the form of sprays to prevent such damage.

Chemical fertilizers not only consume the existing humus more rapidly, but destroy the life of the soil as well as its physical properties. One example is sulphate of ammonia. The ammonia is absorbed by the plant, but the remaining sulphate combines with hydrogen and becomes sulphuric acid, a substance that is deadly to living organisms in the soil.

Too much of certain minerals is harmful to crops, and the proper mineral balance is unlikely to be reached by the use of chemicals. Trace minerals are often missing altogether. Such imbalance invites insects and disease and also impairs the ability of the plants to produce good seeds. The food value of crops grown in such unnatural soil has become increasingly deficient in proteins, minerals and vitamins.

Obviously we must change our attitude toward the soil and restore the humus by extensive green manure cropping and returning other organic material such as animal manures and crop residues to the soil. The soil renews itself from top to bottom. Any practice that is contrary to this process should be stopped. All organic matter should be placed on the surface of the soil and left there. The growing of crops should be encouraged by small farmers, with less emphasis placed on large-scale crop production. These ecological practices must begin soon or man will soon find himself unable to survive!

It was more difficult for us to perform some of these things as we live in an area which is rather arid and full of rocks. However, we found a spot which we thought would make a nice garden area even though it is somewhat shady because of surrounding trees. We spent our first winter pouring on a combination of wood ashes taken from our three wood stoves, chicken and goat manure, pine needles, leaves and compost from our compost pile. Then early in the spring we rototilled the whole area and planted a variety of vegetable seeds, sunflower seeds and berry bushes. Soon, very much to our surprise, there was a "jungle", even though that was the first time a garden had been planted in that particular area, with birds trilling away and a little fish pond in the middle of it fed by a gravity flow watering system from the overflow of a spring which watered the garden as well.

Even in January we are able to dig under the snow into the garden to get carrots and beets from the ground; that garden has become almost a year-round blessing to us.

Many an evening we sit before a warm wood stove or blazing fire in the fireplace cracking sunflower seeds or nuts as a family by the soft illumination of an old-fashioned kerosene lamp.

The reason we use our free organic compost, fertilizer, ashes and similar natural items rather than chemical fertilizers for our garden is that they are much better than chemicals. Another benefit of organically grown, healthy products is their excellent resistance to bugs.

It would be a good idea to store up some vegetable seeds so you will have a supply for future use. It would also be good to plant some fruit and nut trees if you do not already have some.

Be sure to have a good assortment of garden tools: shovels, hoes, rakes, spading forks. Another item you might want to have is a hand-operated cultivator with different attachments to help in preparing and caring for your garden. Rototillers are more efficient and easier to operate, but only as long as you have fuel for them.

There could be greenhouses on the property for year-round production of plants.

Here is a typical menu at our mountain retreat:

1. In the morning: freshly hand-ground grains mixed with nuts, honey and shredded apples, a few slices of home-baked bread with homemade goat butter and homemade jam or honey from our own bees or homemade cheese.

2. At mid-day: a fresh salad of various green, leafy vegetables and some root vegetables, venison from our last hunt, or beef, goat meat or chicken from our own ranch, with homegrown potatoes, gravy and homemade sauerkraut.

3. In the evening: fruit salad and a bowl of homemade yogurt with some honey.

Storage Items

The more self-sufficient we can become, the better off we will be in perilous times. We should learn to raise what we need to be independent of supermarkets or city utilities. It is important to store food for winter use and possible famines: by freezing (while electricity is available), drying, smoking, salting, canning and pickling. Some fruits and vegetables can be kept for months if properly stored in a root cellar. There are several excellent books presently on the market that give much detail on winter food storage.

Nuts, grains and seeds store well and take little space and care in proportion to the nutrients they offer. Be sure to keep them in vermin-proof containers.

Further items to store at your retreat: All kinds of clothing (even though it might not fit you, you can always utilize the cloth to make other suitable clothing out of it.) When I think back to the five years under Communism when we had to dress ourselves with clothes partly made out of potato sacks, then I must say that the bargains a person can obtain from Salvation Army, Goodwill and other second-hand stores are worthy to be considered. All kinds of clothing can also be used as good barter items during the bad times ahead. You might want to get yourself a treadle sewing machine in case there is or will be no power available.

Another important item is footwear of all kinds: shoes for summer and winter, boots and rubbers. Under survival conditions, especially, you will have a great need of footwear as nearly all movement or travelling has to be done by foot. It will wear out your shoes very fast.

You might also want to stock blankets, sheets, towels and various other linens, salt, iodine, water purification tablets, matches, soap, toilet paper, pails, large containers (you will have to use these to heat water on your wood stoves as well as many other uses), animal food, seeds for your garden, bicycle tires and tubes, air pump, pencils, erasers, paper, books, razors, razor blades, nails, screws, nuts, bolts, glue, string, sewing items, shoelaces, candles, kerosene, kerosene lamps and lanterns, wicks, chimneys, lumber, tar paper, roofing cement, plastic bags and sheets, some paint, first-aid items (adhesive tape, etc.). This list is by no means complete. To make it complete would not only make it too lengthy, but different individuals might have a preference for different items and therefore add or subtract from this list as they so desire.

You should store up enough food and other supplies to keep you going for one to two years in case of a complete breakdown.

Farm Animals And Fowl

If you have a cow or some goats, you will be able to have a supply of milk, butter and cheese as well as meat. If you have goats, you would need a cream separator—preferably a hand-operated one—in order to separate the cream from the milk.

You will be able to obtain more leather from goats or sheep you might have. If you have sheep, you will be able to make your own yarn with one of the inexpensive spinning wheels on the market. One of the more reasonably priced and durable spinning wheels which will turn out quality yarn and is widely used in the United States by spinning clubs and spinners in general can be obtained for approximately $52 each (including freight), if you order five at one time, from Ashford Handicrafts, Ltd., P. O. Box 12, Rakaia, New Zealand. My wife uses this with great satisfaction. She even colors her yarn with moss, bark, flowers and berries. Carded wool can also be used for quilt batting.

When you have your own flock of chickens you will find that the meat and eggs are far superior to any you can buy in the store. If your chickens are allowed to forage during the day, they will require a little less grain. Our experience has been that bantam hens are better sitters than larger birds, although both types are prolific layers. The bantams take much less feed than the standard breeds, but the standard breeds are much larger and meatier.

On our small ranch we have practically no food waste whatsoever. The bones are eaten by the dog. Carrion and other portions unusable for human consumption like the innards, small pieces of fur from the head of the animal and the feet can be chopped up with an axe into fine pieces and fed to the chickens and ducks as they relish it. They also enjoy banana peels, carrot pulp and almost anything else. The rest is taken care of by our goats, sheep and cat.

Root Cellar

A root cellar would be very useful for storing vegetables and fruits through the entire year. It can be dug into a bank or into level ground if you have no bank in a convenient location. Choose a site that is out of the sun but still close to your house or garden. You can use scrap lumber to build it. Then cover the boards with tar paper or sheet metal and add about a foot of dirt all around. The door should be a double one to permit an insulating layer of air. If you can have two doors to your root cellar, spaced several feet apart, then you will avoid an excessive air exchange from the outside when you visit the cellar. Be sure the roof and door are slanted so rain and snow melt can run off easily.

Liquid Gold

You can have a fresh, good supply of honey by keeping your own bees. We use honey for sweetening. This is much better than white sugar, which is one of the synthetics and does not contain any nutritive value at all. Honey would also be a good investment as it will keep almost indefinitely and the price has increased within the recent years 300 to 400 per cent. You could use this item in barter or for your own family's needs, including baking and canning of fruit.

Wood Cookstove

If you have a wood stove (which you should), you can heat your water for laundry, dishes and baths in a couple of large containers such as canning kettles by setting them on that stove and find that within a short period of time the water will get extremely hot.

Be sure also to have a wood cookstove that is in good working condition and stove pipes to go with it. You might want one or two wood-burning stoves for heat in other parts of the house. You will need saws and axes to cut wood for the stoves and, as long as gasoline is available, a chain saw is an excellent time and labor saver for this purpose. Prepare and store your winter supply of wood in the summer when the wood is dry so you will not be caught by autumn rains. It is not necessary to cut live trees as fallen logs and branches burn nicely and are safer to handle. It is a good idea to clean your chimney or stovepipe in the early fall, before the season of heavy use begins, in order to reduce the danger of chimney (flue) fire from soot build-up.

Helpful Hints For Gathering Wood

To those who might think it to be an insurmountable problem to supply additional wood for your stoves in the winter time, it might be a comfort to know there are a number of days in many areas when there will be no snow on the ground, but when the temperature will be just below freezing. On those days you can go out with your family and pick up large four- to five-inch-thick branches and crack them on a rock or log lying on the ground. The branches will break up easily as the frost has hardened the wood and made it brittle. You will be able to supply a good amount of wood for your stove in no time at all. This will save you a lot of sawing.

We find that fallen timber and even half-rotten wood makes a very nice slow-burning fire. You will want to have a supply of both thicker and smaller pieces on hand so you can always regulate the flame and heat output of the fire. Especially good burning are knots which will pull out very easily from rotten logs.

Some of the smaller branches will crack up nicely over a rock even in warm weather.

Considering all the above, we find it a great waste when people go out to the forest to get their firewood and cut down some of the beautiful living trees when there is dead wood all around them which will burn well. Certainly this is an area where a lot of waste could be avoided, if people would go by the above points.

Using dead wood will keep up the value of your property and preserve the beauty of the place with its undiminished natural resources left intact. Besides this, the practice of picking up and utilizing dead wood will decrease the potential fire hazard a whole lot.

Independent Energy Sources

Let us talk a little about energy sources for your homestead. The more independent you can be in your energy supply the better it will be. Aside from potential power failures in the future, you also will have the added freedom of not being dependent upon public utilities which most likely will not be available to you as you move away from the population centers.

Alternate energy sources are numerous and varied. Some will take care of several needs; others are more limited. It is possible to use the sun, the wind, water, wood and manure—all either free or relatively inexpensive.

1. The sun can be used to provide heat for your homestead or just to warm water for your house by running it through a system of curved copper pipes, putting them over reflective material and holding the system into the sun. The main requirements are many sunny days, large lenses, reflectors and ingenuity if solar energy will be utilized for a multitude of other purposes.

2. There are three types of windmills on the market today, two require high towers and one does not. The latter type is the Savonius Rotor, which consists of three cylinders (such as 55-gallon drums) split lengthwise and each half offset an amount equal to its radius. Then fasten the pieces to circular plates at each end with a diameter equal to the diameter of a barrel plus the offset length. Place a strong metal rod through the middle of all the plates, set the bottom end in bearings and the newly created S-rotor will be ready to operate in the next wind.   The types that require a high tower are the conventional windmill and the Stuart mill (a big propeller). These are much more difficult to erect and maintain than the S-rotor.   All three require a generator or an alternator and a bank   of   storage   batteries—either   regular   twelve-volt automobile batteries or Ni-Cads (nickel-cadmium) batteries— to store power when the wind is not blowing. Also an inverted rotary converter is needed to transform the current from DC to AC and some type of cutoff should be arranged so the alternator is shut off when there are high winds or no wind.

3. Water can supply electricity by means of a water wheel or turbine, the latter being the more expensive but more compact set-up. One of the main essentials would be a spring, fountain or river. Then you would have a wonderful possibility of installing either one of the two systems for a free supply of electricity aside from the expenses of putting in the installation. Maintenance charges will be negligible if the job has been done properly.

There are several types of water wheels, divided into two classes, overshot and undershot. The undershot wheel is placed in a swift current of sufficient depth to handle the size wheel desired. The current hits the blades of the water wheel and turns it. The overshot wheel receives its water via a sluice which delivers the water from above by falling down upon the wheel in a regulated flow.

Running water can also be put to work to pump itself up a grade by means of a hydraulic ram into a tank some distance away. The force of the flowing water itself powers the ram and provides a steady, continuous supply of water. The tank should be elevated above the faucets and pipes in order to supply sufficient water pressure.

4. Wood can be used for heating your house and also for running your automobile, if desired. The latter requires, among other things, a unit containing a hopper and a combustion chamber. A certain amount of air is pulled through the bed of red-hot coals produced by the burning wood and eventually winds up as carbon monoxide. This is mixed with approximately the same amount of air and burned in the automobile engine in about the same way as gasoline.

5. Manure can be put through a digester to produce methane gas which will work in a manner similar to natural gas or propane to heat one's home, supply electricity or run an automobile.

(Some more details on alternate energy systems can be obtained from various issues of T.M.E.N., P.O. Box 70, Hendersonville, North Carolina 28739.)

In the absence of all of the above, it would be good to have one or two of your own generators with some needed fuel stored, such as gasoline or propane. In our case we run the generator every so often, maybe once every two days for half an hour or so in order to take care of our electric needs, such as running the water pump to fill up our water tank, mixer, record player, vacuum cleaner and blender. In this way a little stored fuel will keep you supplied with electricity for a long time. (Also in this chapter you will find more detailed information along this line in the section entitled "Generators and the Main Power Line".)

Transportation Media

It is important that you begin to economize on your travel equipment at the present time. Try to secure vehicles which will require only a minimum of maintenance and are inexpensive to repair when necessary. Make it a point to keep vehicles which will give the maximum mileage for each gallon of gas, as a further increase in gasoline prices, a further shortage in the supply and perhaps rationing can be expected.

It is definitely advisable to get some bicycles. This formed the only means of travel besides a sled during our years under Communism. They were even helpful in the winter time; even though it was impossible for us to ride them, we could hang a load of baggage or groceries on the bicycle and use it as a transport carrier by pushing it along.

If you can supply enough food from your own land for a horse, that might be a good animal to have. It could plow your land and pull a big sled carrying you and your supplies in the winter time and a wagon in the summer time. You can put a snow plow behind it to plow your access road and utilize it while on hunts and looking over the country. It can also be used for transporting deer from the hunt and bringing in your wood supply.

Beware of Auto Repair Gimmicks

Beware of unscrupulous auto repairmen, many of whom are located along major freeways as well as some in local neighborhoods. They sell used parts at new part prices, bill for "work" that was not done, charge more than the amount of the original estimate and break or cut parts just to be able to sell new ones. Some swindlers try to sell unneeded oil or try to tell you the brakes need to be fixed or the transmission overhauled. Transmission overhaul or replacement runs into hundreds of dollars and often the problem, if any, could be corrected by a band and linkage adjustment or new seals, all of which are much less expensive. Another gimmick is trying to get you to replace ball joints, mufflers, shock absorbers and similar items.

To insure against such shady practices, familiarize yourself with some of the things under the hood of your vehicle. Every week take time to check your oil, water and battery and at the same time look over belts, hoses and wires. You will come to an awareness of the general condition of your engine and be better prepared to deal with swindlers. Another good tip is to find a trustworthy repair garage or a service station in your neighborhood and patronize that one. The people there will soon recognize you as a steady customer and give you good service. Have them check over your vehicle before trips and service the vehicle regularly. If you get an "all clear" before you leave, you can be suspicious if an attendant far from home tells you something is wrong. Women are much more likely to be subjected to shady dealings.

Helpful Hints in Case of Breakdowns

When bringing my car or airplane for repair, I have always made it a practice to be present when the mechanics worked on them for the following reasons:

1. I know exactly what has been done to the motor of the vehicle. When encountering difficulties in the future I will be more likely to know whether it was caused through the work or whether it is a new problem.

2. I will increase my knowledge of how to perform repairs myself.

3. I will receive a better understanding of the engine.

4. I will be able to make sure that I am not charged for repairs which have not been performed or for parts which have not been inserted.

5. I can make sure that broken parts had been broken before that time and not after removal. In connection with this, I make sure that I always get and keep the broken part. In case there is doubt as to whether or not that part is defective, I can seek confirmation by other mechanics.

6. I can see to it that I am not overcharged for labor time and that a good mechanic gets to do the work.

7. I have noticed many times over that the mechanic takes a greater interest by far in doing a good job when he sees that the owner of the vehicle is interested enough to stand and watch what is being done and when he knows that he is being watched.

Any time you need repairs on anything, you might find this a valuable practice to follow.

PART V
OTHER PRESENT DAY
ESSENTIALS

THE

ULTIMATE

IN

EDUCATION

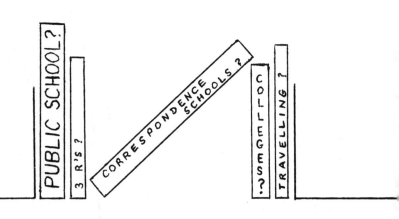

Chapter 16

The Ultimate In Education

Correspondence Schools

Since the national school system has deteriorated to a level where it is practically irresponsible for parents to continue to send their children to public school any longer, I would like to mention a few things about this problem.

We live 33 miles from the nearest town, half of which is snowpacked and treacherous in the winter. It would be impossible for us to send our children to public school even if we wanted to. All of the children are enrolled in a correspondence school. This is a very efficient and economical way of taking care of the children's schooling because there is no waste of time in senseless social activities, travelling back and forth to school and intermissions. There is no slowdown on account of low IQ classmates which would be a waste of time, especially in the case of my oldest son, who is a straight "A" student. We find that two hours of daily work in this program is equivalent to a day in a conventional school.

The student can work at his convenience. He may finish his entire course within a short period of time and get his high school diploma, or he may set his schooling aside if other activities are pressing upon him temporarily and finish it at a later time. This method of schooling is also very appropriate for persons or families who do a lot of travelling as the students can carry this material with them and work at it on their trips.

In addition, we conduct some school on the premises for the children. The subjects are varied. I teach German, mathematics, geography, most of the practical tasks required in this lifestyle and delight the children with globetrotter stories in the evening before the fireplace. Also, I teach them flying, sailing and driving as they reach proper age. My wife teaches Norwegian, homemaking and spinning and a friend of ours teaches English, history and business subjects. We are concentrating on the "3 R's" as in the times of the pioneers. Most of the American children going to established school systems have an extreme lack of knowledge and skill in spelling, mathematics (especially the very important mental arithmetic), reading and writing, which are the most important subjects. A lot of schools in our land presently are in a state of semi-constant turmoil because of dope, riots and various other problems, and it makes a person wonder how much good eduction pupils are able to obtain there besides the considerable amount of bad influence which they receive at such places. The terrible and outright vile textbooks being used to some extent in the school systems make the conditions even worse. This gives us yet another reason to stay away from the conventional school systems. Our public educational system allows atheism to be taught, but forbids prayers to God. We may, therefore, be creating our own grave diggers.

In Canada the government has correspondence courses set up for children of families who live too far away from any school. It is unfortunate that the United States government does not have such a provision, for there are still a fair number of students living in remote areas who could profit from such a program, especially since that could be provided for by the excessive school tax payments (included in real estate taxes) on the part of the citizens. In the United States a person not only pays taxes for the school system but has to pay again for correspondence school fees of the children in cases such as ours. I think, though, it is well worth it in order to save the children. One further asset of a correspondence school is that in addition to a few required subjects the pupil has about two hundred elective subjects to choose from in a high school course.

We find that combining theoretical knowledge with a practical application of that knowledge is a great advantage which, with our set-up, is very easy to accomplish. This way our children get sufficient fresh air, a wholesome environment and a healthy atmosphere away from the city contamination and noise. The student does not have to eat the highly processed, practically valueless and harmful meals served at school. An industrious student who takes a stand for what is good and valuable does not have to see his efforts and time wasted by foolish horseplay and other persecutions on the part of jealous classmates.

Here are the addresses of two fine correspondence schools which you might want to contact if there is a need:

For grade school:
(Kindergarten through 8th grade)

International Institute
P. O. Box 99
Park Ridge, Illinois 60068

For high school:
(Also several college-level courses)

American School
Drexel Avenue at 58th Street
Chicago, Illinois 60637

Also, you can contact the National Home Study Council, 1601 18th St., N.W., Washington, D.C. 20009. They have a directory of all accredited correspondence schools.

Please consider that most states have compulsory school attendance laws and that it will not be legal to keep the children out of public school if they can attend. In such cases the correspondence schools might not enroll your children as they could encounter trouble. This, however, changes when you as a family travel permanently, live in a foreign country or beyond the reach (for some distance) of the school bus route. In the State of Oregon, for instance, your seven- to ten-year-old children do not have to attend public school if you live more than one and a half miles beyond the school bus route. In the case of ten- to eighteen-year-old children, it is three miles. Check with your own state on the law applying there. You can figure on an expense of approximately $90 to $130 per year per child for correspondence courses. There are ways to cut down on this expense through certain discounts (in some cases) and by using the same textbooks again for other children of the same family (allowed by some correspondence schools).

Of interest to persons considering a college education would be an article which appeared in the *Reader's Digest* of October 1975. It deals with college credit being earned through home study and gives names and addresses of places to get complete information.

Travel—A Great Teacher

Let me point out in this connection that one of the best methods of learning practical, always needed and down-to-earth matters is travelling. It is a well-known fact that open-minded children of travelling families (especially if the trips include foreign countries) are usually far ahead of their own age group who attend public school regularly. Most school principals realize this and gladly allow parents to take their children along if they happen to make only a temporary trip abroad during the school term.

With open eyes a person gets confronted with so many varied subjects such as different cultures, languages, customs, foods and mannerisms that he can't help but learn, as he needs to observe and apply himself to those various things in order to be able to get around. There are many problems which he will need to solve for himself, such as the obtaining of visas and many other travelling documents, the intricacies of foreign currencies, the acquisition of at least a small working knowledge of the various languages, the talent of making himself understood by the various people and how to make friends and get along with many different personalities. We could go on and on.

A French experiment was conducted many years ago in which young people were sent out into the world for ninety days on bicycles with only twenty-five cents in their pockets. In this particular instance those young people were asked to travel down to Greece and then return and to be able to maintain themselves for that period of time without any further help from their parents or relatives. Those young people had to call upon their own initiative and inventive minds on such an undertaking. They would usually travel a ways, stop, and perform some odd jobs at a place to earn funds. After this they would continue their journey until they had almost run out of funds and then again take on some type of a job to earn more money to continue their trip. While travelling on a bicycle, they would ride at a pace slow enough to enable them to observe the countryside more thoroughly and have a better contact with the populace. A fair percentage of those young people indeed were able to conduct that far journey, staying away for a quarter of a year. At a later time—many years afterward— those very same young people were interviewed once more and it was discovered that nearly every single one of them had attained some type of greatness in life. Some of them had returned to the areas they had gotten acquainted with during their bicycle journey. They had discovered discolorations and mineral deposits in certain territories and had set up mines and factories for the mining and processing of the various resources. Others had become authors, lecturers, explorers, and so forth. The reason for this success is the fact that they were thrown out of their pre-established environment and comfortable nest and put on their own. This required of them a complete application of all their capacities and a tremendous strengthening and deepening of their capabilities in order to survive. Upon returning to a normal life at a later time they were able to utilize those increased capacities in the attainment of their individual goals.

I myself have found that while travelling, I would learn such a tremendous wealth of things in a lifelike manner—things which I would need in everyday living which would beat school knowledge by a long shot! Persons who have spent more time on school and university benches are by no means usually the more able or intelligent ones.

When my father employed people in his offices and factories, he generally avoided university graduates, for he felt that they were often very impractical, arrogant and thought they had already mastered life. On the other hand, students who had just come from the fundamental schools, still young in life and wanting to improve themselves, made much better employees than the self-esteemed paper carriers.

Whoever studies the lives of successful men will find that they have become something despite their school education. Many were rather average pupils. Edison, the greatest inventor of modern times, was even put out of school by his teacher because of his inability. Knowledge is without profit if you do not know how to use it. There is no sense for a person to accumulate an enormous amount of knowledge unless he is able to digest that knowledge and integrate it into himself; otherwise, that knowledge will remain on the surface. Ninety per cent of our people are using only fifteen per cent of their abilities, while eighty-five per cent is unused which they will thereafter carry into the grave.

There are forever things to learn during our daily life in a more practical and life-related way. Our children, for instance, always have ample opportunity to learn many things on the various trips we are taking them on.

My oldest boy has just in the recent years been with me on a one-month flight by private plane through West Canada and all over Alaska, on a nine-month lecture trip (again with our plane) all over the United States and on a two-month European tour. When visiting public school (before we moved out into the wilderness) in between his extensive trips, he maintained his "A" grades. His intellectual level is above that of others his own age. I receive many compliments about him. What a joy properly to train those young people we are entrusted with and to see them striving for masteries yet unattained. There lies the future of America!

How To Solve Juvenile Delinquency and the Generation Gap

Away from the disruptive influence of cities and public schools, children can be raised in the way they should. The parents will be much better able to control the influences on their children and see that the children learn desirable things. Some very excellent books for children are the McGuffey Readers, available for grammar school ages.

Since, however, so many children are growing up in crime-infested cities spiked with bad movie theatres, pornographic book shops, bars and dance halls, absorbing more smut emanating from a television set in the so-called American home, with both parents probably working, and being brought in contact with more filth in the form of bad textbooks, smoking, dope and cursing in the present school system, it is not any wonder to see where our young generation is ending up. Unfortunately, many parents have not done their part in training their youngsters and in setting the right example. Naturally, young people look for challenges; they want to have an interesting life. They are full of vim and vigor and if their energies are not channelled into the right areas, they will find wrong associations and end up in the wrong direction as so many already have. With a world full of so many wholesome outlets and so many interesting things to do, it is hard to understand how people can choose such a terrible and senseless way of life resulting in disaster.

In our life there is no problem with juvenile delinquency and absolutely no generation gap. Our children are happy with their environment away from the television set, the crime-infested cities and the public school system. They have a multitude of most interesting outlets such as hunting, hiking, flying with their Dad, building projects and other interesting chores connected with a ranch in a wilderness type of life. There are so many interesting jobs waiting for each member of our big family that we do not find sufficient time each day to take care of all the many interesting things. Here is a small list of some of the activities we find ourselves enthusiastically engaged in during the year. You will find that they are mostly related to the different lifestyle we have chosen: Observing the birth of a lamb or goat kids and the hatching of baby chicks or ducklings; feeding the animals and fowl; milking, straining and separating the milk; making butter, cottage cheese, cheese and bread (from flour we have freshly ground); preparing and cutting up our home-raised meat; shearing the sheep; carding and spinning the wool and knitting the yarn; tanning the hides from our animals and making various items from them; cutting our firewood with a chain saw and axe; bringing the wood home with our truck; planting, weeding, watering and harvesting the garden; making cosy fires which keep the house warm throughout the winter; painting the house and other newly constructed buildings; studying a great variety of subjects from correspondence schools; maintaining the vehicles as well as the road; gathering edible mushrooms and plants; visiting national parks and monuments; talking with many interesting old timers; travelling; doing office work; and much more. There is never a dull moment and every day brings fresh and new experiences.

What a thrill our smaller children just had recently when two little goat kids came into this world (nine more have arrived since) and a little lamb appeared! To see the magnificent winter scenery with dazzling snow blanketing the ground and hanging from the trees, to listen to the birds singing on a nice, balmy summer evening and to observe the results of the changing seasons such as the foliage turning bright in the autumn—these are just a few of the joys we have in our country life.

At a time when there are plenty of delinquents being raised, we feel it is a wonderful change and responsibility to raise some good children. While many families seem to have problems keeping their children at home, we find that we have "problems" taking them away from home for even a limited period of time and, when we do, they can hardly wait until they can come back home again. However, this is really not a "problem" for us—we count it a blessing!

During an average year a child aged six to eleven years watches television 1,340 hours and attends school 980 hours. By age eighteen a child has watched television 22,000 hours and attended school 12,000 hours.

One Chinese proverb says that one picture does more than one thousand words. What can you expect of young people, therefore, when they are being influenced by continuous gangster programs night after night? Even if there should be good programs on television, why live second-hand when you can live your own full life, having your own personal rewarding and challenging experiences?

In most homes everyone seems to be going his own way and "doing his own thing." This gap is further widened by the destructive educational pattern in the school system today which, among many other things, discourages a sound family life through such teachings as the new mathematics, the demoralizing, perverted social studies and atheism. The unscientific teaching of evolution which was later repudiated by Darwin himself is another example.

Simple living in itself strengthens the family ties. People again find life pleasant and more rewarding in a genuine spirit of co-operation as everyone applies himself to his particular calling in this type of life, as there is much variety in contrast to most people's specialized lives.

What an encouragement for the youngsters to know parents are there who are interested in them and whom they can call upon when they need help. Young people especially need good guidance for their early lives in the form of other older, experienced persons. Unfortunately, there is very little of that guidance found in our world today. May this book encourage many parents to give their children that right type of guidance.

Learning While Associating

Associate yourself only with people who will have a furthering effect.

In my personal extensive associations with all kinds of people such as pilots, opera singers, industrialists, explorers, world travellers, authors, captains, doctors, professors, and others, I have usually followed a very profitable and interesting custom: First I would find out, if I did not already know, which fields and subjects those people would be authorities in. After this, I would initiate a conversation, leading straight to the most interesting subject in which they are knowledgeable. After this I would become quiet and listen while learning and planning. I always lose little time in sitting or hanging around with people but instead get right to the interesting points.

Many times I would have questions in certain areas of life and when meeting people with knowledge in those areas I would ask them everything I needed to know. My interests in life are just as varied as my friends. I find that they will appreciate me more if I show interest in their fields.

When meeting other people, I will be able to get into closer contact with them faster if I already know much about their fields of knowledge and endeavor. I certainly learn more as a listener than by being a speaker. There are times when I find myself among people—more by accident than by arrangement—who are either untalented in speaking or boring. At such times I assume the role of a speaker rather than a listener, hoping they will learn at this time.

There is much room for continual improvement in life. It is a pity to observe how many people live outright boring and frustrating lives when the world is full of interesting challenges and enticing opportunities. There is nothing more monotonous than to be with a person who is not interested in anything, who doesn't know what to talk about and doesn't want to talk about any worthwhile matter—who, frankly, is just repetitiously dull. I have met many such individuals throughout life and had nothing but pity for them. I was never reluctant always to extend a fast farewell in such instances.

Wisdom vs. Knowledge

When I withdraw into the desert for a period of time, my inner man, including its confusing thought pattern, comes to a wonderful rest and to a reassessment of life's values. Out in the desert without bugs, flies and mosquitoes, without smog, with just the right temperature, I find myself sleeping on the sand looking into a beautiful far-away firmament at night. There is no noise to sidetrack me. I think of the many stars being thousands of light years away from us. I think of the universe consisting of untold nebulae, suns and various other constellations. Then I think of our world just being like a grain of sand in an ocean in one of these nebulae.

Science has proven that our five senses are actually deceiving us. Look at some train tracks and it looks as though they come together in the distance. Listen to a horse cantering on the radio and it will seem to you as if it were happening right there.

In tests performed on a criminal with covered eyes, they have pretended to puncture his vein by just pricking him with a needle on his arm. After this they permitted warm water to drip down his arm, giving him the sensation of losing blood. Not very long afterward, the criminal was dead. After doctors examined him, they found that he had indeed died because of loss of blood.

Most of us judge, think, decide and know things out of the experiences we had with our five senses. This proves that, generally speaking, we are actually sitting in a merry-go-round while relying solely upon our five senses.

At the scene of an airplane accident three witnesses who were present and saw the accident were questioned about the cause. Each of those three witnesses gave an entirely different account. When a movie that had been taken of the accident was played, it was found that each of the three witnesses had been mistaken. This is why it is very necessary in our lives that we do not just depend upon book knowledge and shallow experiences, but that we have periods in our lives when we have quiet and solitude, endeavoring to eliminate much of our own thought patterns; in other words, making our mind temporarily blank and permitting a higher inspiration which will lead us in a more definite way if relied upon.

Then I ask myself, "Who am I, and what are my problems?" I found that in periods such as these I have received many answers which have guided me in my past life in a way no other person could have led me. I have always found that as the unnecessary and banal things of a conventional lifestyle fell away, life took on a new meaning and only truly important aspects became outstanding, while I lost the attachment to things which at one time I thought were very important. Life then arranges itself more along important long-range projects.

Literally millions of people are sick and miserable in their daily grind. They are caught up in a never-ending endeavor to earn not only enough money to meet their current obligations (including their regular monthly payments) but also to provide something for a "rainy day". Many wish they could get away from the cities and jobs they are chained to and long to live a simpler life in the country.

Scientists tell us that even nature planned an outdoor life for humans, but most people only live such a life on weekends and on their annual vacations. There are still many, many open country areas where people could live simply and cheaply—so why not break your fetters and start living the way you want to?

Cities are becoming human beehives of vice, corruption, racial violence and moral decay at an increasing rate. In order to survive the oncoming economic breakdown and the many hardships that will accompany it, people would be well advised to relocate in remote areas principally west of the Mississippi River. Since land is becoming more expensive and more scarce, do not put off such a move too long.

Educational Gems

He is the happiest, be he king or peasant, who finds peace in his home. —Goethe.

The moment passed is no longer; the future may never be; the present is all of which man is the master. —Rousseau.

The most manifest sign of wisdom is continued cheerfulness. —Montaigne.

No one sees the shadows who faces the sun.

Let him who would move the world, first move himself.

Freedom is the last best hope of earth.

Hold out a hand instead of pointing a finger.

All freedoms spring from freedom of the mind.

A wise man will make haste to forgive because he knows the value of time and will not suffer it to pass away in unnecessary pain.

He who chops his own wood is twice warmed.

The humble man is ever ready to overlook the faults of others . . .knowing he has so many.

A great man shows his greatness by the way he treats little men.

If God had intended that man should go backward, He would have given him eyes in the back of his head. —Victor Hugo.

A man who uses a great many words to express his meaning is like a bad marksman who, instead of aiming a single stone at an object, takes up a handful and throws at it in hopes he may hit. — Samuel Johnson.

It matters not what you are thought to be, but what you are.

No one knows what he can do till he tries.

Good health and good sense are two of life's greatest blessings.

"I've captured a politician," cried the South Sea Island cannibal. "Now I can have a baloney sandwich."

If you put off until tomorrow what you should do today, there will probably be a higher tax on it.

Future generations won't be squandering their hard-earned money foolishly—we've already done that for them.

The power which is needed to resist temptations forms only a small part of the power which would later be necessary to bear the consequences of having surrendered to the temptations.

Knowledge is a treasure but practice is the key to it.

Knowledge is of two kinds: we know a subject ourselves or we know where we can find information upon it. —Samuel Johnson.

"Patriotism" is the banner under which you are approached for a donation of time and services even though it is for an unworthy cause and not worth your effort.

Don't give up hope—there is not enough darkness in the whole world to put out the light of one weak candle.

TIMELY

DEFENSIVE

MEASURES

Chapter 17

Timely Defensive Measures

Your chances of becoming the victim of a serious crime are greater today than ever. A number of crimes are committed every minute of the day, involving people of all ages and all walks of life.

There are a number of things you can do to protect yourself, your family, your home and your car.

1. *Yourself and your family*. Do your best to avoid possible trouble. Keep away from lonely city areas, especially at night. Some parks and neighborhoods are dangerous even during daylight hours and should be avoided completely. It is safer to walk in the middle or outer edge of sidewalks as you could be grabbed by a criminal if you walk too close to doorways and alleys. Avoid carrying large amounts of cash with you.

One excellent means of protection for adults that can be used no matter where they are is a small container of chemical (preferably CS tear gas) that can be held in the hand easily and sprayed by depressing a push device into the face of an attacker or burglar. Their chemical spray causes extreme discomfort to the person being squirted but does not permanently harm him. The containers are quite inexpensive and contain enough chemical for quite a number of sprays (50 to 100). Each spray will incapacitate a person for about fifteen minutes. The CS tear gas is being used by the United States Army and many police forces in America. I know a number of the better products along this line and as far as I know, these defensive aerosol tear gas devices are perfectly legal in most areas at the time of this writing (check locally before purchasing).   Projectile-type weapons, pens, revolvers, shotguns and pistols (which have been used to fire live ammunition) that are designed to discharge tear gas by means of a cartridge shell (22, 32, 38, etc.) are subject to the gun control act which started June 1, 1975. As of this writing, this does not affect, control or restrict the aerosol tear gas device. These units have saved many lives. They usually come in a small container with a pocket clip and a bigger police unit.

If, however, in spite of your best efforts, you are faced with a criminal, here are some suggestions: If you are about to be robbed, don't resist senselessly, but do try to observe details that might be of importance in the apprehension of the thief. It would be more wise to lose a little money than risk being injured or killed. If you are physically attacked, try to determine how desperate the criminal is before you cry out. Perhaps you can make him think you are too frightened to move or sound an alarm and then catch him off guard. If, however, you are in good physical shape with your muscles in tone, there are a number of things you can do to help yourself. For the best results, practice them at home until you are familiar with them. Be careful while practicing these techniques, however, as some can kill or injure a person if done too forcefully. *Be sure you are within arm's length of your assailant when making any of these moves*. If you are further away, they will not work and you should do what he says.

When you are ready to make your move, either shout or grunt explosively (this will give you more momentum) and move fast, taking your assailant by surprise. The secret of this unarmed self defense is leverage, not brute strength. There is much greater leverage force at the elbow or on the upper arm than on the lower arm. When you make your moves in turning, be sure to pivot.

Always be ready to use general defensive measures: Bite, butt hard on nose, chop upwards with your hand to strike hard at throat or at bottom of nose, jab hard in the eyes or on the sides of the neck with your thumb nails, chop at the windpipe with the edge of your flat hand, jab hard with one knuckle on the back of his hand or in the ribs, hit hard with cupped hands over the ears (if you hit too hard, you could break his eardrums), bend his fingers backward, knee him sharply in the groin or stomp heavily on his instep. These can be done singly or in combination.

If the assailant is facing you with a gun or knife in his hand, you could slap his inner wrist very sharply with one hand and grab the weapon quickly with your other hand and twist it out of his grasp.   (You can also slap hard with both hands simultaneously, using one hand on his inner wrist and the other on his knuckles. Use this defensive measure with care as long as the pistol is pointed at you.)   Another suggestion is to chop down on his wrist hard, (sidestep as you do so), grab for the weapon with your other hand and wrench it away from him.

If he threatens you with a club upraised, step toward him and block his forearm with the outer edge of your forearm. With your other hand grab either the club or his wrist and twist sharply.

If you are attacked by a straight jab with a knife toward your waist, block with your left arm and step back right away with your right leg. If the knife is at your back, hit hard backwards with your elbow while turning around fast to grab his wrist. Then bring your other arm over the top of his arm and seize the knife and his hand. Twist his hand so he drops the knife. If the knife is across your throat with the assailant standing behind you, clutch the knife quickly with your opposite hand, twist his arm downwards and jab up suddenly with your knee to knock the knife away.

Any coat can be used as a weapon by grabbing each side of the collar in a cross hold and forcing your knuckles into his neck as you pull your hands toward the middle.

If a towel or similiar item is put around your neck, hit assailant's elbows (one up and one down). If something is placed over your head from behind, turn and attack.

If you are on the ground and he is standing near your foot, hook one foot around his heel and kick sideways very hard with your other foot into his leg (above the knee, if possible).

If he stoops down, bring your knee up sharply to hit him in the face and chop him sharply with the side of your hand on the back of his neck.

If he grabs you from behind, lean against him and stomp down hard on his instep.

To prevent a headlock, put your arms up and hit him under the arm with your elbow.

If you are grabbed by the neck from the front, bring your arms up together quickly through his arms and then bring both of them forcefully down over one of his arms to break his grip. If he tries a stranglehold from the rear, grab his elbow hard with both of your hands and bend your knees, still holding his elbow firmly. Next, bend forward, and by then automatically straightening your knees and pulling him, you should be able to throw him over your shoulder if you want to.

If he seizes you with a wrist hold, reach over his hands, grab your own hand and pull up hard.

Ladies, a hatpin carried in your coat lapel where you can get at it easily and quickly is a good weapon.

There are some extra safeguards to remember concerning children. Teach them never to accept a ride with a stranger, to run away from strangers who touch them, to refuse any gift offered by a stranger, not to answer remarks a stranger makes but keep walking away, to keep away from car doors if asked directions by anyone in a vehicle, not to go alone into public rest rooms, if possible. Children should also be instructed to report any strange behavior by an adult to his parents, school teacher or policeman. Know where your children are. If they are not at home, they should be accompanied by a trustworthy adult—trustworthy because often child molesters are either relatives or friends of the family.

If there is no "Block Mother" set-up in your neighborhood, it would be a good idea to form one so children have a place to go in case of need as they walk to and from school. Be sure your babysitter is thoroughly trustworthy and mature enough to be able to handle any emergency that might arise. Be sure she has telephone numbers to refer to in case of need.

2. *Your home.* Be sure all your doors and windows are locked when you go out (including basement windows). The best locks for doors are the kind that are key-operated because those that lock by slamming can quickly be opened. It is a good idea to leave on some lights inside the house (not the porch light), and don't

"hide" a key. Be careful not to let strangers know when you plan to be away from home and don't let strangers in when you are at home unless you have some positive identification from them. A peep hole used together with a chain bolt is an excellent safeguard. A good precaution is to keep extra valuables in a safe place away from your house. Be sure to have a list of the serial numbers of the valuables that you need to have at home, such as typewriters, stereos, cameras, etc.

If you notice your door ajar when you come home or your lock seems to have been "jimmied", quietly go to a neighbor's home or some place where you can telephone the police. If you should enter and surprise a burglar at work inside your home, you could be injured or killed.

When you are planning to be away from home for an extended period of time, be sure to take extra precautions. Make sure all home deliveries are stopped and your mail held at the post office. It is a good idea to have a trustworthy neighbor keep an eye on your property and check to see that no deliveries are made. Alert neighbors can be of great help and you can return the favor when they go on a trip. It would be well worth the money to invest in two or three timers. Set them for various times such as turning lights on and off in the living room during the evening hours and then on and off in the bedroom at your usual bedtime. Another timer could be used to turn a radio on and off. Lights and sounds make it seem as though someone is at home and will very likely steer a burglar elsewhere.

3. *Your car.* Be sure to keep your car locked and all valuables locked in the trunk out of sight. Don't forget to take the key with you. Unless required by law, don't keep registration papers or other identifying papers in the car. If you park in a parking lot or leave your car at a garage for repairs, be sure to give the attendant only the ignition key. When returning to your parked car, look behind your front seats before entering the car. Assailants like to hide out there in order to attack you from behind when you are driving. Ignore strangers hitchhiking; you could lose your life as well as your car. A white rag tied to the radio aerial or a raised hood are signals for help you can use if your car malfunctions on the road. If a stranger offers help, lower your window a little to talk to him.

WISDOM

FOR

PHYSICAL

PROFIT

Chapter 18

Wisdom For Physical Profit

A good condition of physical and dental health is a very important aspect of survival life as there will be no medical facilities available or only in a very limited form during those times. The few medical and dental services which will be at public disposal then would labor under great shortages of needed supplies and also they would be greatly overrun. As times of breakdown are usually accompanied by uprisings, revolutions, civil strifes, riot and gang activities, the run on those facilities would be even greater. It is therefore advisable that you have your teeth checked and maintained while you are still able to do so.

What Type of Diet?

The various parts of this world produce different products, each of which is particular to its own area. It has been claimed and the way of nature teaches that the foods which are characteristic for your own territory are the best suited to sustain you in your own environment and therefore apparently also the healthiest for your body. In other words, if you live in an area such as Florida, grapefruit, oranges, coconuts, guavas, papayas and mangoes would be a healthy part of your diet. Other products which you would import from different weather zones, such as cherries and apples, are not necessarily the healthiest diet for you. Whatever will grow in more northerly zones, such as apples, peaches and pears, would be the right type of diet for you in that area. Just as a certain type of people fit into a certain geographical area because of their particular physical make-up, so a diet composed of food growing in that area is the best type of food for those people.

There has been much material written regarding what is the best diet for people. Some believe that we should all be vegetarians, others believe that we should eat a lot of meat, and still others believe that a mixed diet is the best for us. It seems that there are about as many opinions as there are advocates on this subject. After much research, I have come to understand that the foods we eat should be patterned after the geographical location we live in. If, for instance, I live in a warm climate, I can easily maintain myself with a diet of just fruit and vegetables and stay happy and healthy. If I live in a very cold climate, such as northern Norway, Greenland, Alaska, or Canada, I would freeze to death if I were to try to live on just vegetables and fruit alone. There my body will need a good amount of oils, fats and protein such as we get from fish, meat, seeds, nuts, eggs, cheese, butter and milk. In fact, in places such as Greenland, Iceland and northern Norway, people have to live mostly off the ocean in the form of fish (especially herring and cod), seals, whales and meat. This gives them the needed fuel to heat their bodies and they stay healthy, while a person eating that type of diet in a warmer climate would become seriously ill. I think it is safe to conclude from this that if we were to live in a moderate climate, a sensibly mixed diet would constitute the right type of food for us.

Diet would also have to be adjusted in accordance with the particular job a person has; that is, if a person works at heavy physical labor, such as construction work, he would then need a heavier diet and also be able to utilize it properly. A person doing light clerical work, for instance, which does not require much physical labor, should have a lighter diet.

No two bodies are alike and each person will have to use some common sense to know which particular food pattern to follow in the framework of that general diet in order to suit his individual make-up. A certain type of food which would be very digestible and profitable for one person might just be the opposite for another person. It certainly would be recommendable if people as a whole, particularly for our climatic area, would stick to a diet which contains a lot of unprocessed grains, seeds, nuts, fresh fruits, vegetables and pure water. Naturally it would be preferable if those products could be grown biologically, and in the person's own garden wherever possible. There is a great waste in minerals, vitamins and enzymes by having those products lay around for any period of time in transportation, warehouses and supermarkets. Many of the products being shipped are picked unripe for easier transportation. If we again, in keeping with simplicity, look at the way a wild animal lives, we find that it obtains all its products in the very vicinity in which it lives; it does not import any products and it lives from fresh products which it harvests at the very time of eating. Those animals are still conforming to their natural pattern for they are not as civilized and degenerated as human beings. This once more shows us the advantage of living from products grown in your immediate area.

One of the reasons we have chosen a diet as close to nature as possible is expressed by the saying "you are what you eat".

Also, it is best to eat the products that are fresh in their season since each ripens at the proper time to condition your body and blood for that particular climatic temperature.

Lake Bottom Soil—A Bonanza for Your Diet

When thinking of having an organic garden and growing your own food products, I would like to point out a very important matter. Historical records indicate that before the great flood there were no rains but instead the soil was moistened by the mists in the atmosphere. After that time occasional severe weather outbreaks and frequent rains have been the lot of mankind. Those rains brought about a carrying off of the mineral-rich soil into the ocean by means of the river systems. Much of the fertile soil left has accumulated in lakes; therefore, if you are able to scoop off soil out of nearby lake bottoms and then apply it on your garden spot, you will find a tremendous improvement in your products and in their growth pattern.

A friend of mine has experimented in this field and has grown very large strawberries, carrots and tomatoes which had a great resistance to rot because of their high mineral content. Some of those products would wither before they would ever rot. In comparison tests he conducted with general supermarket products, he found that the supermarket products would rot within a period of a few days while his products stayed fresh and kept their extremely good flavor even after relatively long storage.

Independence From Commercial Foods can be a Life-or-Death Matter

At this point I would like to advise the readers of this book to store up various grains such as wheat and related products. If properly stored, they will last almost indefinitely. You may remember that the wheat found in the pyramids of Egypt still contained life after thousands of years of storage. These foods will be much better for you than artificially prepared storage foods such as those which have been dehydrated, canned or freeze-dried. The latter are all very expensive and overstressed in today's market; however, some persons who live in cities might wish to keep a supply of them on hand in case of emergency or a breakdown when food would be hard to obtain. One danger of having food stored—especially in cities—is the fact that in times of chaos and breakdown there is a great risk of having this food taken away from you. Also, past agricultural buying programs have given the Federal government both the machinery and the authority to buy up food from the general market place quickly, thereby creating a food shortage.

It was our experience under Communism that we were able to manage sufficiently and maybe in an even more healthy way by not having to depend upon such conserved commercial storage foods during that time of collapse and chaos, as we were able to live off the land because we had a practical knowledge of the edible wild foods growing in the area. It would be good for people today to settle in some rural or remote area where they can have some land of their own to utilize for growing their own food and where they are able to roam the open country, study the edible wild foods and practice survival knowledge first hand. If people will take the time to obtain or increase this knowledge about wild herbs, fruits and vegetables, they will benefit in several ways:

1. They can gather a supply of absolutely fresh products daily that are filled with vitamins, minerals and enzymes.

2. Many wild, edible foods are easily available, even near and in some cities, and utilizing them in your diet would save money on grocery bills and cut down on the number of trips to the supermarket besides being much healthier for you.

3. If, under survival conditions, people have to move suddenly from their location without being able to carry stored-up food with them, they will be able to supply themselves with the wild foods they find as they travel. Mobility is a great factor under this type of survival conditions.

4. They will have peace of mind and confidence in any situation knowing they can always find food when they need it. The individual knows he has actually practiced that kind of life and can do it again when necessary.

There are many good survival training manuals and books on the American market. Many are very similar in context and it might be profitable for an individual to browse through some of them in a library or bookstore before buying them. In this book I am endeavoring to bring everything down to the most simple way possible. If we have to rely completely upon manufactured and processed survival foods under emergency conditions, then we would be in bad shape when we run out of those, once the economy has collapsed, as the factories would no longer be able to produce those items. Of course, there is always a lot of personal profit involved, and it is understood that many business interests would get hold of the present and future dilemma of the people even to commercialize on that.

A good way for you to prepare for an emergency is by buying some of the hand-operated grain mills which are available on the market today. We find this a very healthy and economical way of life even now, as each morning we grind our grains and eat those fresh, delicious products uncooked, since they then contain nutritious substances such as vitamins and enzymes which are destroyed to a great extent in processing, cooking and baking. We find that we can nourish our family in a better way for much less money—just a few pennies per meal!

Health and Wellbeing—Exercise

When travelling a lot while lecturing, I meet a lot of different, interesting people. Once, while speaking in Southern California, I ran across a rather interesting individual with a unique personality. He is now 62 years old and looks like a man of 40. He engages in a vigorous plan of exercise, much of his own devising, which keeps his blood freely circulating and causes an aerobic effect. His body does not show any of the typical signs of aging such as baldness, a paunch or a stooped posture. He is full of energy, healthy and very alert and intelligent. He also eats a healthy and natural diet. He mentioned to me how much better he feels every time he does his exercises and trained me in some of those exercises. I felt rejuvenated afterwards, almost like being reborn.

I would strongly recommend that you be in good physical condition for the times ahead. It certainly would be very helpful if you train your body through such activities as extensive hikes, hunting, swimming, and temporary outdoor life, including supplying your own food from nature, so that you will be able to endure adverse circumstances. You will find that you can progress from an initial limited program of exercise to a broader program as your body condition improves. The advantages of living in your homestead in the open country already will give you a chance for many of those exercises in your daily activities. This subject might be of particular need for this country as people sit in their cars to go where they want to go, get out of their cars and sit at another place. They sit at their jobs, sit at meetings and sit before their television sets. There is very little walking being done in America. In fact, it seems that walking is almost a forgotten art—so much so that my wife and myself have been stopped by police while taking hikes in cities, being questioned as if they apparently thought we were vagrants!

A Few Notes On Relaxation

There is a great need for each one of us to relax from time to time, if possible, every day. A good relaxing exercise is just lying flat on the rug listening to good music and having someone give you a massage on the soles of your feet.

It is not the *things* themselves which put us into tense conditions of fear, but rather the *conceptions* we have of certain things which give that fear.

Seek out sympathetic people who appreciate you and who have influence, because their thought waves will benefit you.

Avoid aggravations and running into troubles. Consider them small things in relation to your big life goal.

In our time man comes in contact mostly with things which he builds himself; therefore, he becomes disattached from nature and unhappy.

How peaceful and harmonious everything looks from a cosmic view—a beautiful world. How happy the inhabitants could be if their view would reach a little further than just to the encirclement of walls within which there is so much jealousy, hate and mistrust.

The day will come that the collection of human masses in giant cities will stop and it will not be necessary any longer for people to work in big factories doing jobs which are demeaning to the thinking nature of man and stifling to his spirit.

Take a hike in the forest. You might never have realized what the word "hiking" means, what a volume of unknown blessings it encompasses; the peaceful quietness in the high forest in which at dawn the sunlight often breaks through in brilliant display; the murmuring of small creeks among ferns and moss-covered stones; the mid-day glow on the plateau among wild berries and foxglove in deepest calm, infinite, far from the world, where a bird of prey circles high and clear; evening peace on a forest meadow when the deer are browsing. Only a hiker could experience this!

Many people are prisoners of their own particular habits, such as vanity, and they ask for a Persian carpet for their cell instead of freedom.

Don't pay for a higher life standard with your health. Don't conform your life according to your neighbor, but according to your body. Don't try to "keep up with the Joneses", but rather do that which is right for you and don't overdo your physical capacity.

Even though the absence of a telephone might be an inconvenience in some ways, I count it a blessing as I do not miss it. It interrupts your privacy when you want to relax or listen to some good music. Suddenly the telephone rings and you are in contact with the world. I find it an added blessing not to have any utility bills any longer!

Another blessing is the absence of television. Our beautiful and warm home atmosphere is such a joy that we could consider television a most unwelcome intruder, beside the fact that we have no use whatsoever for the programs which are being televised on it. What peace without that rumble box!

Chapter 19

Emergency Short-Term Survival

It is amazing to see how few people actually have a theoretical knowledge, much less a working knowledge, of how to maintain themselves if they were to get lost suddenly. They would not know how to find their way to the next settlement after getting stuck with their car some place in the mountains, after getting lost on a hunting trip or after crashing with a plane in the wilderness. There is enough food and enough shelter material available at nearly every conceivable location to make it needless for a person to freeze or to starve to death. A person lost in the wilderness will nearly always be able to help himself if he knows just a few main guidelines.

Survival Foods

Many times I travelled alone and had to rely upon myself to survive any conditions I would find myself in. I learned how much a body can actually endure if properly trained. I also found out how little food the body actually needs and still be strong and healthy. I ate very little and there were many days without food, yet I kept on at a very stringent pace.

A person will be able to survive for an extended period of time without food as long as he has water. The number of days he will be able to live without food depends upon his physical condition, his activity and the elements. People have been known to exist up to sixty days without food. There is food in plenty all around you in the forest. You can eat the needles (rich in Vitamin C) and leaves of most trees. You can peel off the bark of many live trees and eat the sap layer, or peel back the bark of decaying logs and eat the insects, such as ants and termites.

As there is enough wholesome food in the wilderness to keep you in excellent shape, it would be nothing short of suicide through gross ignorance if you were to die out in the wild country. Rather than dying, you should get well in body and soul while being in such a setting—this is where the animals stay well, healthy, strong and free of civilization's diseases. Some of these creatures of the wilderness are so strong that you can hardly kill them with a bullet.

All grasses, for instance, are considered edible. When young, grass is one of nature's most nourishing foods high in Vitamins A, C, K, G and some factors of the B complex. A great amount of vegetables and fruits (340 pounds)—which usually a person could not eat in a year—does not contain, by estimation, as many vitamins as 13 pounds of powdered dry grass. Tests have been conducted feeding people dehydrated grass in addition to other food. They did exceptionally well. You can, for instance, grind the dry grass in a sausage grinder when at home or eat the softer selections the way they are when out in the wilderness.

Many so-called weeds, for instance, contain more vitamins and minerals than a lot of garden vegetables. Dandelion contains more than twice the amount of iron, calcium and phosphorus and six times that of Vitamin A as garden lettuce. Water cress has almost three times as much calcium as spinach and three times as much Vitamin E as lettuce.

Most of the vegetation, berries and many mushrooms are edible. When in doubt, stay away from mushrooms.

If not familiar with the area and the plant life in that area, a person can survive by testing the edibility of such.

Depending upon where you live, 60% to 85% of your diet will consist of plant foods. The kingdom of plants is divided into two main subkingdoms, known as thallophyta (primitive plants such as fungi, algae and one-celled bacteria) and embryophyta. Two groups divide the embryophyta division; they are known as bryophyta (simple plants such as liverworts and mosses) and tracheophyta, which has a subphylum (subgroup) we are most concerned with as it includes seed-bearing plants such as flowers, vegetables, common grasses, shrubs and most trees. This subgroup is called pteropsida. Most of our plant food comes from this group. In this world there are more than 335,000 different species of plants. Common sense would indicate that even though a person would spend his entire life studying the edibility of plant foods, he still would not master the entire subject. Even though he should arrive at the last species, he would have forgotten much of what he learned previously.

In today's cosmopolitan world, a person can never know where he might be at the time when he has to call upon his survival knowledge. Obviously, it will be impossible for him to study all the plants of this world and even then it would only be a part of his survival know-how. In most cases a person will only have a small portion of his time available for this subject, as there are many other tasks he has to perform in life.

There is a definite need in this all-important subject matter, therefore, to find a simple general test procedure which will enable a person *to know for sure* what he can eat and what he must stay away from. Fortunately, there is such a test and most good survival manuals agree on the procedure with only minute, insignificant variations. I will give you in a moment the best and most comprehensive version I have arrived at from my own experience and the study of the various survival manuals on this subject. I believe this combination of personal and other reference material should offer safest application.

First, you must realize that the sense of smell is so closely associated with the sense of taste that it is believed much of our taste comes from what we smell by association. A person who has a cold and plugged-up nose does not have a keen sense of taste. You can arrive at the same phenomena by closing someone's nose, blindfolding him and then letting him differentiate by taste such items as potatoes, apples, red wine and coffee. Sweet, sour, salty and bitter are the four taste sensations. Odors and tastes arise when liquid-dissolved chemicals touch the sense organs. The taste center is near the smell (olfactory) center and right below the brain center. A feeling of pain expresses itself as sharp and biting to the taste buds. The back part of the tongue is sensitive to bitterness, the sides to sourness, the frontal side edges to saltiness and the very front to sweetness. Because of this, you should make sure that in case of a taste test you mix the food well all over in your mouth. The taste and smell senses are so delicate that infinitesimal amounts of chemicals still can be detected. Much more of the brain is taken up in animals by the olfactory lobes (part of the smell organ) than in man. This probably accounts for the fact that animals usually test their food by sniffing it. Also, their taste plays an important part in their food selection. Why should it not be possible for man to do likewise in modified form (because of his duller senses)?

An understanding of the above will show you the reasons behind the food test which follow. It will prove to you how important a keen set of senses in combination with a healthy body are to you, especially under survival conditions.

1. *Visual Test:* Examine the food to see if it looks healthy and uncontaminated (just what is easily visible with the eye). The chances for pollution are slim, as you most likely will be some distance from a defiled civilization. After gathering more experience, you will be astounded to find out how much you can tell concerning the edibility of foods by visual inspection. When picking fruits and herbs while travelling, stay away from roadsides. They are at times polluted by lead poisoning from car emissions and from sprays designed to kill vegetation and insects.

2. *Smell Test:* Smash, crush or otherwise mash up the fruit, root, stem, leaf, flower, or other food substance under consideration and smell the same. Just as nearly all plant foods have a taste, so nearly all of them also are odoriferous. If the odor is acrid, nauseating or otherwise offensive, then stay away from this product. I have applied this test many times throughout the years of my wilderness travels before I had ever learned the more important taste test, and it kept me alive. However, it was coupled with good common sense. By conducting a smell test, you can avoid an oral test of outright obnoxious products.

3. *Taste Test:* This is the most important and final test. *Do not apply these three tests to mushrooms and other fungi. Poisonous fungi cannot be detected by unpleasant taste or disagreeable odor.* The ones which are edible could also easily

be confused with poisonous types. The little food value they contain, aside from other dangers, makes it advisable to disregard them as food sources unless you are very sure about them.

a. Put a small raw portion of the plant in your mouth and chew it. *Don't swallow!* Then spit it out after about five minutes and wait to see if there are any ill effects on the mouth or tongue. If not, then proceed to the next step.

b. Take a teaspoonful of the raw plant food and hold it in your mouth for about five minutes. If by this time no burning sensation, disagreeable, offensive, odious, repugnant, nauseating, bitter, sharp taste or other unpleasant effect has occurred, swallow a *little* of it. If after eight hours no ill effects as mentioned below have occurred, swallow a little more (about a teaspoonful) and then wait eight hours. If no ill effects such as nausea, cramps, diarrhea, stomach or intestinal pains occurred, take the next step.

c. Take a little more of the plant food, prepared in the way it will be used (raw, boiled, baked—do not add any foreign substance such as salt, etc.) and eat it (about a handful). Wait another eight hours; if no ill effects have taken place, then you can consider that food edible. Do not eat other substances while making this test, as it could upset the reliability of the experiment. Also, keep in mind that any new or strange food should be eaten with restraint until you have become used to it. Remember that olives are bitter and grapefruit is sour, so an unpleasant taste does not, in itself, necessarily mean poison; but a burning, nauseating or bitter taste is a warning of danger. Never eat strange food without first testing it.

A disagreeable taste in a food item which is otherwise safe to eat may sometimes be removed by leaching; i.e., pouring cold or hot water through the chopped, crushed or ground material. If cooking is possible, boiling in one or more changes of water may remove the unpleasant taste.

In general, it is safe (with some exceptions) to try foods that you observe being eaten by birds and mammals. Food eaten by rodents (mice, rats, squirrels, muskrats, rabbits and beavers) or by monkeys, baboons, bears, raccoons and various other omnivorous animals (vegetable eaters) usually are safe for you to try. Cook all foods when in doubt about their edibility. Some poisons may be removed by cooking. Avoid eating untested plants with milky juice or letting the milk contact your skin—there are good ones among them, but be sure you know them.

All parts of some plants are edible, but often it is necessary to choose the most palatable part, such as fruits, seeds, bark, tubers, buds, leaves, flowers, sap, pods, nuts, stems, root stalks, shoots and bulbs.

If time is of the essence, you could abbreviate the above-mentioned edibility test and might want to use, for instance, the following versions as taken from the Air Force Manual 64-5—Survival: Take a teaspoonful of the plant food, prepared in the way it will be used (raw, boiled, baked, etc.), hold it in your mouth for about 5 minutes. If, by this time no burning sensation, or other unpleasant effect, has occurred, swallow it. Wait 8 hours. If no ill effects such as nausea, cramps, or diarrhea come about, eat a handful and wait 8 hours. If no ill effects show up at the end of this time, the plant may be considered edible. (Keep in mind that any new or strange food should be eaten with restraint until you have become used to it.)

Again, I would like to stress that it would be very important for you to develop such an understanding of plants and berries so you can be self-sufficient and mobile rather than storing a large amount of artificial, processed food. There is a great need to go into a simple life, divorcing ourselves from the fancy things which in the oncoming crash will soon be destroyed by vandals and will not be maintainable in bad times ahead.

Unfortunately, most people always look for an easy way out. To them it seems easier to *buy* a quantity of storage food than to acquire a working knowledge of how to identify the food nature provided so plentifully. They are missing out on a great and wonderful challenge. Their lack of initiative along this line can easily prove fatal some day, especially in the times we are living in.

Some of the wild edible plants of our forests are: pine nuts, huckleberries, elderberries, miners lettuce, wood sorrel, salmonberries, cattail roots, new fern leaves and roots, inner bark of trees, wild plum, wild rose flowers and fruits, Oregon grape berries.

Some of the poisonous plants of our forests are: buttercup, larkspur, water hemlock (in parsley family), poison oak, milkweed, locoweed and certain mushrooms.

Most streams in mountainous areas are pure enough to drink, but if in doubt boil drinking water three to four minutes or add purification tablets before using. You can obtain water by digging a two-foot hole covered by a plastic sheet. Place a stone in the middle to form a concave (V-shaped) depression. Moisture from the ground will condense and run down the plastic sheet and drop from the lowest point into a can.

Disoriented? Then What?

It would be wise to prepare now, so you could also deal with a situation an experienced trapper in British Colombia encountered a few years ago. He became lost in the wilderness as he checked his trap lines. He knew something about the terrain he was in and searched for an old, abandoned telegraph trail that was in the vicinity which would lead him to the nearest settlement. In a short time the food he had brought with him was eaten and he then lived on green berries and leaves of the edible Solomon seal plant. He shot a moose with his rifle but could not carry much of the meat with him. "I should have taken a hand gun with me," he said, "because I saw hundreds of squirrels but couldn't shoot them without blowing them apart."

The underbrush was so thick in that part of the country that sometimes he could scarcely crawl through it. He lost the trail a couple of times but eventually found it again and followed it ninety miles out to safety. His comment on this experience was thought-provoking: "That's the one thing this experience did for me," he said. "It's given me the guts to quit my job pounding ties, collect my pension, and start all over again—in the bush."

The best thing is *not* to get lost, so before going on your trip, study a map of the area, learn the direction in which the streams and drainages flow, where the trails are located, names and location of prominent peaks and other important items pertinent to the area.   Learn how to use your map and compass.   When you are travelling in the area, pinpoint your camps and locations on the map.   Orient your map to land features every chance you get.

If you do become lost, do the following:

1. Keep calm. Do not walk aimlessly; trust your map and compass.   Shelter and warmth are much more important than food.
   a. To find your positions, climb to a place where you can see the surrounding country.
   b. When you reach a road, trail, power or telephone line, follow it.   As a last resort, follow a stream downhill.
   c. Before being caught by darkness, select a sheltered spot and prepare camp,   shelter and firewood.   Stay in this camp all night.

2. If you are injured and alone, keep calm. Stay where you are. Clear an area down to mineral soil and build a signal fire with green boughs on it. Usually someone will find you.

3. Signal by three blasts from a whistle, three shots from a gun, three regulated puffs of smoke or three flashes from a flashlight or mirror.   (The following can be substituted for a mirror: a sliver of glass or ice, or a piece of shiny metal.) Repeat at regular intervals.   If your signal is recognized by a searching party, it will be answered by two signals.   Three signals of any kind, either audible or visible, is the nationwide SOS call. Use it only when in need of help.

4. Notify the County Sheriff's office if a member of your party is believed to be lost or in trouble and if it is beyond your resources to find or assist him.   Forest Rangers co-operate with the Sheriff in rescue work.

If you are lost, don't get frantic; keep a clear head.   Try to figure out where you are.

Here are a few more details on the two cardinal rules I have used many times:

1. Climb the nearest hill, mountain top or other elevation and see if you can find your directions by scanning the countryside. If you can, then choose a point of reference close

enough that you will be able to reach it, and keep it in sight most of the time while approaching it. Just before arriving at that point, sight it up with the next one and follow this system until you reach your destination. If there is no such elevation in sight or that system is not feasible, then go downhill until you come to a creek.

2. Follow that creek downstream until it leads you to a bigger stream and continue to do so until you finally reach some settlement or help.

If necessary, you can use a watch as a compass. Point the hour hand at the sun if north of the equator, and then south will be just halfway between the hour hand and the figure 12 on the dial. Be sure the watch is set for standard time for the time zone you are in.

Travel in poor visibility without the aid of a compass may compound your problem. Find suitable shelter and await better conditions.

A simple shadow stick compass will show you north on any day with enough light to cast a faint shadow line. Select a straight stick three feet long and five small pegs. Place the stick upright in a cleared area. Place a peg into the ground at the end of the stick's shadow line. Wait fifteen minutes; place another peg at end of new shadow line. Repeat until five pegs are in. Place a straight stick alongside the pegs. This stick points east and west. To find north, place a stick at the base of the upright shadow stick and place it 90 degrees to the east-west stick. This stick now points north. Check for possible errors. (Redo if doubtful.)

It is possible to determine directions on a clear night by the North Star as has been done for centuries. The two pointer stars which form the front of the Big Dipper (Dubhe and Merak) are nearly in direct alignment with the North Star. Merak forms the lower front of the Big Dipper and Dubhe forms the upper front. The North Star is approximately five times as far from Dubhe as Dubhe is from Merak.

Shelter And Heat

Under temporary survival conditions, you should never underestimate the necessity of conserving your body heat and energy. Shelter from the wind, rain, blizzard and sun will help.

In cold climates you can keep warm by building a fire in a deep hole, cover six inches of coals with six inches of soil and sleep on the warmed earth. Leaves or branches could serve as a blanket.

A cave dug in deep snow will keep you warmer because it is a 32-degree insulation from the colder outside temperatures.

In the desert, you should find or make some shelter from the sun during the day to avoid excessive loss of body moisture, and during the night dig yourself into the sand to stay remarkably warm. If you need to travel, do so only at night, using the stars to find directions.

When lost in the woods, there are enough branches, needles, leaves, rocks and soil from which a person can build himself a shelter. The kind of shelter you make depends on whether you need protection from rain, cold, heat, sunshine or insects and on the expected duration of your stay. Use care in picking the location. Try to be near water. Don't set up camp in a wash where flash floods could suddenly get you, or in areas of avalanches, floods, rockfalls or battering winds. You can quickly improvise a tent by placing a pole or rope between two trees or stakes and hanging a plastic sheet over it, fastening its corners with stones or knotting them around pegs.

Avoid sleeping on the bare ground. Provide some kind of insulation under yourself—soft boughs are good. Pick a bed site on level, well-drained ground free from rocks and roots. If you have to sleep on bare ground, dig depressions for your hips and shoulders and try out the site before you set up your shelter or spread your bedding.

During the winter a lean-to is a good shelter if in timbered country. Lay the covering bough shingle-fashion, starting from the bottom. If you have a canvas, use it for the roof. Close the ends with fabric or boughs. Build the fire before the open side. Keep the front openings of all shelters crosswind. Don't build a shelter under large trees or trees with dead limbs. They may fall and hurt you or wreck your camp.

For fire making you can use the following in the absence of conventional methods:

1. Use flint and steel. If you have no flint, look for a piece of hard rock from which you can strike sparks.

2. Any convex lens can be used in bright sunlight to concentrate the sun's rays on the tinder and get it burning. Carry some dry tinder with you in a waterproof container and collect more wherever you find it. Keep some firewood dry under shelter and dry more wood near the fire for future use.

You could also carry along some charred wood to help in starting your next fire. Another helpful suggestion is the use of a candle under a tepee-shaped collection of small, wet branches to help them dry.

Survival Hunting

The following would constitute ideal ways of obtaining meat in times of need: A bow and arrows with enough poundage to kill a deer would be good equipment. You can find ample use for the bow during each year's archery season. Be sure to practice a lot before you go hunting so you will be sure to kill the deer quickly and humanely. A crossbow might also come in handy.

A slingshot can be used with stones, metal pellets (B-Bs) or fence staples. Under Communism we found a good use for slingshots with just a straight, thin rubber band on which you put fence staples. During survival conditions you will always be able to find a forked stick and then you can cut a narrow strip of rubber tubing which you fasten by knotting the two ends of the rubber and inserting those ends into slots on each prong. Then you can shoot those staples by laying the fence staples over the rubber just as you would put them over a strand to fasten the fence. Pull at the ends of the staple and aim at small animals. Be sure to insert the staple in the center of the rubber and then pull back with an even draw. Aim right through the middle of the forked stick before releasing. If you don't do it properly, the sharp staple and rubber can catch on the stick and hit the back of your hand. When proper rubber is used, you will find that this simple little weapon has a tremendous killing power which will come in handy for the obtaining of much-needed game during times of food shortage.

Old-Time Remedies And First Aid

It is advisable for people to gain as much knowledge along this line as they can. Attendance at a Red Cross First Aid course, which is generally conducted free of charge in any good-sized community, will be very helpful. Obtain the FIRST AID TEXTBOOK prepared by the American National Red Cross for the instruction of first aid classes. It is well worth its modest price (around $1.00), being one of the best general first aid courses available. Even if you never need this knowledge under survival conditions, it may one day save someone's life, including your own and your family's.   Already the confidence and self-reliance this knowledge and practical experience will give you is worth a lot.   Practice the obtained skills every so often so you won't be rusty when called to help.   Hunting, camping, wilderness travel and Red Cross work can do much to improve your skill. Always make sure that you proceed in the following manner:

1. Administer the necessary first aid which is urgent.
2. See to it that the victim lies down.
3. Check for injuries, and while you do this figure what to do.
4. Then carry out what needs to be done.

Fortunately, aid for the main emergencies such as heart failure, stoppage of breathing, poisoning and massive bleeding is relatively simple.

Once I drove along the world-famous Tamiami Trail built through the middle of the vast Everglades in Florida.   As I drove along this Trail which extends for over a hundred miles between Tampa and Miami, I marvelled at the multitudes of beautiful white birds such as the egret, ibis and flamingo which literally covered the trees.   At times I would step out of my car and when those birds heard my voice they would take wing and rise in a mighty cloud of feathered finery.

In this area live the Seminole Indians, whose formidable resistance for seven years cost the United States $20,000,000 and 1,500 men. Their resistance lasted over one hundred years and finally ended in 1934. The Seminoles withdrew into the depths of the Everglades and were able to live very nicely from the bountiful wildlife found there, such as alligators, birds, fish, snakes and frogs, as well as fruits and vegetation in great abundance. They were able to hide easily when pursued and had all they wanted to eat. This wild food provided a means of survival for those Indians and in the more isolated portions of the reservations some of the Seminoles still live as they did a couple of hundred years ago.

While spending some time with the Tribal Chairman of the Seminole Indians, Billy Osceola (who, by the way, is a direct descendant of the famed Chief Osceola who led the desperate warfare of the Seminoles against the United States troops), I was told of some rather secret emergency hints. The Seminole Indians did not have much trouble with rattlesnakes, alligators and crocodiles apparently because of certain body odors on account of their way of life. When a white man came into their territory, however, he would be bitten and attacked very easily.

I questioned Billy Osceola as to what the Indians would do when bitten by rattlesnakes and he told me that they would cut out the meaty area around the anus of the snake and put that on the bite. For some time I wondered about the practicality of that treatment. I spent some time talking with some old Texas Rangers and was told by them that a person if possible should take a chicken and cut it open right in the middle and lay that on the snake bite. They believed that the warm meat sucks the poison right out of the bitten area.

Naturally, a person would want to have a snake bite kit with him. In the absence of one, however, it will not hurt to know what old timers did in such emergencies. Much depends upon your faith. A treatment which works for one does not necessarily work for another. It is important that you stay calm; many people have died of shock because of panic rather than from the snake bite. If you have confidence in your remedy, then this will help you to stay calm.

One of the Texas Rangers told me how he was hit by a stingray. The stingers of the stingray emit a poison which often gives its victims trouble for years because of deep, festering wounds which literally will not heal. This Texas Ranger caught the stingray, killed it and scraped off all the slime from the body of that stingray. After having removed the stinger of the stingray from his leg by pushing it through and pulling it out on the other side, he took that slime and pressed it into the sore. He left it in that sore until the slime dried and eventually fell out. The wound healed up quickly without any trouble then or later.

I have been told and read that it is possible to check up on the different parts and organs of the body for trouble by pressing upon the soles of one's feet; the various areas of your feet represent the different areas of the body. It is claimed that if there is pain in any place, just keep pressing and massaging that portion of the foot and, because of many nerve endings in the feet, the portion of the body affected by that particular nerve will be stimulated into restoring itself to health. Also, pressing on the portions of the body may reveal problems. If you keep pressing for a few moments, the pain should be relieved and the organ stimulated into action to overcome the problem. (See STORIES THE FEET CAN TELL and STORIES THE FEET HAVE TOLD, by Eunice D. Ingham, P. O. Box 948, Rochester, New York 14603).

Carbon monoxide poisoning can be caused by a fire burning in an unventilated shelter. Usually there are no symptoms; unconsciousness and death may occur without previous warning. Sometimes, however, there may be pressure at the temples, headache, pounding pulse, drowsiness and nausea. Treat by getting into fresh air at once; keep the person warm and have him rest. If necessary, apply artificial respiration.

The dangerous sun exposure in the desert can cause heat exhaustion, heat cramps and heat stroke. Treat the patient by cooling him off. Loosen his clothing; lay him down flat but off the ground, in the shade. Cool by saturating his clothes with water and by fanning. Do not give stimulants.

If you are totally immersed in cold water for even a few minutes, your body temperature will drop. The same will occur under long exposure to severe cold on land. The only remedy for this severe chilling is warming of the entire body. Warm by any means available. The preferred treatment is warming in a hot bath. Severe chilling may be accompanied by shock.

If you should injure yourself in the wilderness away from any medical help or supplies, you can cleanse your wound by simply sucking and spitting out the material until the wound is cleansed or by licking the sore such as a dog would. I have practiced that many times with excellent results.

Make sure you get plenty of rest. Don't worry, and try to take it easy. Keep as clean as possible under the circumstances. Restrict your movements to necessities as then you will conserve vital energy you will need.

When you are stranded or under primitive circumstances, it is especially important to keep well. It will be a life-or-death matter to you and a deciding factor of your pulling through. Protection against heat and cold and a knowledge of how to find water and food will be very important to keep your health. Drink enough water to avoid dehydration and avoid excessive dehydration from sweating. If you are walking a lot, rest ten minutes each hour. Give your feet special attention. You won't be worth much without a good pair of feet. If you develop troubles with your feet, stop and take care of them.

For your convenience, I am including a list of essential items for survival and a list of recommended survival manuals with a few explanations.

Essential Items for the Survival Kit

Waterproof matches

Flint bar

First aid items

Sewing items

Knife

Compass

Fishline, hooks, sinkers

Assorted safety pins (strung
    on the largest)

Aluminum foil

Plastic bags

Assorted rubber strips and leather
    (for slingshot)

Geological survey maps

Lightweight rope and string

Plastic sheet

Powerful magnifying glass

Whistle

Steel mirror

Extra food and clothing

Some Possible Supplemental Items

Light wire for snares, etc.; nested screwdrivers with plastic handles; tinder; rubber patches and a tube of liquid rubber; cutting pliers; sunburn protection; a small can of assorted screws; six- and eight-penny nails; rawhide lacing; flashlight; small saw, extra saw blades (for cutting bone and metal); small axe; small file; candle; all-purpose cement; plastic tubing and narrow adhesive tape which can be used for mending articles (especially if warmed a little in cold weather.)

List of Survival Manuals

There are many good survival books on the market, such as the AIR FORCE SURVIVAL MANUAL (for sale by the Superintendent of Documents, U.S. Government Printing Office, Washington, D.C. 20402). From these a person can get additional knowledge.

The above-mentioned AIR FORCE SURVIVAL MANUAL (AFM 64-5, Search and Rescue, Survival), by the Department of the Air Force, Headquarters, U.S. Air Force, Washington, D.C. 20330, comes in the format of six by nine inches and consists of about 140 pages. Its price a few years ago was $1.50—an excellent value and one of the best investments you will ever make. This manual is designed to aid your survival and rescue regardless of geographical location or climatic condition. It describes the proper use of the equipment in your survival kit and, just as important, it will aid you in recognizing and using the natural resources at hand.

Another book specializing in nuclear attack and natural disaster is IN TIME OF EMERGENCY—A CITIZEN'S HAND-BOOK ON NUCLEAR ATTACK—NATURAL DISASTER (H-14), given out by the Department of Defense, Office of Civil Defense.

Other excellent books describing various plants and their uses are:

BACK TO EDEN, by Jethro Kloss (no plant description).

USING PLANTS FOR HEALING, by Nelson Coon.

EDIBLE WILD PLANTS OF EASTERN NORTH AMERICA, by Merritt L. Fernald and Alfred C. Kinsey, revised by Reed C. Rollins.

WILD EDIBLE PLANTS OF THE WESTERN UNITED STATES, by Donald Kirk.

CONCLUSION

America was once a mighty nation, looked up to by the entire world. Fearless, valiant men and women began migrating to her shores from various parts of Europe over 200 years ago and soon a new nation was born. From a group of small colonies she grew to become states and in 1776 the states were united in a single cause. Freedom! The very word struck to the hearts of the stalwart inhabitants and challenged them to shake off the remains of the shackles that bound them. The United States grew to be a colossus among the world family of nations. The people who lived within her borders were God-fearing, honorable people of a common racial and ethnic background.

For centuries European nations fought one another for "elbow room," but America had enjoyed more tranquility due to her almost complete isolation with oceans to the east and west and non-aggressive, weaker neighbors on the north and south. Partly because of this, many—if not most—Americans have developed a placid composure during the decades.

Sinister elements, however, eyed this rich prize across the sea. A gigantic plot was conceived and, little by little, the hard-won liberty of the American people began to be eroded and lost. Congress was deprived of the right under the Constitution to coin money. Free enterprise choked as more and more controls insinuated themselves upon the economy. Taxation began—small at first, but soon growing into tremendous proportions that crippled individuals and businesses alike. People began to be chained to city jobs as they needed to earn money in a futile effort to fill the ever-expanding maw of governmental budgeteers. No-win wars drained the country of its intelligent young men, wasted national wealth and disheartened the entire populace. Infiltrated communications media hypnotized the majority of the people into believing the distorted information that was given to them. Chemicalized food replaced wholesome fresh fruits, vegetables, grains and nuts in the diet and soon sickness filled the land, further devitalizing the people. Welfare and other "get something for nothing" agencies swelled their ranks with more enrollees as unemployment skyrocketed,and soon almost everyone would be on the books, leaving few productive workers to pay the bills. Crime increased at a staggering rate and soon lawlessness was the order of the day. Criminals were free to prey upon helpless people while law-abiding citizens were jailed. Now inflation is spiralling and eventually will bring about a complete economic collapse even though government spokesmen tried to soothe the frustrated citizens by assuring them that the situation was under control and soon would improve. However, under the grip of monopoly interests and bombarded with many confusing and conflicting viewpoints, this nation is struggling between inflationary recession and deflationary depression. Most likely we will end up with an *inflationary depression*, if the aftermath of the monetary contraction which has been upon us for some time does not dump us into a crash before the last-initiated, super-inflationary waves can temporarily avert it. Also, America is still finding itself in the midst of a raging sea of political and general confusion through planned give-aways, crime-infested cities, massive welfare and other socialistic programs, riots and drugs in the schools and universities, anti-liberty legislation galore and a complete economic collapse right ahead of us.

Even though the cumulative consequences of fatal blunders in American political and financial manuevers have been hitting home, therefore, with increasing strength and accuracy, bringing this fair land in catastrophic proportion to the brink of disaster and thus the attitude of many Americans has slowly been changing for some time, all of this has still caught most people unprepared, having been used to a life of relative ease. They have been unaware of the underlying trends in evidence for a very long time which have caused this dilemma. The general American populace, especially the middle class, is in dire need of immediate and practical help in the desperate and tragic times now upon us. It is a well-known fact that without proper knowledge and a vision, people will fail.

Getting out of a vulnerable society and back to essentials of nature is a "must". Simple things such as fresh eggs, milk, meat, fruits, nuts, and garden produce from your homestead not only are more nutritious, tastier and less expensive than their store-bought counterparts, but will mean much more to you when our economy worsens and eventually fails altogether. Gold, silver and barter items will provide the indispensable media of exchange when a dollar is worth only as much as the paper it is printed on. This new way of life will make you look forward to the dawning of each day and give you strength and confidence to face a challenging future.

Just as winter brings a long period of dormancy over the land, when it seems at times as though all life had come to an end, spring finally heralds a great awakening. The sun melts off the snow blanket to expose new life sprouting forth from the earth. Animals suddenly are in evidence everywhere. The birds return and bring gladness to our hearts with their melodious songs as they turn the surrounding countryside into one big concert hall.

As nature all around us begins to live again in the springtime, so will we also experience a new and fresh uplift in our lives. There will once again be an awakening expectation of the eventual fulfillment of man's God-given hopes and dreams.

May this book do its part to move many a person from the death and dreariness of a long, wintery existence into the bright and joyful sunlight of a new spring in life. May your soul find the courage to seek a free and better life overflowing with glorious experiences, excitement and challenges as outlined herein. May there be a fresh song in your heart and a joy in your soul to make living the most beautiful endeavor imaginable, as it was meant to be.

In this book I have covered numerous important aspects of life. It would not be possible to go into minute detail on every subject discussed as this would produce many volumes. For the reasons of the reader's convenience, time, expense and practicability, I have kept to the main issues in a brief manner. A good number of readers, therefore, might desire more detailed personal counselling. If you have such a need, you may write to me for terms (be sure to include a stamped, self-addressed envelope): P.O. Box 105, Ashland, Oregon 97520, USA. Please understand, however, that I cannot promise to be available or provide follow-up consultation or supervision, as I travel a lot and much of my other time is occupied.

But for the most part, now that you have read this book you have the knowledge necessary to meet whatever the future holds with assurance. No government agency can or will help—you must do it yourself. City, State and Federal government agencies are deeply in debt and unable to stave off the inevitable disaster. New York City's financial problems are well known; not so well known is the fact that the Federal Government's indebtedness (according to a survey made by the reputable private firm, Arthur Anderson Accounting Agency) at the end of fiscal year 1975 totalled $812 billion rather than the reported $486 billion arrived at by bookkeeping magic. Also, according to this survey, the debt incurred in fiscal 1974 amounted to $95 billion, 30 times the acknowledged deficit. With listed government assets of $330 billion, our liabilities are almost three times as large as our assets with worse things ahead. Except in "Federalese," it means staggering insolvency. Indeed we are living on borrowed time.

The ship of state on which we are sailing and in which we have trusted so long has been mortally torpedoed and is sinking fast. Soon there will be a mad scramble for the rapidly vanishing portions of the quickly sinking ship in order to escape a deadly, encroaching sea. Now it will be only those who have learned how to swim who stand a chance. If you have prepared a lifeboat for yourself, the better off you will be and also can joyfully extend help to others in deep trouble. If you are wise, you will leave the doomed ship early, for if you cling to the drowning wreck to the last as your only hope with foolish trust, the whirlpool created by the disappearing vessel will drag you down into the depths of destruction. So don't make the present perishing Babylonian system your only hope—get yourself on a sounder base long before the old system collapses. Soon you will be glad for this most important move in your life.

Above all, get hold of eternal values. The fast-fading fashions of a world in anguish show the dire need for them. Could it be, dear reader, that this is the ultimate purpose of it all? A turning of men from those things which are seen to those things which are not seen—for the things which are seen are temporal, but the things which are not seen are eternal.

And it was the ETERNAL ONE Who uttered through His prophet Isaiah the following comforting words:

> "And the work of righteousness shall be peace; and the effect of righteousness quietness and assurance for ever. And my people shall dwell in a peaceable habitation, and in sure dwellings, and in quiet resting places." (Isaiah 32:17, 18).

APPENDIX
Recipes from
Our Mountain Home

BUTTER

Skim cream from raw milk or, in the case of goat milk, use a cream separator. The cream should be at room temperature before churning. Fill a butter churn, mixer, or a glass container (with a tight seal) one-third to half full with cream. Churn the cream (in the case of a glass container, you should shake it) until tiny granules of butter form a clump and separate from the buttermilk. Pour the buttermilk into a container for use in bread, pancakes, waffles, etc. Then, to remove any remaining milk, wash the butter repeatedly in cold water until the water becomes clear. Drain completely and knead the butter to remove the last water. Add salt to taste and distribute it in the butter. Shape into a ball or square and refrigerate. It takes about 2½ gallons of milk to make one pound of butter.

NOTE: Goat butter is white. Most dairy products bought in the store are loaded with chemicals. Butter has food coloring added to give it "a rich golden" appearance. Ice cream, being no exception, can contain as many as 30 additives without listing the ingredients.

YOGURT

Heat ½ gallon of whole milk in a (heavy) steel pot until it reaches a temperature of 195°F. Cool the milk to 110°F. Put in ½ cup of plain yogurt from the grocery store. Stir well. Let it stand in a warm place until it sets. My wife makes her yogurt in the evening and places the whole pot on the pilot light overnight to set.

COTTAGE CHEESE

¼ rennet tablet
½ cup water
1 gallon raw skim cow milk or whole goat milk

½ cup yogurt or buttermilk
1½ teaspoons salt
1/3 cup cream

Disperse rennet tablet by crushing in water. Heat milk to 70°F. Add yogurt or buttermilk and rennet tablet solution and stir well. Let stand at room temperature until a firm curd forms.

Cut curd in ½" pieces using a long knife. Heat curd slowly over hot water until temperature reaches 110°F. Hold the curd at this temperature for 20 to 30 minutes. Stir at five minute intervals to heat curd uniformly. When curd has firmed sufficiently, pour mixture on fine cheese cloth in a colander and allow whey to drain off. Shift curd on cloth occasionally by lifting corners of cloth. After whey has drained, lift curd in cheese cloth and immerse in pan of cold water 1 to 2 minutes working about with a spoon. Then immerse in ice water 1 to 2 minutes. Drain the curd until all liquid is gone and put cheese into a bowl. Add salt, caraway seeds (optional) and cream and mix thoroughly. Chill.

MAYONNAISE

1 large egg
½ teaspoon mustard
¾ teaspoon sea salt
½ teaspoon raw sugar
  (or 1 teaspoon honey)

Dash of cayenne
2-3 tablespoons apple cider vinegar
  or lemon juice or ½ of each
$1/_3$ cup safflower oil
$2/_3$ cup safflower oil

Place all ingredients (except oil) into blender or beat with mixer until smooth. Continue beating as you add the $1/_3$ cup oil, a drop at a time. Then add remaining oil slowly, a tablespoon at a time.

In order to make good mayonnaise, it is important to add the oil slowly to the other ingredients, mixing it well. Makes about 1¼ cups.

MOUNTAIN BREAD

$1/_3$ cup unsulfured molasses
2 packages active dry yeast
4 cups whole wheat flour
  (freshly-ground red hard
  wheat is best)

1 cup soy flour
2 teaspoons sea salt
3 tablespoons safflower oil
1 slightly beaten egg
Sesame seed

Mix molasses and 2 cups lukewarm milk and dissolve yeast in the mixture. Stir in one half of the flours and beat until smooth. Add sea salt, oil and remaining flour, or enough to make dough easy to handle. Turn out on floured board and knead 8 to 10 minutes or until smooth and no longer sticky. Put dough into greased bowl, cover and let rise in warm place 1¾ to 2 hours or until doubled in bulk. Divide in 2 equal portions and shape into loaves. Put them in greased 9" x 5" x 3" loaf pans. Brush top of loaves with egg, then sprinkle with sesame seed. Let rise 1 hour, or until doubled in bulk. Bake in preheated 375°F oven about 50 minutes.

NOTE: Store-bought bread may have up to 16 chemicals added to keep it "fresh" (or rather to keep it from spoiling). One type of bread, the so-called balloon bread, goes through a rigor mortis treatment with the addition of plaster of Paris.

CAROB-ZUCCHINI BREAD

3 eggs	¾ cup oil
1 cup raw sugar	1 teaspoon vanilla
½ cup honey	2 small ripe bananas

Mix these ingredients together. Then mix together and sift the following items:

3 cups whole wheat flour	3 teaspoons cinnamon
1 teaspoon sea salt	3 tablespoons carob
2 teaspoons baking powder	

Add dry ingredients to the egg-oil mixture and mix well. Then add 2 cups shredded zucchini, 1 cup chopped dates and 1 cup walnuts. Bananas and zucchini provide the moisture needed. Bake in 3 small or 2 large loaf pans for 50 minutes at 350°. This bread is also very good without the dates and nuts. It is delicious fresh, and keeps for several months in a freezer.

SPRING SANDWICH

Slice whole wheat bread. Spread with butter. Put ½ inch homemade cottage cheese on the bread. Cover with a layer of sprouts. Decorate with finely cut green onions and slices of radishes.

WHOLESOME BREAKFAST CEREAL

In a large container, mix well equal weights of these unrefined grains, seeds and nuts: Buckwheat, rye, oat groats, millet, sesame, brown rice, flax, corn, alfalfa, almonds, barley, wheat berry, and sunflower. Each night grind (finely) enough of this mixture in a hand mill for your family's breakfast. Mix with water or fruit juice and allow to soak at room temperature overnight. In the morning add honey, yeast, and sliced raw fruit. Eat this cereal raw—do not cook it.

GRANOLA

Mix 5 cups old-fashioned oatmeal and 1 cup each of cut almonds, unrefined sesame seeds, sunflower seeds, shredded coconut, soy flour, non-instant powdered milk, and wheat germ. In a separate pan combine 1 cup each of honey and vegetable oil. Combine moist and dry ingredients, spread on three cookie sheets and bake at 250°F for 1 hour or until slightly brown. To vary, use cinnamon and ground-up dry apple.

NOTE: Tests that were made of some breakfast cereals showed the box to have more nourishing value than the contents.

GREEN DRINK

Pour 3 cups pineapple or apple juice into a blender. Add several large handfuls of green leaves from plants like alfalfa, parsley, spinach, comfrey, purslane, dandelion, lambs' quarter and malva. Liquify in a blender. We just use water and green leaves, but the fruit juices do improve the taste.

LEMON JUICE

Peel 2 lemons. Cut into quarters and put into blender. Add 4 to 6 cups water, depending how diluted you want it. Then blend. Honey may be added. Lemons and lemon juice are good for cleansing the body.

Final Health Tips

When I see what people eat, I am not surprised that sickness abounds everywhere. It drives me to finish this section with a few health hints in a nutshell.

Stay away from refined, dead foods. Eat living, raw, organically-grown leafy and root vegetables, fruits, grains, seeds and nuts. Partake of the Wholesome Breakfast Cereal, Green Drink, and Lemon Juice given in the above recipes. I prefer to eat the vegetables the way they are, uncut and unshredded.

If you need to eat meat or seafood, then raise and slaughter livestock, or hunt and fish yourself. Bake your own bread and make dairy products from raw goat's milk.

Drink fresh, pure water. Avoid city water wherever possible.

If sickness has diminished your body reserves, you may need a high mineral-vitamin intake supplied by such items as sprouted seeds, carrot juice, yeast and blackstrap molasses (immediate cleaning of your teeth after the consumption of molasses is imperative).

In order to enable your body to properly absorb the nourishment in the food, it is necessary that a person uses comfrey, Luvos Heilerde (volcanic soil) or other natural intestinal tract cleansers. They clean out the excessive mucus from your bowels.

Growing an organic garden will profit in many ways. Proper nutrition, good elimination, plenty of exercise in fresh air and sunshine, a positive attitude (happy people rarely get cancer) and, not at last, peace with God by prayerfully reading and applying His Word go a *long* way. To achieve this, you may need an environmental change—a simpler, more active life without stress. And that's what this book is all about.

Schneider writes manual to help 'troubled Americans' live better

By STU WATSON
Mail Tribune Staff Writer

Sympathy and concern for an American populace headed toward what he feels is another period of "hard times," prompted Hans J. Schneider to write "Timely and Profitable Help for Troubled Americans."

Schneider, who lives with his family on a self-sufficient farmstead about 33 miles southeast of Ashland, described his book as a manual to help Americans "live better today and be more prepared for tomorrow.

"I wrote the book because I feel the U.S. is heading toward the same times here as I experienced as a child in Europe," said Schneider. "I feel sorry for the American people because they have lived in relative prosperity."

Hans J. Schneider

All that soon may come crashing down around our heads again, much as it did in 1929, according to Schneider.

"The loan-deposit ratio in our banks is similar to that just prior to the Great Depression in this country," Schneider said. "In the last 18 months, the federal debt has increased 22 per cent. Between late 1971 and late 1974, the federal debt increased about 3.7 per cent each year."

He says the accelerating trend toward deficit spending and the upward spiral of interest payments augers ill for the U.S. economy.

"The is only the lull," Schneider said. "We are in the eye of the storm. The worst is still to come."

Schneider tells readers how to beat inflation, protect and increase savings through proper investment, choose an occupation unlikely to be affected by unemployment, become self-sufficient, educate your children—legally—outside the school system and avoid various societal ripoffs and work woes.

"And agricultural real estate is valuable to invest in," he said. "If times turn bad, no matter how much land you have—one, two or more acres—you'll be able to produce your own food."

Born in Breslau, Germany, in 1935, Schneider was weaned on Hitler's fascism, witnessed the economic chaos which forced people to buy bread with wheelbarrows full of money and saw his industrialist father's millions dwindle to the point that his family was forced to forage for food.

Subsequent world travels provided Schneider with much

Book On Help In Troubled Times

of the practical experience from which he draws in counseling his readers. He says the land beckons but offers persons seeking a rural lifestyle to follow three guidelines to sound investment.

"People would be better off to get away from the technocracies," Schneider said, "and lead a simple life. If they can learn to provide for themselves, they'll be better off."

One recommended escape which Schneider has tried personally is yachting.

"You can anchor anywhere, food is cheaper, fuel is less expensive when you use the wind and you can sample the lifestyles of many countries," he said. "If things get bad, you move on."Schneider's book includes chapters on diet, emergency short-term survival, electrical generation without gasoline, food preservation and coping with drought.

Hans J. Schneider and his family live on a ranch off the Greensprings Highway near Ashland practicing what he preaches in a new book calling for a return to a simpler kind of life.

Schneider says his book

Schneider says Americans should be more versatile and develop a full repertoire of job skills. "They shouldn't be too specialized," he said. "Look what happened in Seattle when Boeing started having problems?"

Schneider says he isn't "theorizing" in offering advice.

"I speak from practical experience," he said. "I'm putting down what actually happened to us and helped us survive."

draws somewhat of a comparison between the U.S. and what happened in Germany in pre-World War II days with its runaway inflation. Runaway inflation is demoralizing and paves the way for dictatorships, he says.

"In the book I advocate a return to a simpler way of life...A way in which people can insure themselves against the things that are coming," Schneider said.

For instance, there is a chapter on how to make investments which will not be eaten up by inflation, the kinds of lifestyles which can be led to protect oneself against coming crises, types of jobs that are not suscepti-

ble to unemployment and so on.

There is even a section on how one can legally educate one's children at home as Schneider did.

Schneider says he has travelled under "survival conditions on pennies a day" through nearly 100 countries.

"I am practicing the things I write about," Schneider says. "I live in a beautiful place situated in the mountains by a spring-fed creek without utility bills, polluted air and water, chemicalized food and noise.

"Are you sick of it all? The rat race, pressures of modern-day living?"

Schneider's book may provide some answers.

Author's Book Counsels Independent Lifestyle

By STEVE TAYLOR
(Enterprise-Record Staff Writer)

"A person dependent on swollen government bureaucracy and modern conveniences such as electricity and supermarkets could be in big trouble when the U.S. economy tumbles," predicts author and world-traveler Hans J. Schneider. He cautions, "Live within your means. Become self-sufficient and you will survive."

Schneider has come to Chico and Northern California to lecture and promote his book, "Timely and Profitable Help for Troubled Americans" — a manual to "help Americans live better today and be more prepared for tomorrow."

Born in Breslau, Germany, in 1935, Schneider witnessed the social and financial chaos of war-torn Europe. "We were a very wealthy family before Hitler came into power," he said. Our family had modern conveniences then that even today are considered extravagant luxuries."

But he explained that the war ended all that. His family was dispossessed and for five years wandered through the forests, foraging for whatever food they could grub from the wilderness.

By 1950, the Schneiders had moved to West Germany and started to put their lives together again. Schneider attended school, worked as an apprentice ship's broker and became one of the first Germans licensed to fly commercial planes.

He then adopted a gypsy's life, traveling the world as an importer, pilot and evangelist. The theories he espouses in his book are the culmination of more than 20 years of survival. On his travels, he noted that the world economy is complex and interwoven. "Mexico," he said, "will have big trouble if the U.S. dollar keeps falling in value. Canada, Europe, Japan. If trouble hits the U.S., it will engulf the whole world."

Schneider endorses self-sufficiency and the development of many abilities. "Don't specialize," he warns. "And don't get caught depending on big government contracts which could fall apart when political opinion changes." He mentioned Seattle, Wash., and the troubles they had when the aerospace industry was curtailed by decisionmakers in the Capitol.

A contemporary Thoreau, Schneider is an advocate of the rural life. He lives near Ashland, Ore., and speaks with

Chico (Calif.) Enterprise-Record pride of the farmstead he has built on 25 acres of land. He claims to spend only $20 a month to feed his family of seven. Although he is building a generator, they live now without a major power source.

Schneider admits this lifestyle is not for everyone. "I offer an alternative," he says. "Many people need the social contact and interaction they find in the cities. They could not survive and be happy in an isolated situation. My book was written for another type of person — one who is tired of being dependent on government and society."

The book combines biography, anecdote and economic observations and focuses on "how-to" become self-sufficient. One section deals with life on a yacht and gives sailing tips.

"You can anchor anywhere," he said, "food is cheaper, fuel is less expensive when you use the wind and you can sample the lifestyles of many countries. If things get bad, you move on."

Liberty Baptist Church to Host Guest Lecturer

Liberty Baptist Church, Seventh Avenue and The Esplanade, will host guest lecturer Hans J. Schneider of Ashland, Ore., at 7:30 tomorrow night.

Schneider an evangelist, author and world traveler, will discuss his book, "Timely and Profitable Help for Troubled Americans", which details his personal plan for freedom and survival in the midst of economic turmoil.

Born in Breslau, Germany, in 1935, Schneider feels that many of the symptoms of disaster he witnessed in that country in his youth — inflation and overdependance on a swollen, bureaucratic government — are being repeated in the United States.

Chico (Calif.) Enterprise-Record

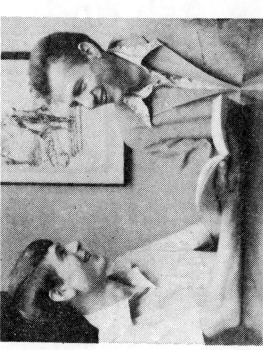

WORLD TRAVELERS — Hans J. Schneider (right) and his oldest son, Roy, 19, confer over Schneider's book, "Timely and Profitable Help for Troubled Americans." Young Schneider acts as his father's press agent and adviser, has a pilot's license and has found time during a busy lecture schedule to earn a high school diploma from a correspondence school. He favors travelling with his father to more academic forms of education because he feels college students can "lose touch with reality." (Enterprise-Record Photo by Oz Mallan)

Schneider's lectures, like much of his book, are filled with involved analysis and projection of world economic trends. He draws many comparisons between the inflation he has seen in other hard times and the situation that he finds today in the U.S.

He said, "the loan deposit ratio in our banks is similar to that just prior to the great depression in this country."

He said, "I feel sorry for most American people because they have lived in relative prosperity."

Schneider offers advice on beating inflation by making wise investments in such things as the low denomination bulk gold coins, rare jewels and rural land which can produce food and shelter.

The Daily Tidings

People

Book by Ashland resident offers various advice

Economy, investments and lifestyles are the main subjects Hans J. Schneider of Ashland explores in his recently-published book "Timely and Profitable Help for Troubled Americans."

Much of the book covers Schneider's own life experiences in the form of actual accounts as well as suggestions and predictions based on his experiences.

Schneider was born and raised in Breslau, Germany, behind what is now the Iron Curtain. His father had been a multimillionaire industrialist before World War II, and after the communists took over the area, the family's life changed drastically to the point of looking for food in the forests and wearing clothes made from gunny sacks.

Five years later the family moved to West Germany, and there Schneider studied extensively. In the following years he held several jobs, became a licensed private pilot and later traveled through nearly 100 countries under survival conditions on pennies a day, he said.

After coming to the United States in 1958 and living in big cities from New York to Los Angeles, he chose to return

to a simple lifestyle with his wife and five children. They moved from Salem to the Ashland area in 1973 and fixed up a 25-acre ranch about 33 miles southeast of Ashland, located beyond telephone and electric service. They provide their own energy and food there, and the children are enrolled in educational correspondence courses.

Schneider says his book has suggestions on successful employment, personal applications to save time and money, and investments that are safe from inflation. For those who want to "get out of the rat race," there are suggestions on buying land, how to provide your own food and energy, education, and survival in cases of emergency, he said.

The book also has a section giving warning hints to the American who has thoughts of moving to foreign lands, Schneider said. Another section covers the subject of living on boats and the lifestyle it entails.

Although Schneider is an evangelist, he says the book is not concerned with religion, but rather with the general economy, investments and lifestyles.

"It is concerned with the total life and how to live better today and be more prepared for tomorrow. And I am speaking about the joys and awards the simple life has to offer," he said.

• Your book did indeed bring out a great many vital facts . . . What will take place in this nation when crash occurs will make the war in Germany in the late thirties and early forties look like a Sunday School picnic. —H. C. V., Gainesville, FL.

• I agree with what you say as I can see what's ahead for Americans. I can heat my home entirely with wood although I have electric heat too. I have food in the basement and I'm planting a garden right now.—Mrs. A. D., Puposky, MN.

• I appreciate your sending two more TIMELY AND PROFITABLE HELP . . . After hearing your discussion on Channel 5, I bought a copy and wish to congratulate you on its excellence. I found it highly informative and interesting. And this in spite of the fact that my wife and I have been studying the subject for some twenty years, and I have read certainly a majority of the major books dealing with the intrigue and betrayal by the government and the International Bankers, as well as those on ultimate survival.
—M. C. B., Cave Junction, OR.

• "We are on the way to hyper-inflation, more governmental control and finally to total control by a dictator," says author, world traveller, evangelist, pilot, economist and lecturer Hans J. Schneider.—Red Bluff Daily News.

• I want more of your books. I am over half way through TIMELY AND PROFITABLE HELP FOR TROUBLED AMERICANS. Very good.
—Christian Mission, Georgia.

• I have really enjoyed the book. I have read it through and started again and I read different parts all the time. I find it a book of much, much wisdom. I have really got a lot out of reading it, and am thanking God for a man of God like you and for giving you a deep concern for his people in telling them what we are facing in this world. I have learned much. It was really thoughtful of you, to write "be sure before you buy a place . . ." I wish I had heard those words before we ever sold our home.
—Mrs. W. M., Bowling Green, KY.

• Thanks for making your tracts and books available to us here at the church after your inspired message. We just enjoyed it so much.—Pastor E. Z., Arcata, CA.

• After reading your book we have to agree that you have truly compiled an interesting and informative book of history, experience, logic and of much common sense.—R. T. K., Palos Verdes Estates, CA.

• I think your book has much merit. My son and I have changed some savings accounts into gold and silver and my son and wife as well as myself have perhaps two years food on hand. I raise most of my food and use much of it raw. I do very little cooking.—E. W. S., Museum Director, California.

• Thank you very kindly for the prompt service of filling my order for the two books, MASTERS OF LEGALIZED CONFUSION AND THEIR PUPPETS and TIMELY AND PROFITABLE HELP FOR TROUBLED AMERICANS. From a "bird's eye view," these are very good books, and are well written.—Dr. E. W. Perry, Baltimore, MD.

• . . . You appear so brilliant with that fabulous logic you display in your book and your great knowledge in economics. I have great admiration for you—your mind. Great book, am only to page 100 so far.—G. F., Roy, UT.

• I appreciate the concise chapters that cover subjects in which we are not knowledgeable, especially the warning economic forecasts. Your little booklet on religion interested me particularly.—C. P., Wilder, ID.

• I have this book and find it covers the various subjects better than anything I have read. It should be a great help in facing the troublesome times we are now experiencing and preparing for the future. I have many of the things listed in your book as we started preparing a long time ago. I couldn't stand to live in a city again. I like the picture of you and the family and think it so nice you can raise the children as you are doing. I am sending the leaflets on your book to people I correspond with, recommending it, and think you will get some orders.—Dr. M. F., Editor, Castle Rock, CO.

• I have just completed reading your recent book, TIMELY . . . . a birthday gift from my parents . . . I would be interested in talking with you personally. . . . Your subject matter has been of considerable interest to me for many years.—A Northwest Publisher, Portland, OR.

• I was glad to receive your book advertisements and am enclosing an order. Your background fits my interest.—R. C. M., School President, Jasper, AR.

• We have just read all of your very interesting advertisement, and although we have had much "survival" literature, all good, you seem to offer more in the way of personal experience and research, so we ask that you send us: TIMELY AND PROFITABLE HELP FOR TROUBLED AMERICANS and MASTERS OF LEGALIZED CONFUSION AND THEIR PUPPETS for which a check is enclosed.—Mr. and Mrs. R. M., Hamilton, MT.

• Praise God for making it possible for you to write TIMELY AND PROFITABLE HELP FOR TROUBLED AMERICANS. It sounds like one of the most exciting books I have ever heard of. I do want to get a number of them.—H. D., Grand Ronde, OR.

• Would you please be kind enough to send me a copy of your new book, TIMELY AND PROFITABLE HELP FOR TROUBLED AMERICANS. I heard about your book from one of my clients. It looks very interesting.—S. D. L., Financial Planner, Arcadia, CA.

• Your books sound wonderful and much needed. Please send information to the friends listed below.
—T. U., Chicago, IL.

• Yes, I do want the book you mentioned and am enclosing a check. Am looking forward with fond anticipation to reading and digesting it. I know it will be wonderful. God bless you!—Mrs. A. S., Boones Mill, VA.

• I believe you wrote the Right books for the Right time.—J. I. P., Gengapuram Village, South India.

• We received your offer of two wonderful books. You sound like a very experienced man. We have a friend we will try to interest in your books. They sound so interesting.
—J. J. R., Bicknell, IN.

• I thoroughly enjoyed the reading material you sent our way recently, and as a result of reading it, I would like very much to receive your two books as described on the enclosed order form. Check enclosed. May God bless your every effort in the cause of His Kingdom, as well as for the freedom of our beloved America. Most cordially.—J. N., Amarillo, TX.

• Thanks for remembering me. I will be eagerly awaiting my copy.
—B. B., Evans City, PA.

• I am enclosing an order for two more books and I think you will get orders for more from those I have shown the books to.—E. S., Trinity Center, CA.

• It will be a privilege and a real pleasure to give your wonderful book a 3 or 4 page review that I am sure will bring you thousands of orders.
—E. L. M., Editor and Owner of TTC, Harrisonburg, VA.

• I was delighted to hear from you. Please rush your books to me.—J. A. M., Memphis, TN.

• I received your mailing concerning survival in the end times now upon our nation. You are making a very great contribution to the cause . . . We would be honored to have you as a featured speaker and to bring your books for sale to the people of our area. We can arrange for accommodations and can even fly over for you to meet your timetable.—R. G. B., Pastor, Idaho.

• I have read your little booklet MASTERS OF LEGALIZED CONFUSION and enjoyed it very much, as well as your superb tract, "The Incomparable Shepherd." Now I see you have written a new book, which sounds to me like it will be very good . . . TIMELY AND PROFITABLE HELP . . .—O. A. J., Coulee City, WA.

• We are highly interested in your writings. We would also like to have you as our guest speaker. What is it that would bring you here and would you be available? You are probably a busy person and possibly have little spare time. If you can see your way to give us a few hours of that time we would be highly honored.—G. D., Eagle Point, OR.

• My, your life sounds exciting and I do intend to order your books by all means.—C. S., Evans, WA.

• I don't know how you found my name and address, but I sure am glad you did and let me know about your books. Please send me both. Money order enclosed.—A. P., Lubbock, TX.

• I noticed the ad regarding your book . . . Would you please autograph a copy and send it to me. Enclosed is my check.—R. M. O., Airline Captain, Hayward, WI.

BOOKS BY HANS J. SCHNEIDER

TIMELY & PROFITABLE HELP FOR TROUBLED AMERICANS

If you anticipate monetary collapse, a dictatorship and gun confiscation, you **must** read this book. In it Survival Expert Hans J. Schneider reveals his proven plan for **your** freedom and **SURVIVAL** during economic and civil turmoil! 288 pages cover: Self-Sufficiency • Locating **Your** Place of Refuge • Independent Energy Sources • Inflation-Proof Investments • Alternate Weaponry/Defense Tactics • Wilderness Survival Techniques • Food Tests • Yachting for Survival • Barter Items • Food Preservation/Storage and **much** more. Written by one who learned the art of survival from **first hand experience** and travels in nearly 100 countries, this manual could mean the difference between life and death during the coming social chaos.

288 Pages. Softcover. $8.95.

MASTERS OF LEGALIZED CONFUSION & THEIR PUPPETS

An undisputed eye-opener written without compromise about the spiritual confusion so prevalent today! Read this astonishing, frank work by one who grew up under godless Communist occupation when religious worship was taboo, who struggled with a near-fatal sickness, and for many years intensively studied philosophy and religions of mankind (especially Buddhism and Yoga) until he found the simplicity of the Gospel. Written from an uncompromising Biblical standpoint, this expose has led many from man-made religions into the truth. This book has been translated, read and studied throughout America and the world. Many letters of appreciation have been received recommending it.

Over 65,000 copies in print! $1.45

MASTERS OF
LEGALIZED CONFUSION
AND THEIR PUPPETS

by
HANS J. SCHNEIDER

FLYING TO BE FREE

"Destined to become a classic in the annals of flying literature!" The day: April 3, 1958. The place: Brussels, Belgium. "One, two, three—contact!" . . . the beginning of one of the most exciting aviation stories ever written.

Hans J. Schneider, among the first German pilots licensed after WWII, flew 4000 treacherous miles in a dangerous aviation mission around Europe and into Africa. With an overloaded 65-h.p. Aeronca Chief and inaccurate maps, he narrowly escaped death a dozen times. Here is Mr. Schneider's **personal**, never-before-told story of years of barnstorming in war-torn Europe, his passionate love for flying, **and** the dramatic events which changed the rest of his life! This book is a must for everyone who loves to read real-life adventure.

256 pages. Full-color cover. Over 100 photos/illus. $7.95.

With my order, please send me:

☐ Information on subscribing to Mr. Schneider's **financial/survival** newsletter.

☐ Your present catalog of books, reports, and tapes.

☐ Information on having Mr. Schneider speak at a conference, church or seminar.

☐ I have enjoyed **Timely and Profitable Help for Troubled Americans.** Please read my comments on a separate piece of paper. **OVER...**

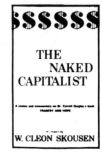